# DC SUPER HEROES
# ORIGAMI

## JOHN MONTROLL

CAPSTONE YOUNG READERS
a capstone imprint

Published by Capstone Young Readers in 2015
A Capstone Imprint
1710 Roe Crest Drive
North Mankato, Minnesota 56003
www.capstonepub.com

Library of Congress Cataloging-in-Publication Data

Montroll, John, author.
  DC super heroes origami : 46 folding projects for Batman,
Superman, Wonder Woman, and more! / by John Montroll.
    pages cm
  Summary: "Provides instructions and diagrams for folding
origami models of characters, objects, and symbols related
to Batman, Superman, Wonder Woman, and the Justice
League"— Provided by publisher.
  ISBN 978-1-62370-217-5 (paperback)
1.  Origami—Juvenile literature. 2.  Superheroes in art—Juvenile
literature. 3.  Handicraft—Juvenile literature.  I. Title.

TT872.5.M6487 2015
736'.982—dc23                              2015003760

**EDITORIAL CREDITS**
Editor and Model Folder: Christopher Harbo
Designer: Lori Bye
Art Directors: Bob Lentz and Nathan Gassman
Contributing Writers: Donald Lemke and Michael Dahl
Folding Paper Illustrator: Min Sung Ku
Production Specialist: Kathy McColley

**PHOTO CREDITS**
Capstone Studio/Karon Dubke, all photos

Printed in China.
032015    008846NORDF15

# DEDICATED TO MATT, JAN, BRIAN AND NICOLAS

## ABOUT THE AUTHOR

John Montroll is respected for his work in origami throughout the world. His published work has significantly increased the global repertoire of original designs in origami. John is also acknowledged for developing new techniques and ground-breaking bases. The American origami master is known for being the inspiration behind the single-square, no cuts, no glue approach in origami.

John started folding in elementary school. He quickly progressed from folding models from books to creating his own designs. John has written many books, and each model that he designs has a meticulously developed folding sequence. John's long-standing experience allows him to accomplish a model in fewer steps rather than more. It is his constant endeavor to give the reader a pleasing folding experience.

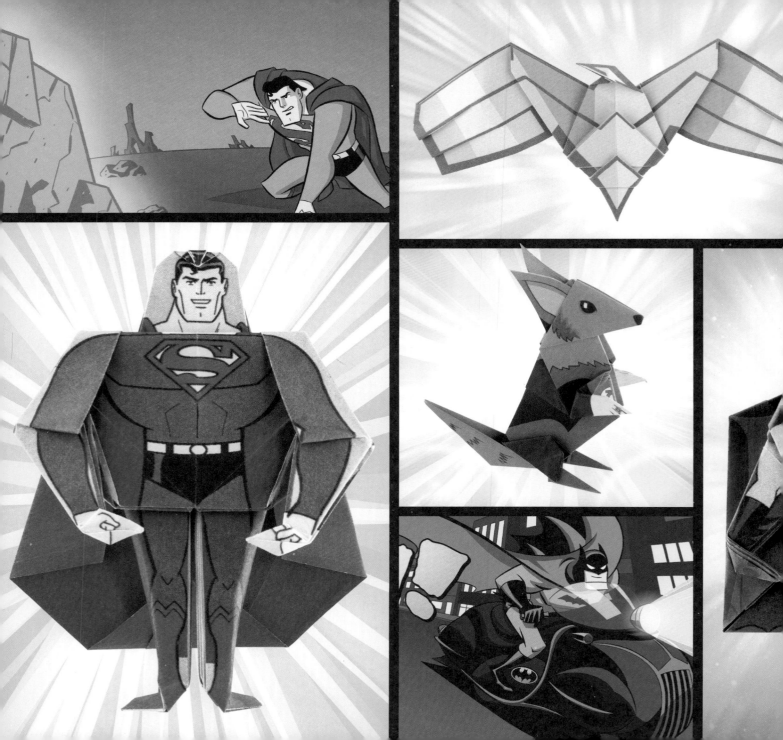

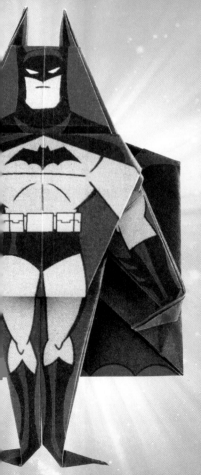

# CONTENTS

# SECTION ONE:
# THE BATMAN COLLECTION

Batarang
**36**

Batwing
**52**

Nightwing
Symbol
**40**

The Penguin's
Umbrella
**28**

Clayface
**58**

The
Riddler's Cane
**20**

Batcycle
**46**

Bat-symbol **32**

Batman
**70**

Robin
**64**

Mad Hatter's Top Hat **24**

# SECTION TWO:
# THE SUPERMAN COLLECTION

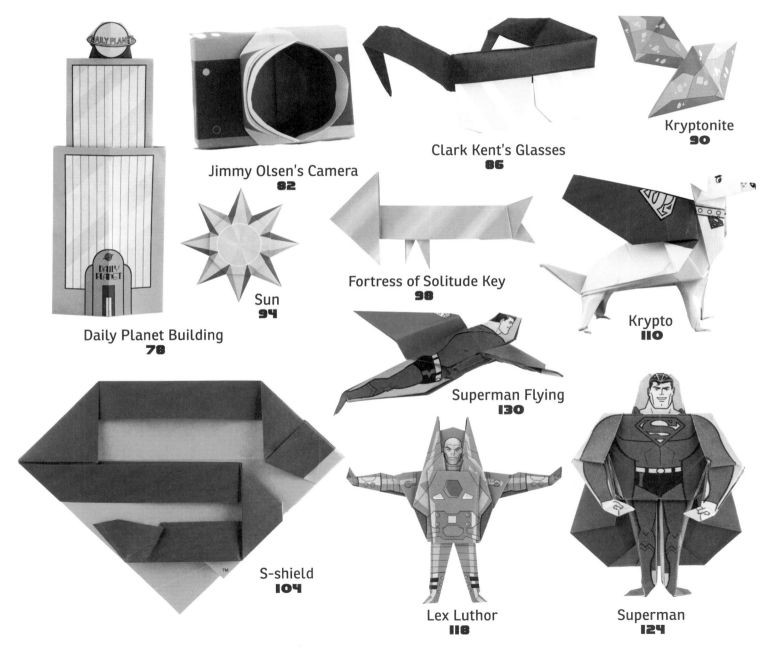

Daily Planet Building
**78**

Jimmy Olsen's Camera
**82**

Clark Kent's Glasses
**86**

Kryptonite
**90**

Sun
**94**

Fortress of Solitude Key
**98**

Krypto
**110**

S-shield
**104**

Superman Flying
**130**

Lex Luthor
**118**

Superman
**124**

# SECTION THREE:
# THE WONDER WOMAN COLLECTION

Wonder Woman's Tiara
138

Eagle
162

Wonder Woman's
Sword 158

Wonder Woman's
Arrow 154

Wonder Woman's
Boot 146

Wonder Woman
Symbol 168

Star
150

Silver Bracelet
142

Jumpa the Kanga
180

Invisible Jet
174

Wonder
Woman
184

# SECTION FOUR:
# THE JUSTICE LEAGUE COLLECTION

Martian Manhunter
Symbol **192**

Green Arrow's Hat
**204**

Shazam!
Symbol **196**

The Atom
**250**

Green Lantern B'dg
**212**

The Flash
Symbol
**200**

Storm
**222**

Green Lantern Symbol **208**

Green Lantern
Hal Jordan **216**

Hawkgirl's
Mace **238**

Hawkgirl
**244**

Aquaman's
Trident
**226**

Aquaman
**230**

# SECRET IDENTITIES

DC Super Heroes have one very important thing in common: a secret identity. Bruce Wayne is Batman. Clark Kent is Superman. Princess Diana is Wonder Woman. During the day, these secret super heroes live plain, ordinary lives—well, at least as plain and ordinary as the life of your average billionaire! But when danger strikes, they transform. Donning cowls, capes, or crowns, they become the World's Greatest Heroes. They fight for truth and justice in their constant quest to save the planet from the world's worst super-villains.

Origami, the Japanese art of paper folding, also has the power to transform. It changes plain, ordinary sheets of paper into extraordinary creations. This book contains instructions for 46 amazing transformations. From a single square of paper, you will create dynamic models of vehicles, weapons, symbols, and super heroes from the DC Comics universe. Make a Batarang to fling at imaginary enemies. Fold and wear Wonder Woman's silver bracelets. Even create Superman's iconic S-shield to display on your bedroom wall. With 96 sheets of specially designed DC Super Heroes Origami paper included inside, you can make each model come to life with bold, colorful comic book details.

The diagrams in this book are drawn in the internationally approved Randlett-Yoshizawa style. This style is easy to follow once you learn the basic folds outlined in the pages to come. The models are also ranked as simple (one star), intermediate (two stars), and complex (three stars), and they are organized in each chapter to help you improve your folding skills. Remember, Bruce Wayne didn't become Batman in one day. He trained his body and mind for years to become the World's Greatest Detective, the Dark Knight. With a little patience and practice, you'll become an origami super hero!

So, choose a favorite project, tear out a sheet of paper, and discover its secret identity!

# Symbols

## Lines

— — — — — — — — — —        Valley fold, fold in front.

—·—··—··—··—··—··        Mountain fold, fold behind.

————————————        Crease line.

····························        X-ray or guide line.

## Arrows

Fold in this direction.

Fold behind.

Unfold.

Fold and unfold.

Turn over.

Sink or three dimensional folding.

Place your finger between these layers.

# Basic Folds

## Pleat Fold

Fold back and forth. Each pleat is composed of one valley and mountain fold. Here are two examples.

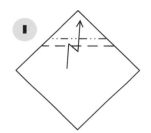 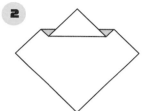

Pleat-fold.

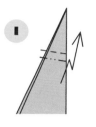 

Pleat-fold.

## Squash Fold

In a squash fold, some paper is opened and then made flat. The shaded arrow shows where to place your finger.

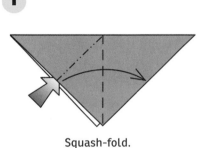 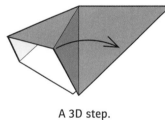 

Squash-fold.　　A 3D step.

## Petal Fold

In a petal fold, one point is folded up while two opposite sides meet each other.

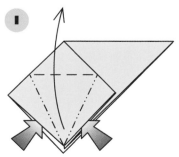 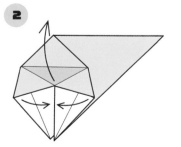 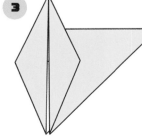

Petal-fold.　　A 3D step.

# INSIDE REVERSE FOLD

In an inside reverse fold, some paper is folded between layers. The inside reverse fold is generally referred to as a reverse fold. Here are two examples.

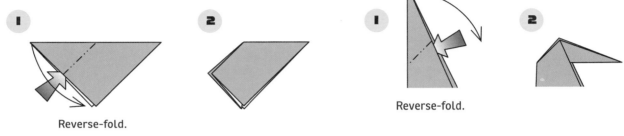

Reverse-fold.

Reverse-fold.

# OUTSIDE REVERSE FOLD

Much of the paper must be unfolded to wrap around, in order to make an outside reverse fold.

Outside-reverse-fold.

# CRIMP FOLD

A crimp fold is a combination of two reverse folds. Open the model slightly to form the crimp evenly on each side. Here are two examples.

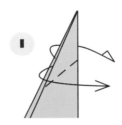

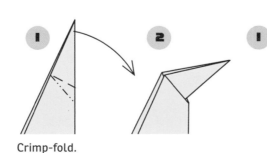

Crimp-fold.

Crimp-fold.

A 3D step.

# Rabbit Ear

To fold a rabbit ear, one corner is folded in half and laid down to a side.

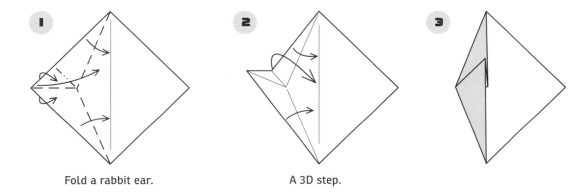

Fold a rabbit ear.

A 3D step.

# Sink

For a sink, some of the paper without edges is folded inside. To do this fold, much of the model must be unfolded.

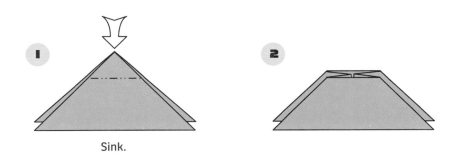

Sink.

# Spread Squash Fold

A cross between a squash fold and sink fold, some paper in the center is spread apart and then made flat.

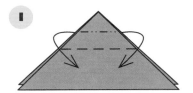

Spread-squash-fold.

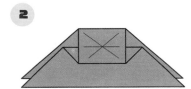

# PRELIMINARY FOLD

The preliminary fold is the starting point for many models. The maneuver in step 3 occurs in many other models.

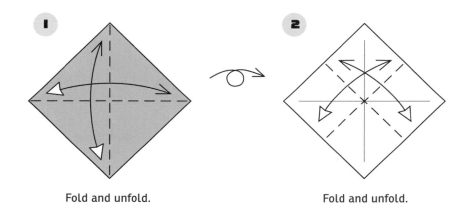

**1** Fold and unfold.
Turn over.

**2** Fold and unfold.

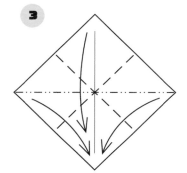

**3** Collapse the square by bringing the four corners together.

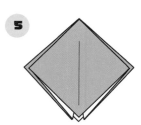

**4** This is 3D.

**5** Preliminary Fold

# WATERBOMB BASE

The waterbomb base is
named for the waterbomb
balloon which is made from it.

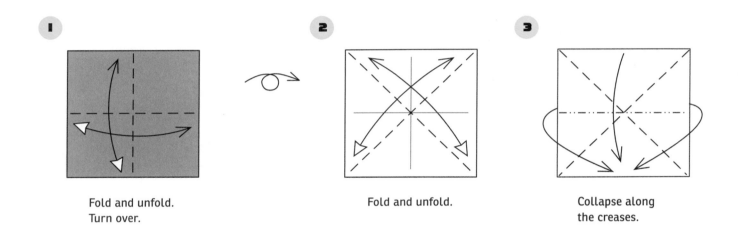

**1** Fold and unfold.
Turn over.

**2** Fold and unfold.

**3** Collapse along
the creases.

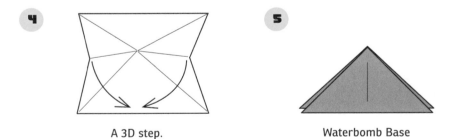

**4** A 3D step.

**5** Waterbomb Base

# THE BATMAN COLLECTION

# THE RIDDLER'S CANE

Even as a little boy, Edward Nygma loved riddles and puzzles. When he grew up, Nygma turned his passion into a career. He became a video game designer and soon invented a popular game called *Riddle of the Minotaur*. The game sold millions of copies, but Nygma didn't receive a dime from the manufacturer. To get his revenge, Nygma became the Riddler, a cryptic criminal who leaves clues about his crimes. The super-villain carries a cane shaped like a question mark. This weapon can deliver a shocking blast—the Riddler's answer to his toughest problems.

**LEVEL:** ★ ★ ☆

**1**

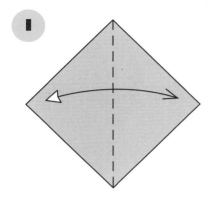

Fold and unfold.

**2**

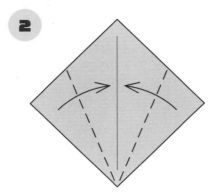

Fold to the center.

**3**

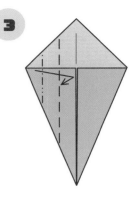

Fold in thirds.

**4**

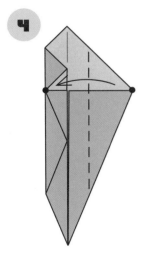

The dots
will meet.

**5**

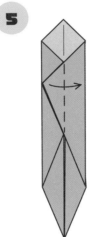

Fold to
the right.

**6**

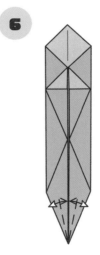

Fold and unfold
at the bottom.

**7**

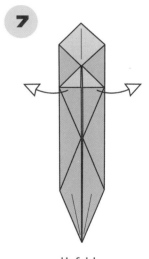

Unfold.

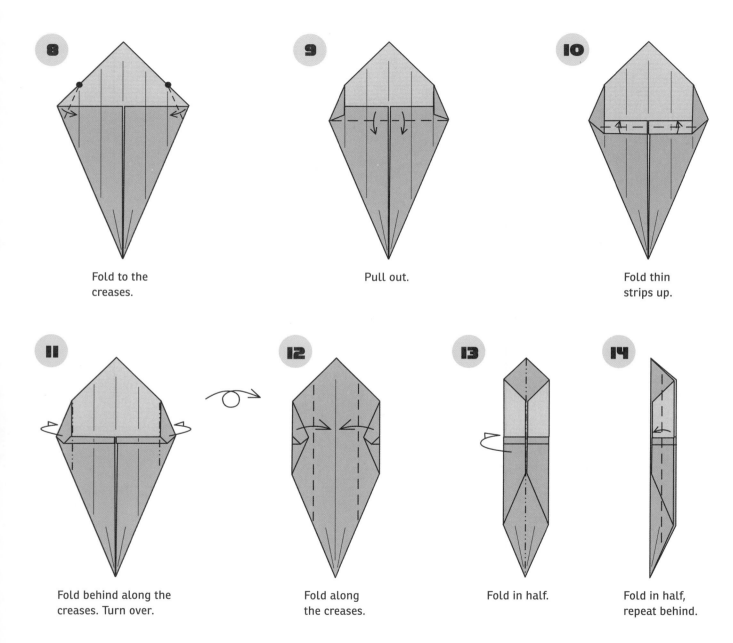

**8** Fold to the creases.

**9** Pull out.

**10** Fold thin strips up.

**11** Fold behind along the creases. Turn over.

**12** Fold along the creases.

**13** Fold in half.

**14** Fold in half, repeat behind.

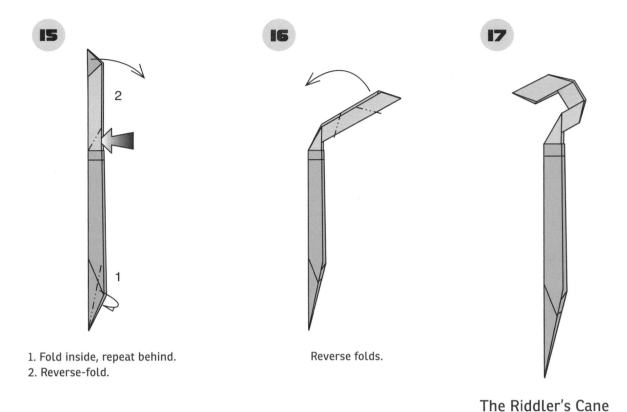

**15**

2

1

1. Fold inside, repeat behind.
2. Reverse-fold.

**16**

Reverse folds.

**17**

The Riddler's Cane

# MAD HATTER'S TOP HAT

Jervis Tetch is obsessed with Lewis Carroll's famous book, *Alice's Adventures in Wonderland*. He believes himself to be the Mad Hatter, taking Carroll's crazy hatmaker's name as his own and donning a top hat. Tetch thinks a former coworker named Alice is the main character from Wonderland and that she is destined to marry him. This belief has led Tetch to create mind-control technology in order to brainwash Alice, and the rest of the world, into living out his crazy fantasy.

LEVEL: ★★☆

**1**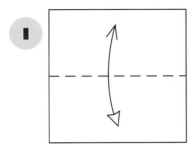

Fold and unfold.

**2**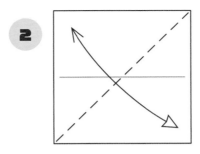

Fold and unfold.

**3**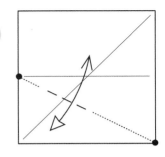

Fold and unfold
by the diagonal.

**4**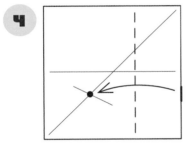

Bring the edge
to the dot.

**5**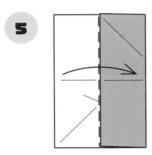

Fold to the right.

**6**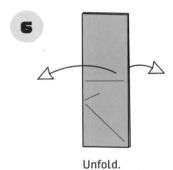

Unfold.

**7**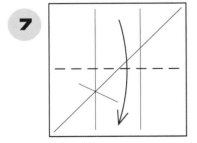

Fold in half.

**8**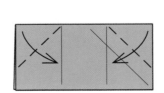

Fold to the creases.

**9**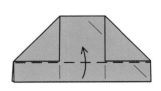

Fold the top layer
up. Repeat behind.

**10**

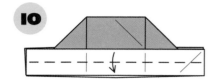

Fold down.
Repeat behind.

**11**

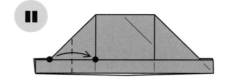

The dots will meet.

**12**

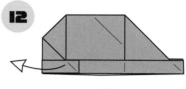

Unfold.

**13**

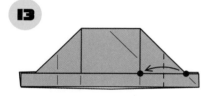

Repeat steps 11–12
on the right.

**14**

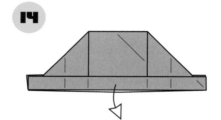

Unfold and repeat behind.

**15**

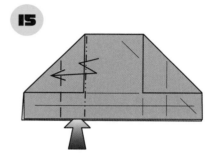

Crimp-fold along
the creases.

**16**

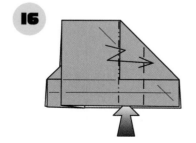

Crimp-fold along
the creases.

**17**

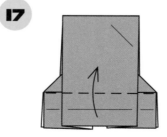

Fold up along the
crease. Repeat behind.

**18**

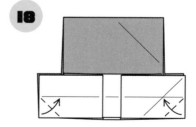

Fold all the layers
on the left and right.

**26** Mad Hatter's Top Hat

**19**

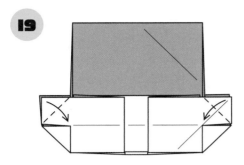

Fold the top layer on the left and right. Repeat behind.

**20**

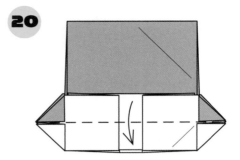

Fold down. Repeat behind.

**21**

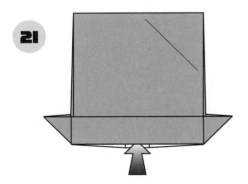

Round the hat at the bottom.

**22**

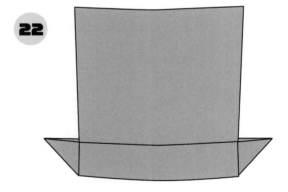

**Mad Hatter's Top Hat**

# THE PENGUIN'S UMBRELLA

Oswald Cobblepot, known as the Penguin, is an emperor of Gotham City's business world—and its criminal underworld. Although often protected by hired goons, the Penguin does have a few rainy-day weapons hidden up his sleeve, including his infamous umbrella! This high-tech device can hide a variety of tools, including a machine gun, a flamethrower, or a blade. The umbrella can also double as a parachute or helicopter, allowing the super-villain to fly away from situations gone afowl.

**LEVEL:** ★ ★ ☆

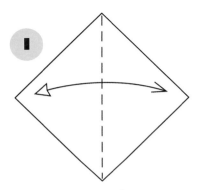

**1**

Fold and unfold.

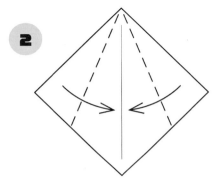

**2**

Fold to the center.

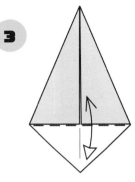

**3**

Fold and unfold.

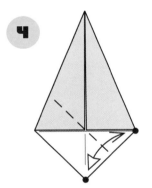

**4**

Fold and unfold.

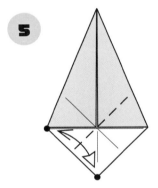

**5**

Fold and unfold.

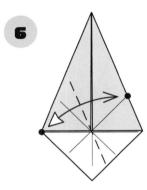

**6**

Fold and unfold.

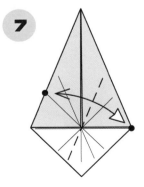

**7**

Fold and unfold.

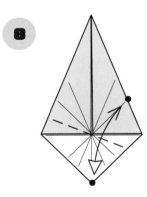

**8**

Fold and unfold.

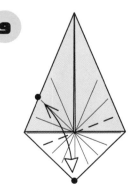

**9**

Fold and unfold.

**10**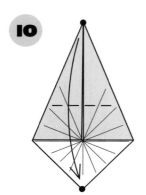

Fold down so
the dots meet.

**11**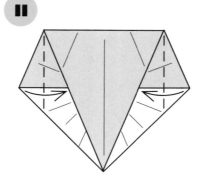

Fold on the left and right.

**12**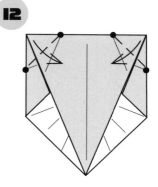

Fold at the dots.

**13**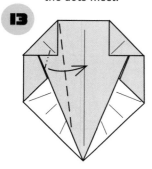

Pull out.

**14**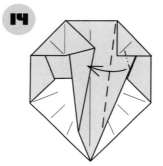

Pull out and rotate
model 90°.

**15**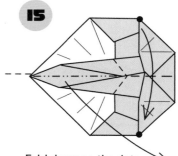

Fold down so the dots
meet and allow the
handle to swing
outward. Rotate model.

**16**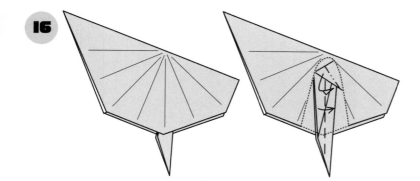

View of the inside. Thin the
handle, repeat behind.

**17**

Shape the handle
with reverse folds.

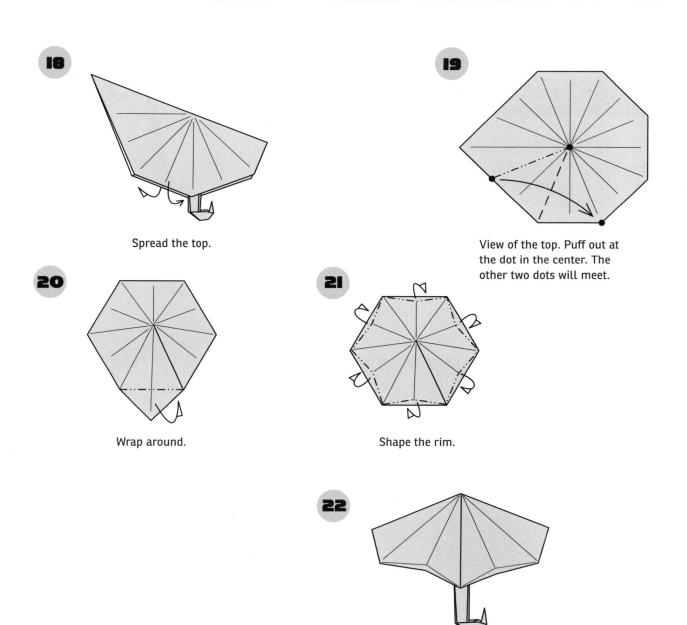

**18**

Spread the top.

**19**

View of the top. Puff out at the dot in the center. The other two dots will meet.

**20**

Wrap around.

**21**

Shape the rim.

**22**

## The Penguin's Umbrella

# BAT-SYMBOL

The bat-symbol strikes fear into the hearts of Gotham City's worst villains, but the symbol originated from Batman's greatest fear—bats! As a child, billionaire Bruce Wayne fell into a well that was swirling with a colony of terrifying bats. After the death of his parents, Bruce transformed this lifelong phobia into a new identity. He became Batman, the Caped Crusader. Although criminals now fear him, Batman and his symbol represent hope to the citizens of Gotham City.

**LEVEL:** ★★☆

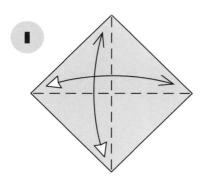

**1**

Fold and unfold.

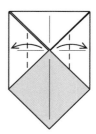

**2**

Fold three corners
to the center.

**3**

Fold the corners
to the edges.

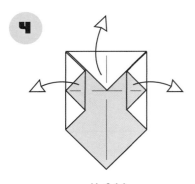

**4**

Unfold.

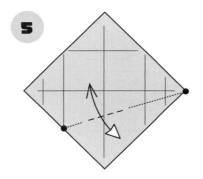

**5**

Fold and unfold
by the diagonal.

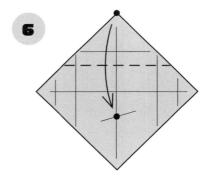

**6**

The dots will meet.

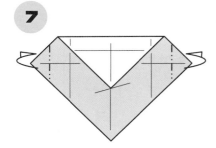

**7**

Fold along the creases.

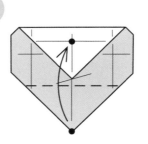

**8**

The dots will meet.

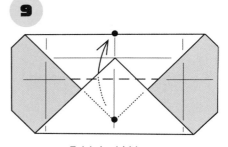

**9**

Fold the hidden
corner to the top.

**10**

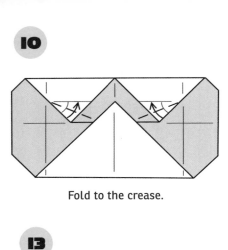

Fold to the crease.

**11**

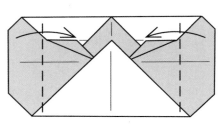

Fold along the creases.

**12**

The dots will meet.

**13**

Fold down.

**14**

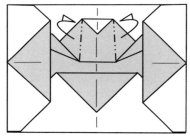

Unlock the layers
to fold behind.

**15**

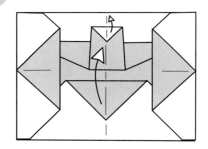

Unfold both corners.

**16**

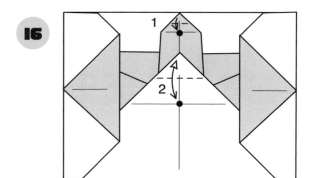

1. Fold down.
2. Fold and unfold.

**17**

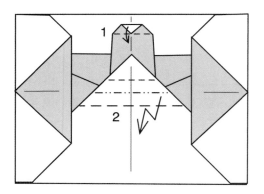

1. Fold down.
2. Pleat-fold. Valley-fold along the creases.

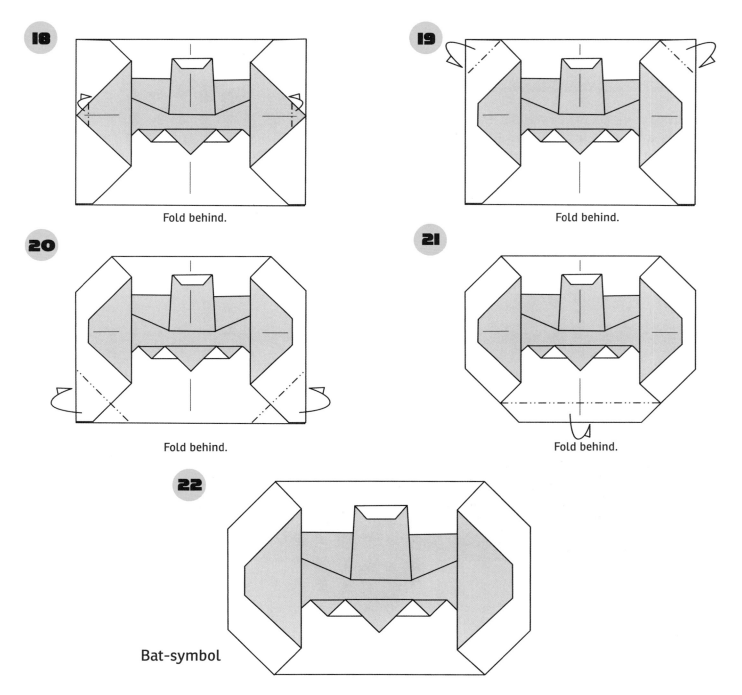

18

Fold behind.

19

Fold behind.

20

Fold behind.

21

Fold behind.

22

Bat-symbol

# BATARANG

Batman takes on the world's worst criminals without using a gun. Instead, the Dark Knight equips himself with non-lethal gadgets, including his all-time favorite weapon, the Batarang! With the flick of Batman's wrist, this razor-sharp metal throwing device zings through the air at high speed. Although lightweight, a precisely thrown Batarang can take down any villain in Gotham City, even hulking brutes like Bane and Clayface.

**LEVEL:** ★★★

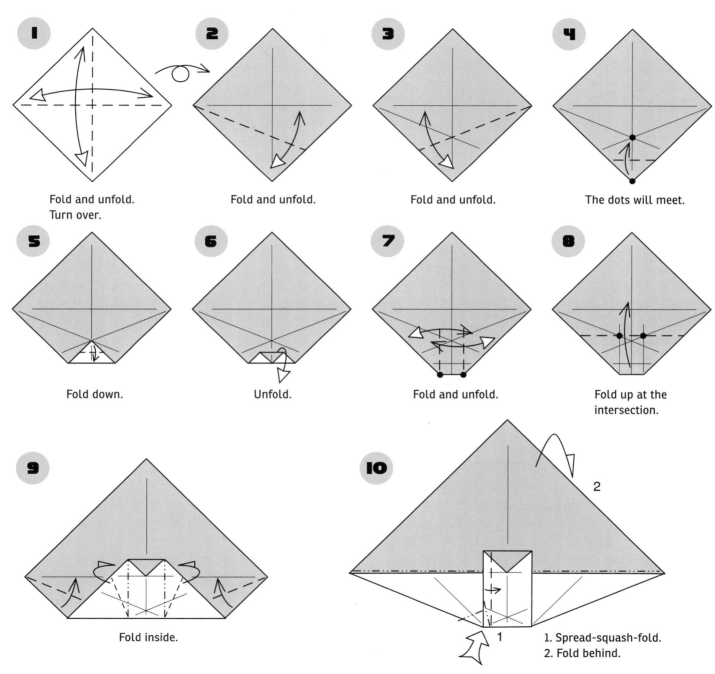

**1** Fold and unfold. Turn over.

**2** Fold and unfold.

**3** Fold and unfold.

**4** The dots will meet.

**5** Fold down.

**6** Unfold.

**7** Fold and unfold.

**8** Fold up at the intersection.

**9** Fold inside.

**10**
1
2
1. Spread-squash-fold.
2. Fold behind.

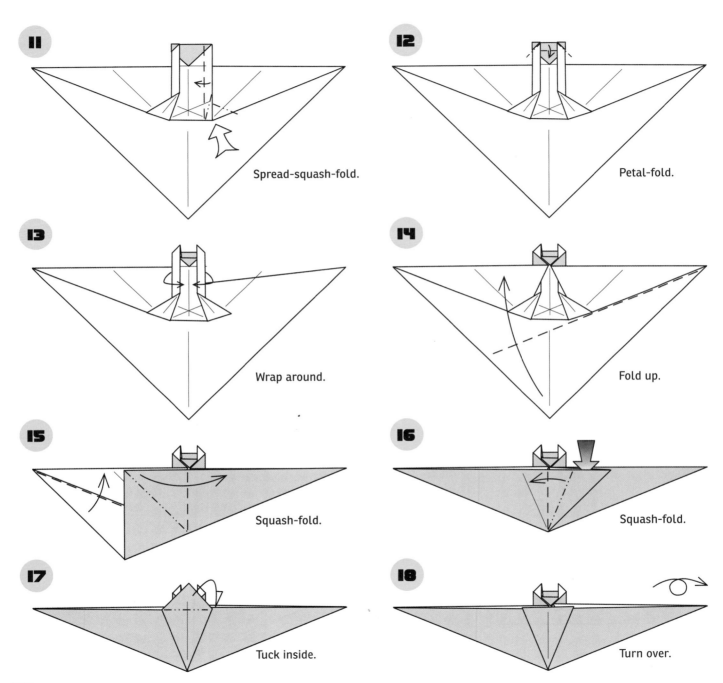

**11** Spread-squash-fold.

**12** Petal-fold.

**13** Wrap around.

**14** Fold up.

**15** Squash-fold.

**16** Squash-fold.

**17** Tuck inside.

**18** Turn over.

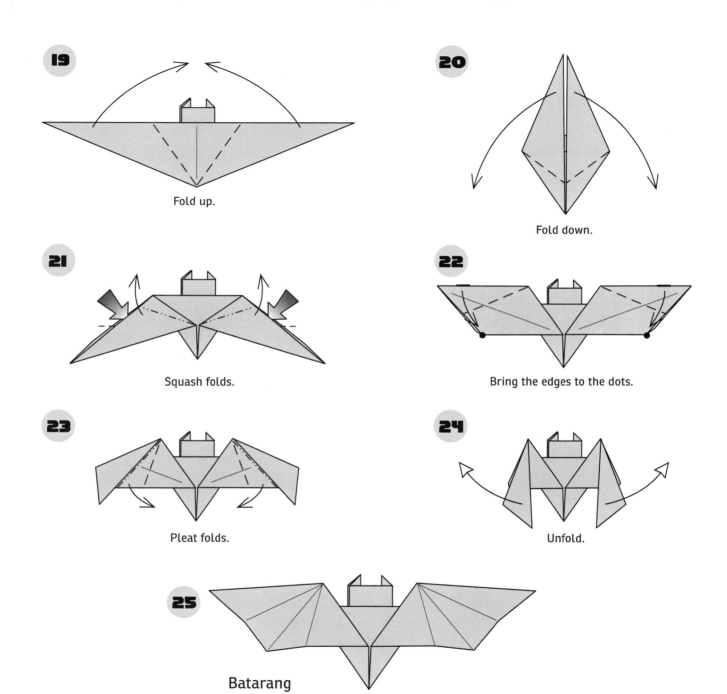

**19** Fold up.

**20** Fold down.

**21** Squash folds.

**22** Bring the edges to the dots.

**23** Pleat folds.

**24** Unfold.

**25** Batarang

# NIGHTWING SYMBOL

A seasoned pro at protecting the innocent, Nightwing once worked with the World's Greatest Detective, Batman. Now the fearless fighter flies solo. He graduated from his former role as Robin to become a stronger, sleeker creature of the night. Whether creating a fearsome threesome with the Dynamic Duo or surprising crooks on his own, Nightwing dons his blue emblem to dart from darkness when least expected.

**LEVEL:** ★★★

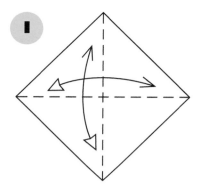

**1**

Fold and unfold.

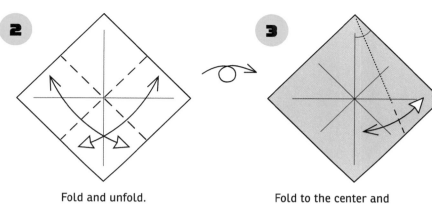

**2**

Fold and unfold.

**3**

Fold to the center and unfold. Crease at the edge.

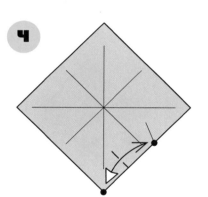

**4**

Fold and unfold by the edge.

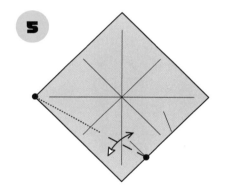

**5**

Fold and unfold by the diagonal.

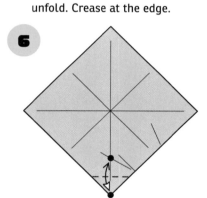

**6**

Fold and unfold so the dots meet.

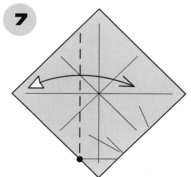

**7**

Fold and unfold.

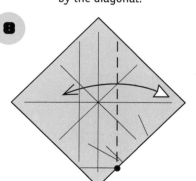

**8**

Fold and unfold. Turn over.

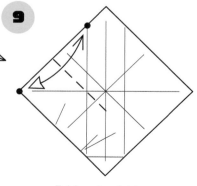

**9**

Fold and unfold on part of the line.

**10**

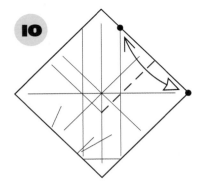

Fold and unfold on
part of the line.
Rotate model 180°.

**11**

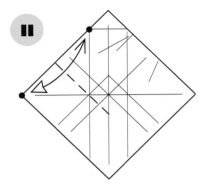

Repeat steps 9–10.
Rotate model 90°.

**12**

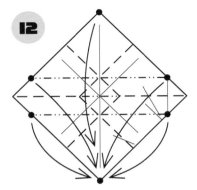

Fold along the creases. The
dots will meet at the bottom.

**13**

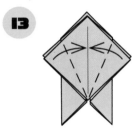

Fold to the center.
Repeat behind.

**14**

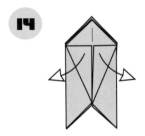

Unfold. Repeat behind.

**15**

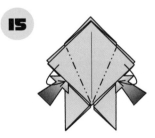

Reverse folds. Repeat
behind. Rotate model 180°.

**16**

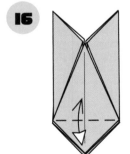

Fold and unfold.
Repeat behind.

**17**

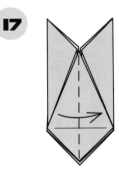

Fold to the right.

**18**

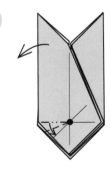

Push in at the dot and
fold to the crease.

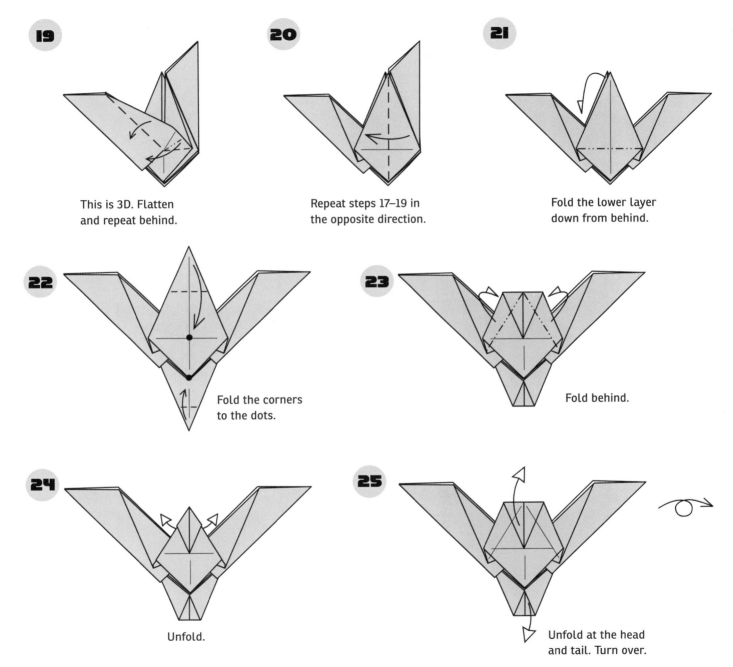

**19** This is 3D. Flatten and repeat behind.

**20** Repeat steps 17–19 in the opposite direction.

**21** Fold the lower layer down from behind.

**22** Fold the corners to the dots.

**23** Fold behind.

**24** Unfold.

**25** Unfold at the head and tail. Turn over.

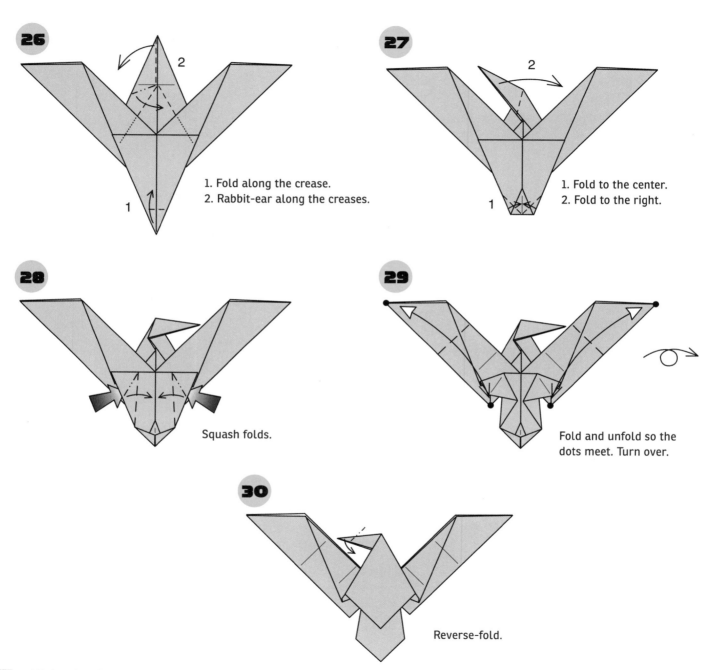

**26**

1. Fold along the crease.
2. Rabbit-ear along the creases.

**27**

1. Fold to the center.
2. Fold to the right.

**28**

Squash folds.

**29**

Fold and unfold so the dots meet. Turn over.

**30**

Reverse-fold.

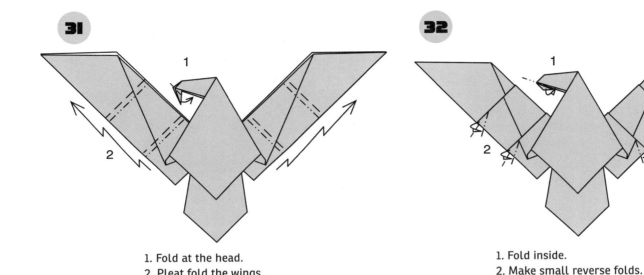

**31**

1

2

1. Fold at the head.
2. Pleat fold the wings.
   Mountain-fold along the
   creases.

**32**

1

2

1. Fold inside.
2. Make small reverse folds.

**33**

Nightwing Symbol

# BATCYCLE

Batman's secret headquarters, the Batcave, is filled with dozens of high-tech vehicles, including the Batcycle. This quick, responsive motorcycle is the Dark Knight's preferred method of transportation on narrow and crowded roadways or when the Batmobile is under repair. Like the Batmobile, the Batcycle is a technological wonder. It sports a bulletproof wind-guard, computerized controls, and a 786 cc liquid-cooled V-4 engine.

LEVEL: ★★★

**1**

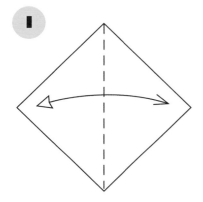

Fold and unfold.

**2**

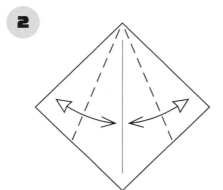

Fold to the center
and unfold.

**3**

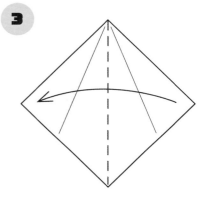

Fold in half.

**4**

Fold and unfold so the
dots meet. Rotate model.

**5**

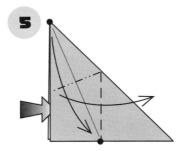

Squash-fold.

**6**

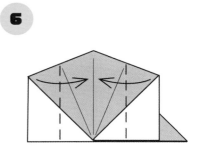

Fold to the center.

**7**

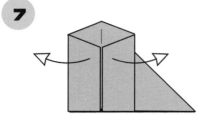

Unfold.

**8**

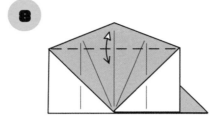

Fold and unfold.

**9**

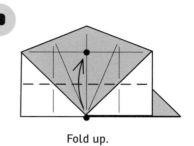

Fold up.

**10**

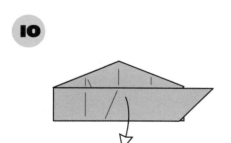

Unfold, turn over,
and rotate model.

**11**

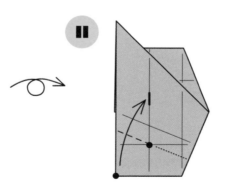

Bring the corner to the
line. Crease on the left.

**12**

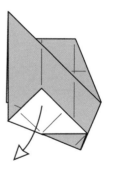

Unfold.

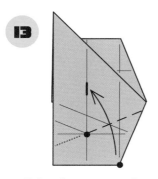

**13** Bring the corner to the line. Crease on the right.

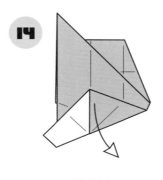

**14** Unfold.

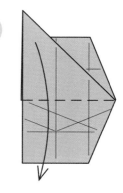

**15** Fold down. Rotate model 180°.

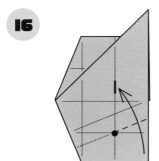

**16** Repeat steps 11–14 in the opposite direction.

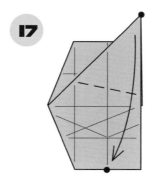

**17** Fold down so the dots meet.

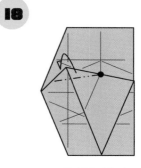

**18** Fold behind.

**19**

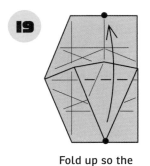

Fold up so the
dots meet.

**20**

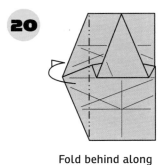

Fold behind along
the crease.

**21**

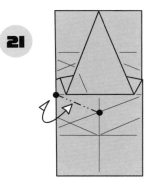

Fold and unfold.

**22**

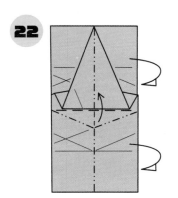

Lift up in the center and fold
in half. This is similar to a
crimp fold. Rotate model.

**23**

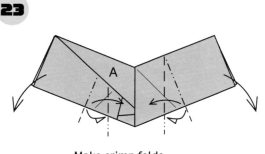

Make crimp folds
along the creases.
Fold under region A.

**24**

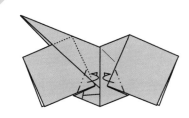

Fold behind.
Repeat behind.

**25**

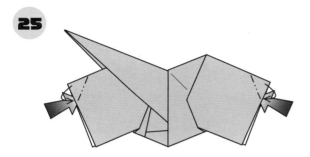

Reverse folds.

**26**

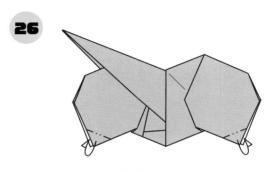

Fold inside and
repeat behind.

**27**

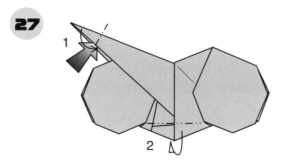

1
2

1. Reverse-fold.
2. Fold inside and repeat behind.

**28**

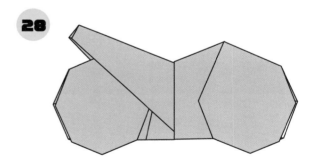

Batcycle

# BATWING

When the Dark Knight needs a bat's-eye view of Gotham City, he lifts off in the Batwing. This high-tech aircraft rockets through the sky at supersonic speeds, but it is also capable of stealth takeoffs and landings. The Batwing includes many comforts of Batman's secret headquarters, the Batcave, such as a Batcomputer, a state-of-the-art communications system, and room for up to six passengers. The Dark Knight most often utilizes the Batwing for long-distance travel, air-to-air combat, and keeping up with his high-flying friends in the Justice League.

**LEVEL:** ★★★

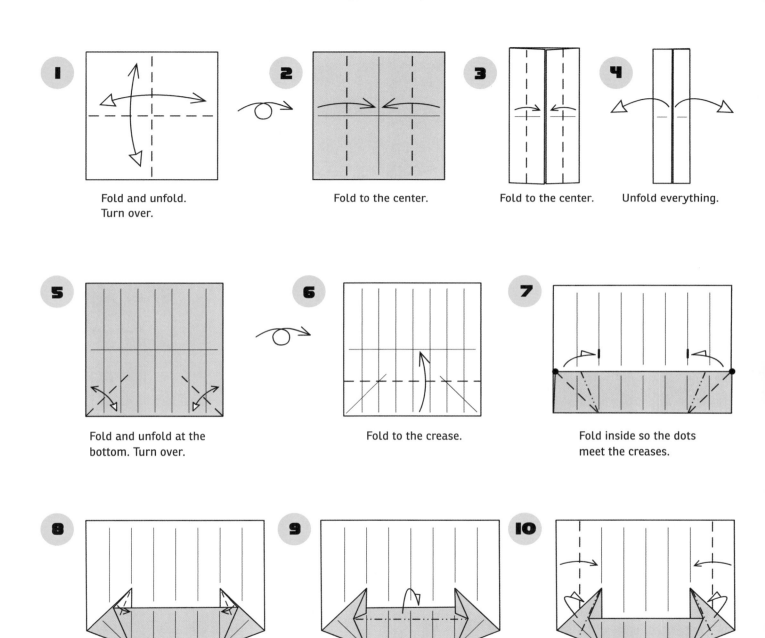

**1** Fold and unfold. Turn over.

**2** Fold to the center.

**3** Fold to the center.

**4** Unfold everything.

**5** Fold and unfold at the bottom. Turn over.

**6** Fold to the crease.

**7** Fold inside so the dots meet the creases.

**8** Fold the top layers.

**9** Fold inside.

**10** Reverse folds. Valley-fold along the creases.

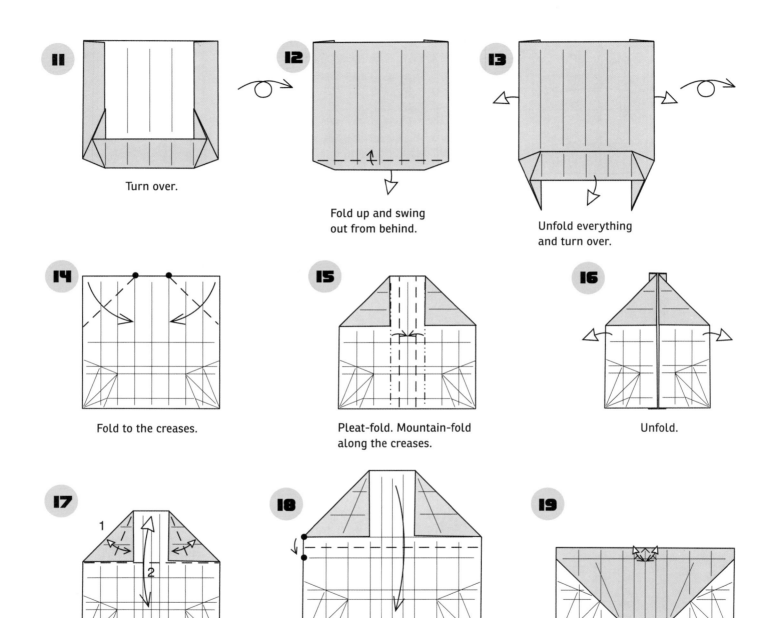

**11**

Turn over.

**12**

Fold up and swing
out from behind.

**13**

Unfold everything
and turn over.

**14**

Fold to the creases.

**15**

Pleat-fold. Mountain-fold
along the creases.

**16**

Unfold.

**17**

1. Fold and unfold both layers.
2. Fold and unfold.

**18**

Fold down so
the dots meet.

**19**

Fold and unfold.

**20**

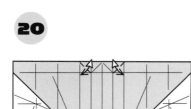

Fold and unfold.

**21**

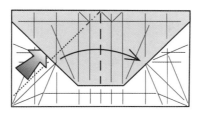

Squash-fold but only crease at the top.

**22**

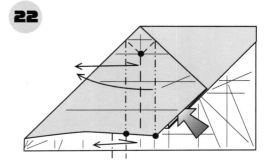

Push in at the upper dot. Bring the two mountain fold lines together, and pleat at the bottom.

**23**

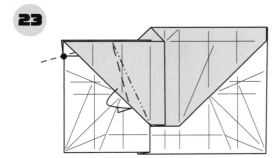

Fold inside. Begin with the mountain fold along the crease and continue to the dot.

**24**

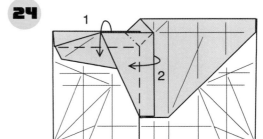

1. Fold down while ...
2. ... folding to the left.

**25**

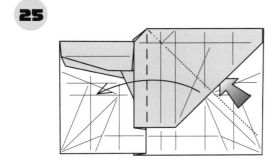

Repeat steps 21–24 on the right.

**26**

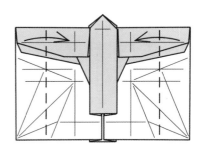

Fold along the creases.

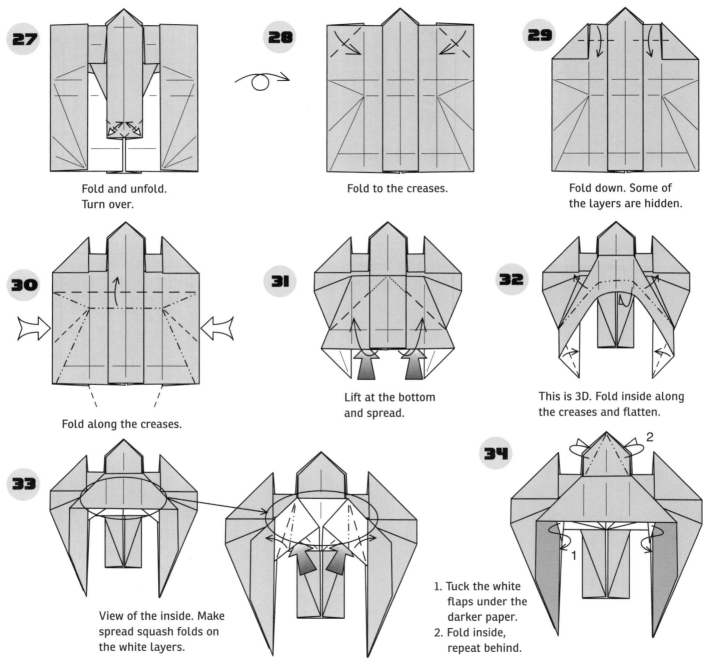

**27** Fold and unfold. Turn over.

**28** Fold to the creases.

**29** Fold down. Some of the layers are hidden.

**30** Fold along the creases.

**31** Lift at the bottom and spread.

**32** This is 3D. Fold inside along the creases and flatten.

**33** View of the inside. Make spread squash folds on the white layers.

**34**
1. Tuck the white flaps under the darker paper.
2. Fold inside, repeat behind.

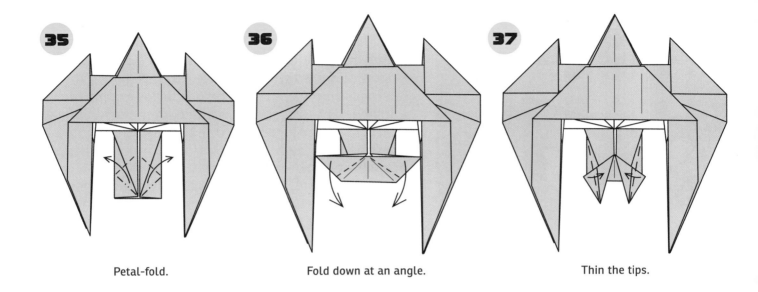

**35** Petal-fold.

**36** Fold down at an angle.

**37** Thin the tips.

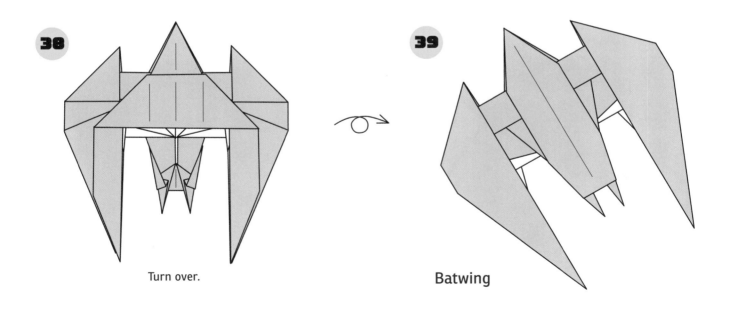

**38** Turn over.

**39** Batwing

# CLAYFACE

Half-man, half-muck, Clayface is a monster with a human heart and brain. Formerly a famous film actor, Matt Hagen's face, and career, were ruined in a tragic car accident. Hoping to regain his good looks, Hagen accepted the help of Roland Daggett. The slimy businessman gave the actor a special cream that allowed him to reshape his face as though it were made from clay. But Hagen became greedy and wanted more. Then he got caught stealing the ominous ointment. As punishment, the angry Daggett forced him to consume an entire barrel. But the supposedly deadly dose didn't kill Hagen. It turned him into a shape-shifting creature with only one thing on his muddy mind: revenge!

**LEVEL:** ★★★

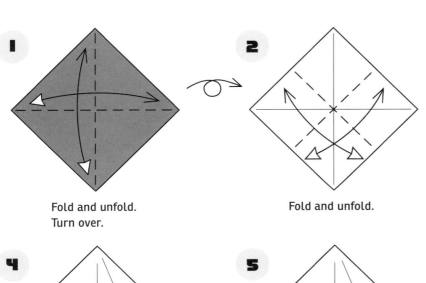

**1** Fold and unfold.
Turn over.

**2** Fold and unfold.

**3** Fold and unfold
on the right.

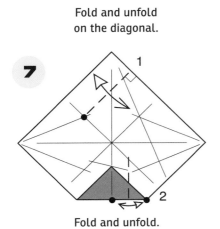

**4** Fold and unfold
on the diagonal.

**5**
1. Fold to the dot.
2. Fold and unfold.

**6** Fold and unfold.

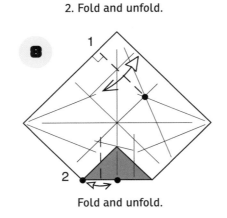

**7** Fold and unfold.

**8** Fold and unfold.

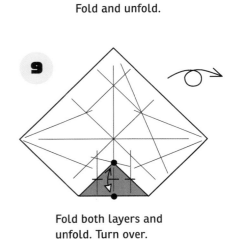

**9** Fold both layers and
unfold. Turn over.

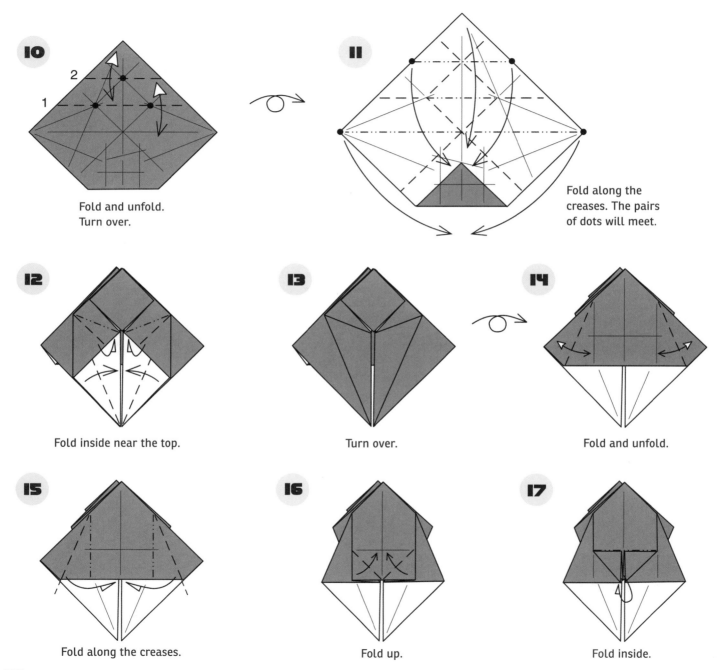

**10** Fold and unfold. Turn over.

**11** Fold along the creases. The pairs of dots will meet.

**12** Fold inside near the top.

**13** Turn over.

**14** Fold and unfold.

**15** Fold along the creases.

**16** Fold up.

**17** Fold inside.

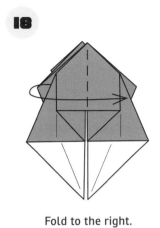

**18**

Fold to the right.

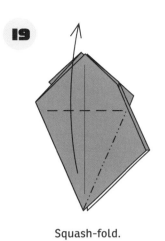

**19**

Squash-fold.

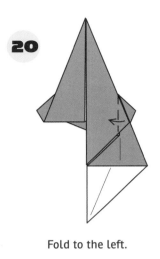

**20**

Fold to the left.

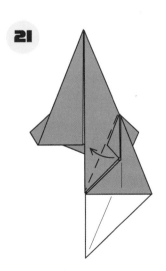

**21**

Fold to the left.

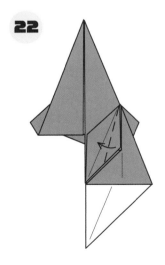

**22**

Fold to the left.

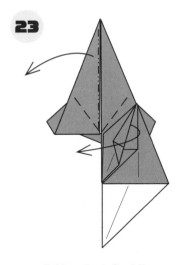

**23**

Fold to the left while folding the arm.

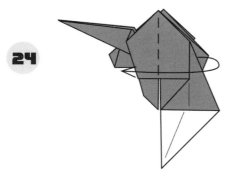

**24**

Repeat steps 18–23
on the right.

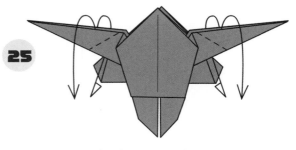

**25**

Outside-reverse folds.

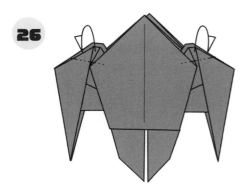

**26**

Fold inside, repeat
behind. Turn over.

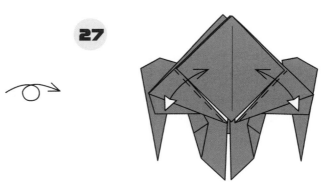

**27**

Fold and unfold.

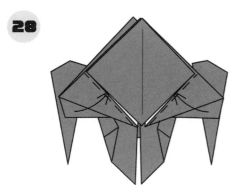

**28**

Tuck inside.

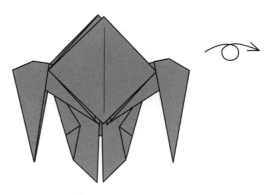

**29**

Turn over.

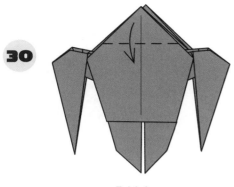

**30**

Fold down.

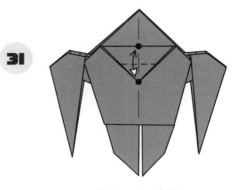

**31**

Fold and unfold.

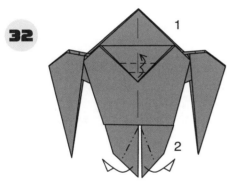

**32**

1. Fold along the crease.
2. Mountain folds.

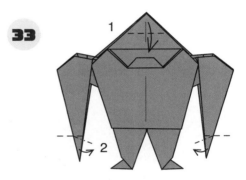

**33**

1. Fold down.
2. Squash folds.

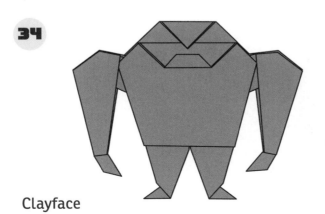

**34**

Clayface

# ROBIN

Robin, the Boy Wonder, battles alongside Batman to rid Gotham City of evil and corruption. No hero can go it alone, and among crime fighters, Robin is the best wingman around. Once a member of a world-famous family of circus acrobats, Robin was orphaned as a child. He soon signed on with the Dark Knight, using his awesome athletic skills against big-time baddies. Robin's symbol reminds Gotham City's citizens that, like his namesake, he too can swoop down and snap up a crooked worm or two for the city jail!

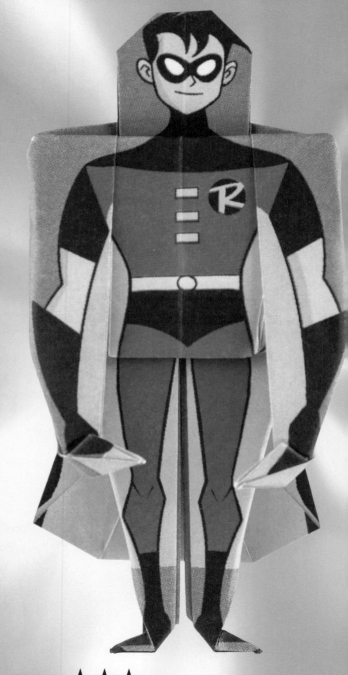

**LEVEL:** ★★★

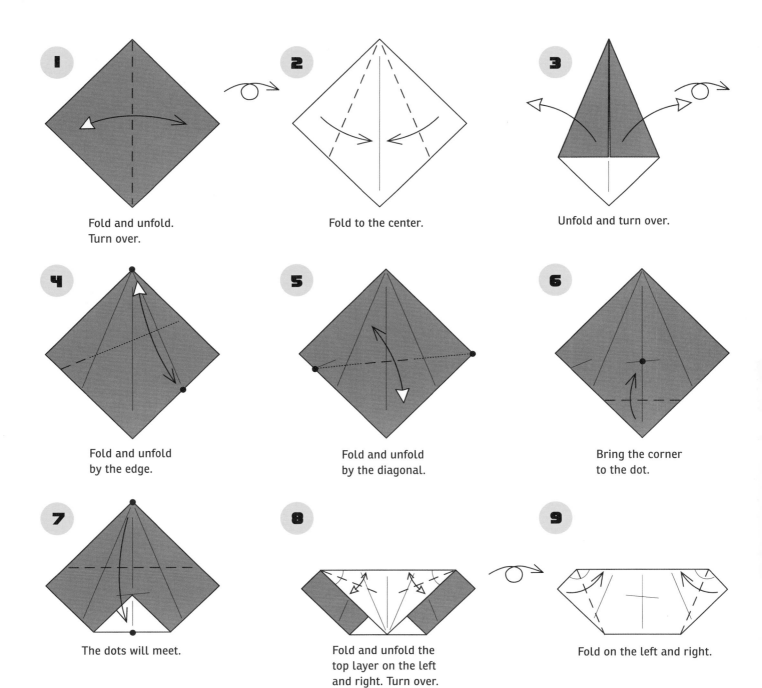

**1** Fold and unfold. Turn over.

**2** Fold to the center.

**3** Unfold and turn over.

**4** Fold and unfold by the edge.

**5** Fold and unfold by the diagonal.

**6** Bring the corner to the dot.

**7** The dots will meet.

**8** Fold and unfold the top layer on the left and right. Turn over.

**9** Fold on the left and right.

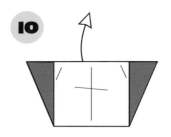

**10**

Unfold from behind.

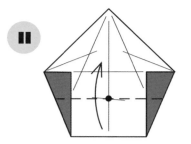

**11**

Fold by the dot.
Rotate model 180°.

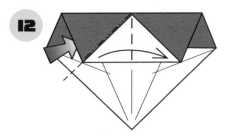

**12**

Squash-fold.

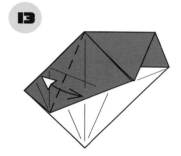

**13**

Fold and unfold.

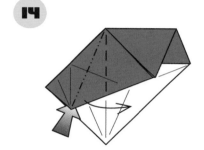

**14**

Squash-fold.

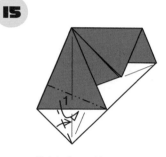

**15**

Fold along the creases
and tuck inside at 1.

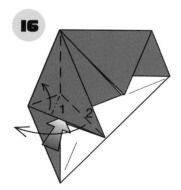

**16**

Lift up at 1 while
folding to the left at 2.

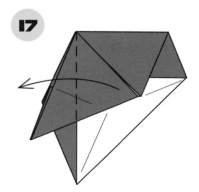

**17**

Fold to the left.

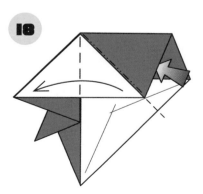

**18**

Repeat steps 12–17
on the right.

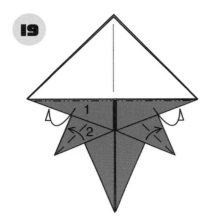

**19**

Fold behind at 1 while folding in half at 2.

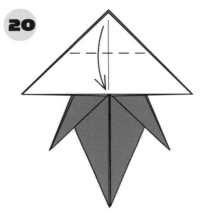

**20**

Fold down.

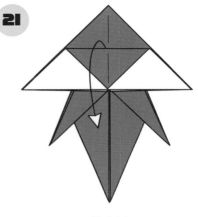

**21**

Unfold.

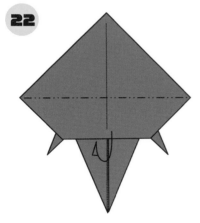

**22**

Tuck inside.

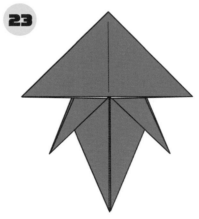

**23**

Turn over.

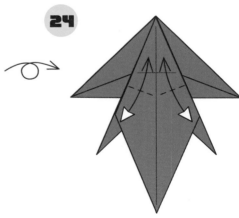

**24**

Fold and unfold along hidden edges.

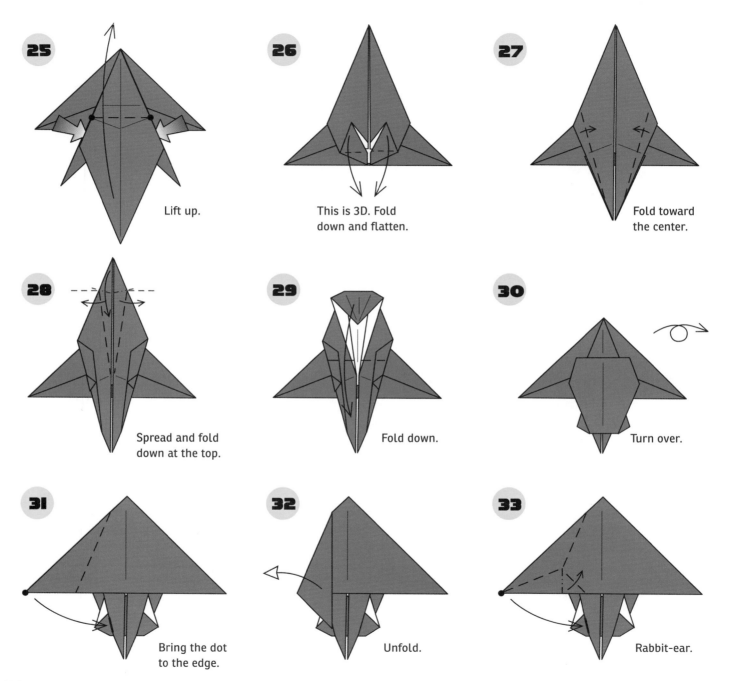

**25** Lift up.

**26** This is 3D. Fold down and flatten.

**27** Fold toward the center.

**28** Spread and fold down at the top.

**29** Fold down.

**30** Turn over.

**31** Bring the dot to the edge.

**32** Unfold.

**33** Rabbit-ear.

**34**

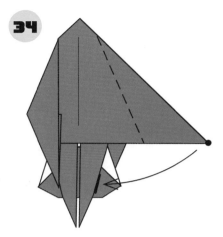

Repeat steps 31–33
on the right.

**35**

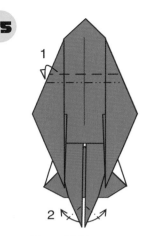

1. Pleat-fold between
   the body and cape.
2. Reverse-fold and
   spread the feet.

**36**

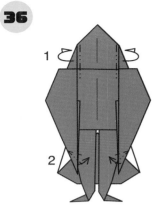

1. Fold behind and make
   small hidden squash
   folds at the neck.
2. Squash folds.

**37**

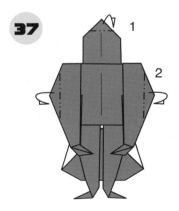

1. Fold behind.
2. Fold behind.

**38**

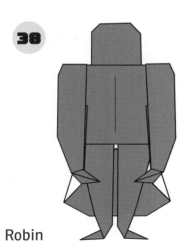

Robin

# BATMAN

The world's worst criminals prowl the streets of Gotham City, including the Joker, the Penguin, Catwoman, Poison Ivy, and Mr. Freeze. Thankfully, the city is protected by the World's Greatest Detective—Batman! While on a case, the Dark Knight protects himself with a flame-resistant cape, a high-tech cowl, and a Utility Belt filled with dozens of gadgets and weapons. Together, these items complete Batman's super hero uniform, known as the Batsuit.

LEVEL: ★★★

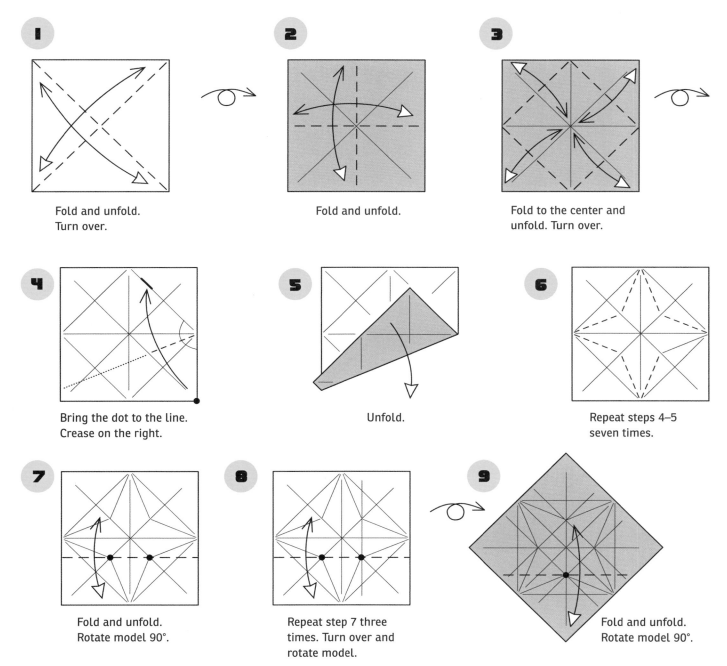

**1** Fold and unfold. Turn over.

**2** Fold and unfold.

**3** Fold to the center and unfold. Turn over.

**4** Bring the dot to the line. Crease on the right.

**5** Unfold.

**6** Repeat steps 4–5 seven times.

**7** Fold and unfold. Rotate model 90°.

**8** Repeat step 7 three times. Turn over and rotate model.

**9** Fold and unfold. Rotate model 90°.

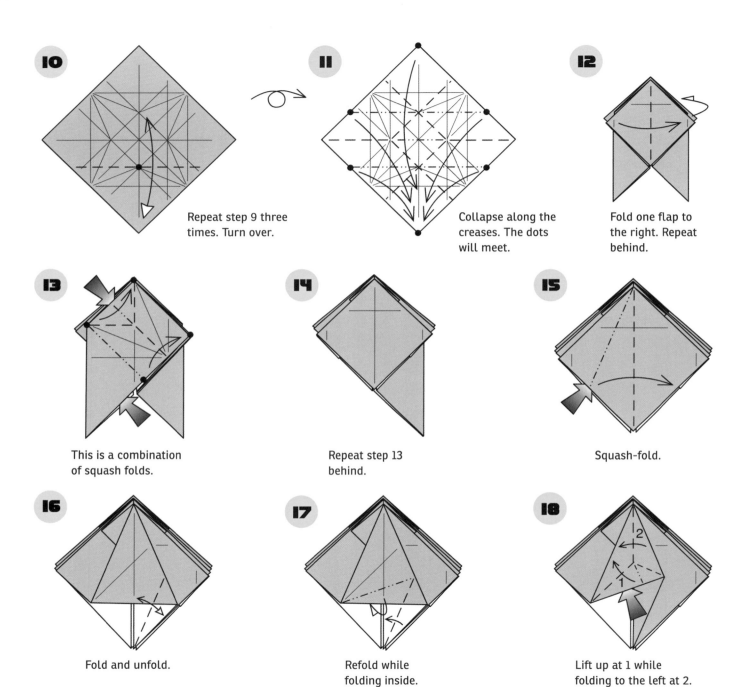

**10** Repeat step 9 three times. Turn over.

**11** Collapse along the creases. The dots will meet.

**12** Fold one flap to the right. Repeat behind.

**13** This is a combination of squash folds.

**14** Repeat step 13 behind.

**15** Squash-fold.

**16** Fold and unfold.

**17** Refold while folding inside.

**18** Lift up at 1 while folding to the left at 2.

**19**

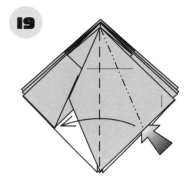

Repeat steps 15–18 on the right.

**20**

Repeat steps 15–19 behind.

**21**

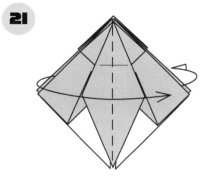

Fold the flaps to the right and repeat behind.

**22**

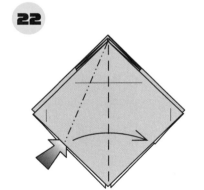

Repeat steps 15–19.

**23**

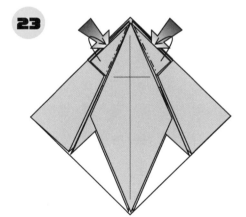

Reverse folds.

**24**

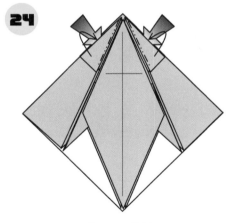

Reverse folds.

**25**

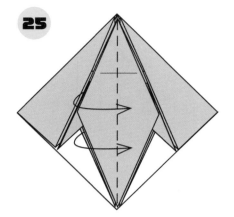

Fold a few layers
to the right.

**26**

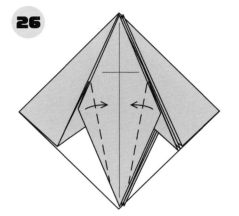

Fold toward the center.

**27**

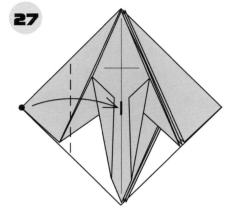

Fold to the center.

**28**

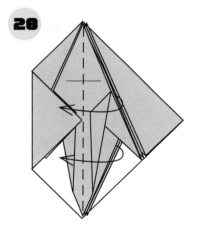

Fold a few layers
to the left.

**29**

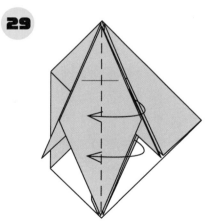

Repeat steps 25–28
on the right.

**30**

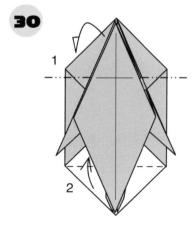

1. Fold behind.
2. Fold up.

**31**

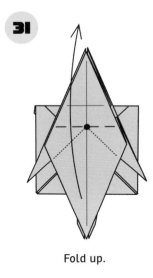

Fold up.

**32**

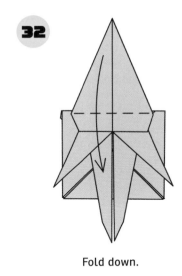

Fold down.

**33**

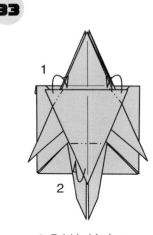

1. Fold behind on the left and right.
2. Fold behind.

**34**

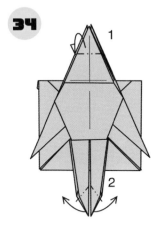

1. Fold behind.
2. Reverse folds.

**35**

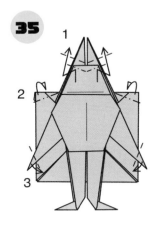

1. Crimp folds.
2. Fold behind.
3. Fold the hands.

**36**

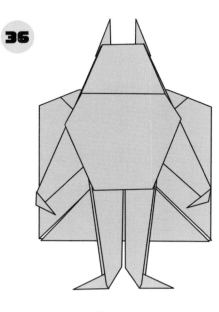

Batman

# THE SUPERMAN COLLECTION

™

# DAILY PLANET BUILDING

An icon of the Metropolis skyline, the Daily Planet Building is home to the city's most reputable newspaper, the *Daily Planet*. Beneath the building's distinctive globe, the World's Greatest Hero, Superman, hides in plain sight as mild-mannered reporter Clark Kent. Alongside fellow reporter Lois Lane, Clark gets the scoop on the day's top stories—when he's not too busy saving the day, of course!

**LEVEL:** ★☆☆

**1**

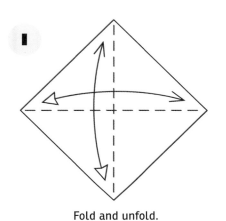

Fold and unfold.

**2**

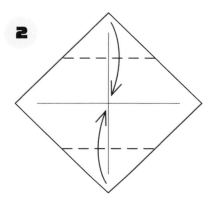

Fold to the center.

**3**

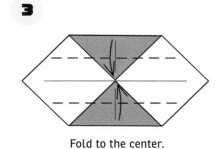

Fold to the center.

**4**

Fold to the left.
Rotate model 90°.

**5**

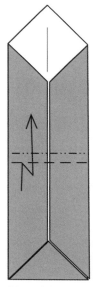

Pleat-fold.
Valley-fold along
the crease.

**6**

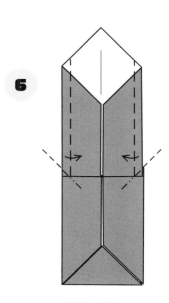

Make thin
squash folds.

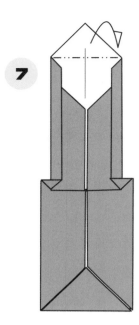

**7**

Fold behind.

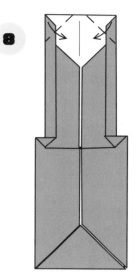

**8**

Fold toward
the center.

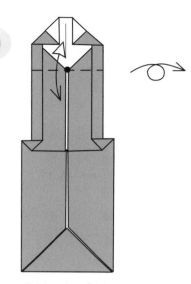

**9**

Fold and unfold.
Turn over.

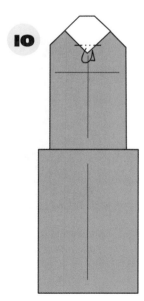

**10**

Fold behind.

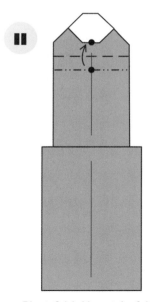

**11**

Pleat-fold. Mountain-fold
along the crease.

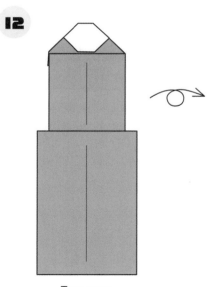

**12**

Turn over.

**13**

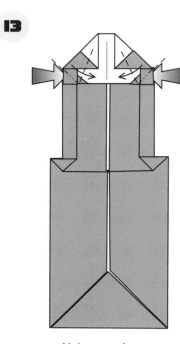

Make squash
folds under the
white layers.

**14**

Bend slightly so the
building is 3D and
can stand. Turn over.

**15**

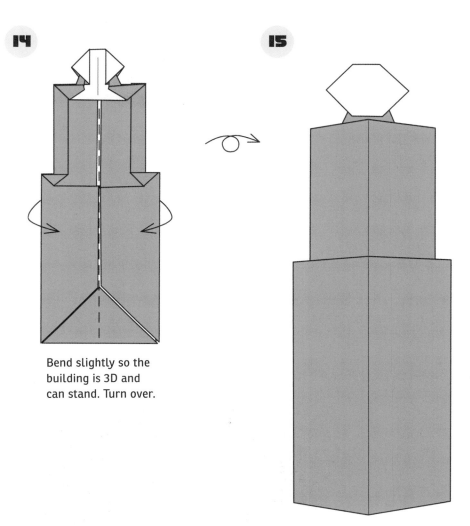

Daily Planet Building

# JIMMY OLSEN'S CAMERA

Jimmy Olsen, cub reporter for the *Daily Planet*, has no idea that his coworker Clark Kent is also his hero, Superman. Nonetheless, the red-caped champion and his redheaded buddy make a terrific team. Whether the Man of Steel battles Lex Luthor's latest evil invention or rescues the victims of a natural disaster, Jimmy is on the scene. With his trusty camera, he snaps perfect pics for fast-breaking scoops. And when the inquisitive kid's photos land him in hot water with crime lords or alien invaders, never fear! Jimmy signals his super-friend with his special wristwatch. Faster than a camera flash, Superman swoops in to protect his pal.

**LEVEL:** ★☆☆

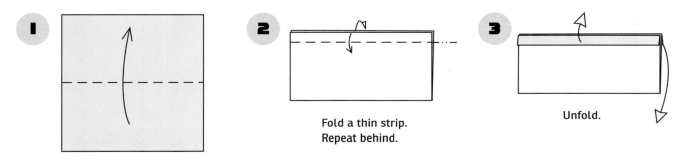

**1** Fold in half.

**2** Fold a thin strip.
Repeat behind.

**3** Unfold.

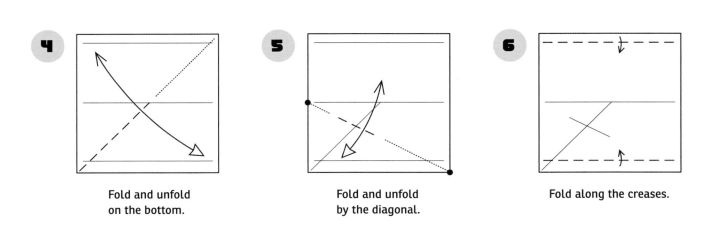

**4** Fold and unfold
on the bottom.

**5** Fold and unfold
by the diagonal.

**6** Fold along the creases.

**7**

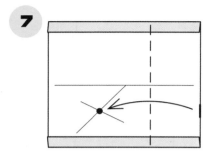

Fold to the dot.

**8**

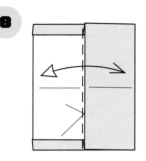

Fold and unfold.

**9**

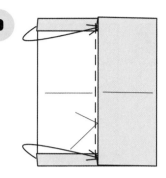

Tuck inside.

**10**

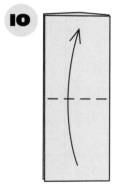

Fold along the crease
and rotate model.

**11**

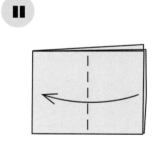

Fold the top flap.

**12**

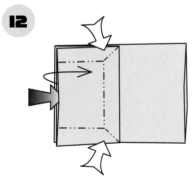

Open the flap on the
left, bring it to the center,
and make the rim round.
The model will be 3D.

**13**

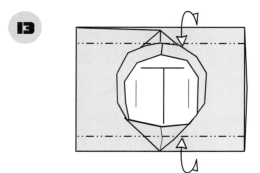

Fold and unfold all
the layers together.

**14**

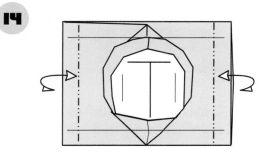

Fold and unfold all
the layers together.

**15**

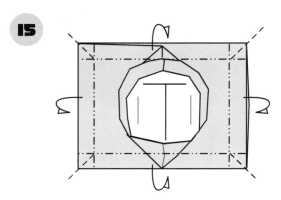

Fold the edges to
make the camera 3D.

**16**

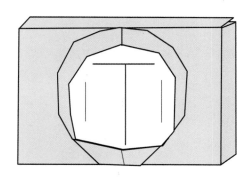

**Jimmy Olsen's Camera**

# CLARK KENT'S GLASSES

Superman's alter ego as mild-mannered reporter for the *Daily Planet*, Clark Kent, allows him to keep an ear and eye on breaking news. From natural disasters to criminal activity, the Man of Steel stays tuned in to major emergencies around the globe. Part of his disguise is a simple pair of glasses. People who see a guy with specs would never guess that he has X-ray or heat vision. Or that a quiet man like Kent could transform into the World's Greatest Hero in the blink of an eye!

**LEVEL:** ★★☆

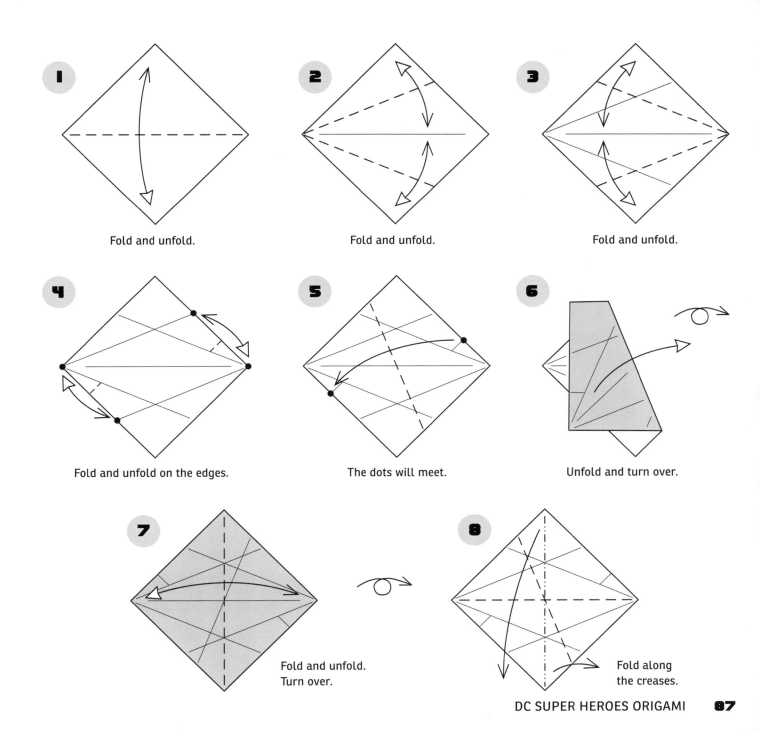

**1** Fold and unfold.

**2** Fold and unfold.

**3** Fold and unfold.

**4** Fold and unfold on the edges.

**5** The dots will meet.

**6** Unfold and turn over.

**7** Fold and unfold. Turn over.

**8** Fold along the creases.

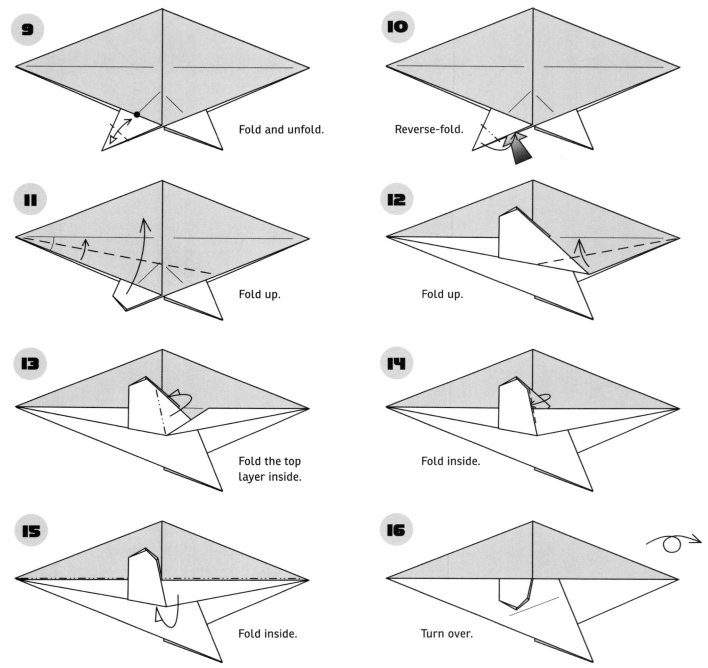

**9** Fold and unfold.

**10** Reverse-fold.

**11** Fold up.

**12** Fold up.

**13** Fold the top layer inside.

**14** Fold inside.

**15** Fold inside.

**16** Turn over.

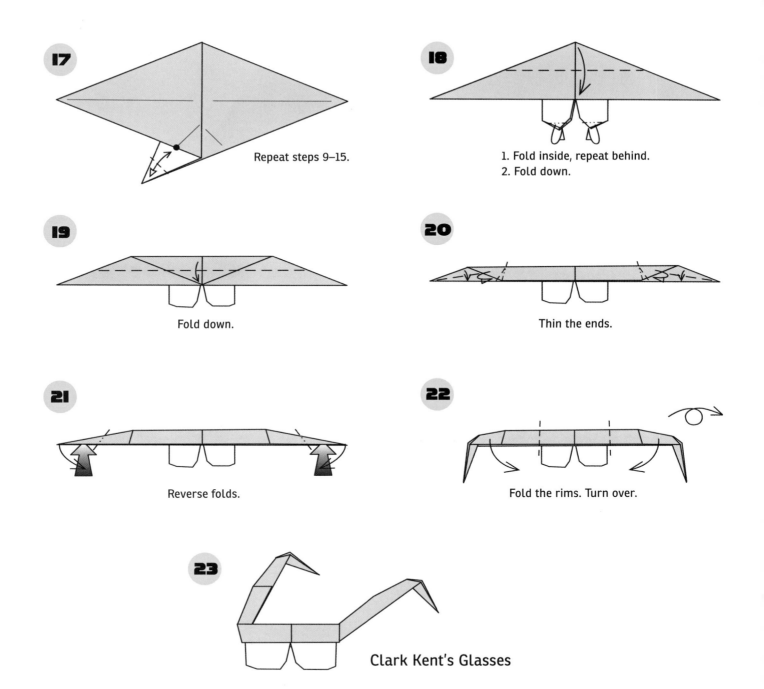

**17**

Repeat steps 9–15.

**18**

1. Fold inside, repeat behind.
2. Fold down.

**19**

Fold down.

**20**

Thin the ends.

**21**

Reverse folds.

**22**

Fold the rims. Turn over.

**23**

Clark Kent's Glasses

# KRYPTONITE

The Man of Steel has many superpowers: flight, freeze breath, heat vision, X-ray vision, and super-strength. He also has one terrible weakness—Kryptonite! When Superman's home planet exploded, fragments of Krypton scattered throughout the universe. Some shards even landed on Earth in the form of meteorites. These glowing, radioactive rocks come in a variety of colors, each having a unique effect on the Man of Steel. The most common form, Green Kryptonite, drains many of his superpowers, leaving him dangerously vulnerable to his vilest enemies.

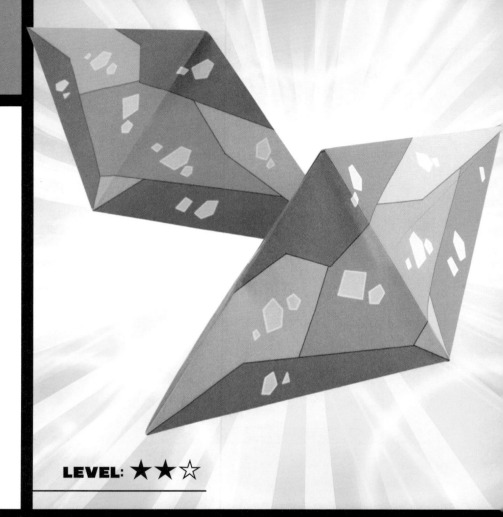

LEVEL: ★ ★ ☆

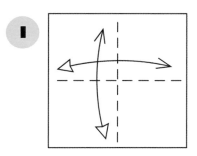

**1** Fold and unfold.

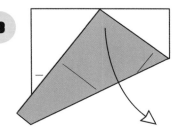

**2** Bring the lower corner to the dot. Crease on the left.

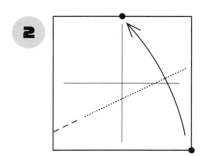

**3** Unfold and rotate model 180°.

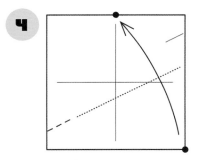

**4** Repeat steps 2–3.

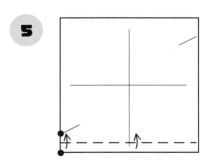

**5** Fold a thin strip up so the dots meet.

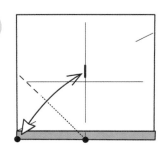

**6** Fold and unfold. Crease on the left.

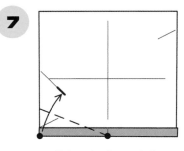

**7** Bring the lower left dot to the crease.

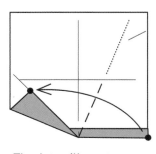

**8** The dots will meet. Crease on the lower half.

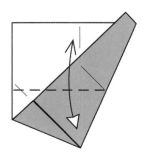

**9** Fold and unfold all the layers.

**10**

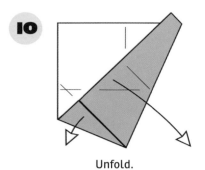

Unfold.

**11**

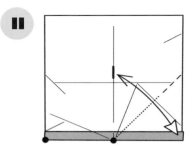

Repeat steps 6–10 on the right. Rotate model 180°.

**12**

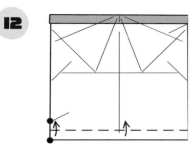

Repeat steps 5–11.

**13**

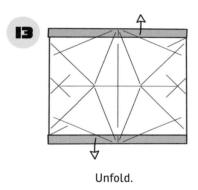

Unfold.

**14**

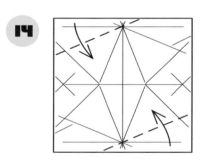

Fold along the creases.

**15**

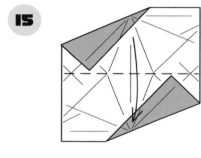

Fold in half.

**16**

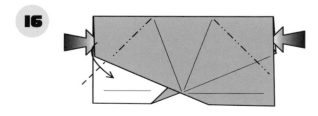

Reverse folds.

**17**

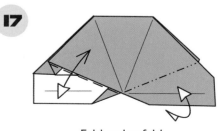

Fold and unfold.

**18**

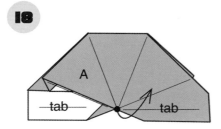

The dot will go to the right and the same below will go to the left. Follow region A.

**19**

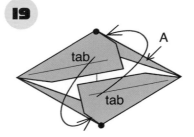

This is 3D. Tuck and interlock the tabs. The dots will meet.

**20**

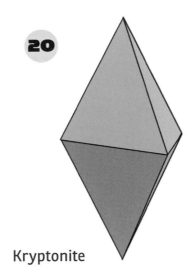

Kryptonite

# SUN

Moments before his home planet exploded, young Superman escaped by rocketing to Earth aboard a small, high-tech spaceship. After his arrival, Jonathan and Martha Kent, a loving couple in Kansas, adopted the child. Soon they discovered their growing boy's extraordinary abilities of flight, freeze breath, heat vision, X-ray vision, and super-strength. Little did they know, the Earth's yellow Sun actually fueled each of these superpowers. In fact, all Kryptonians experience the same benefits from Earth's Sun, including the Man of Steel's cousin, Supergirl.

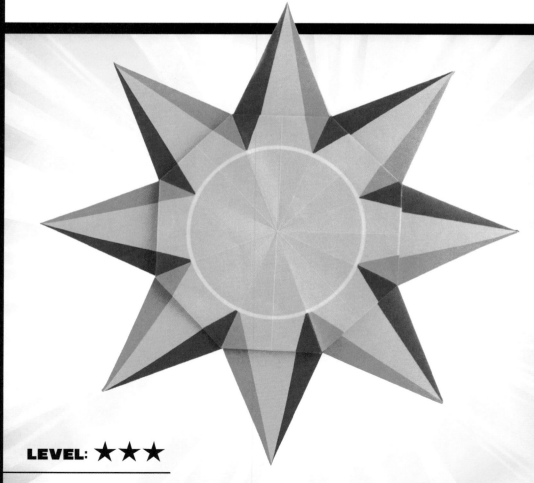

LEVEL: ★★★

**1**

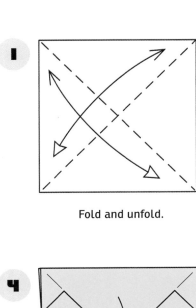

Fold and unfold.

**2**

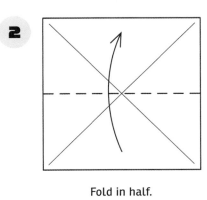

Fold in half.

**3**

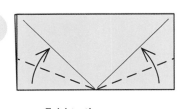

Fold to the creases.

**4**

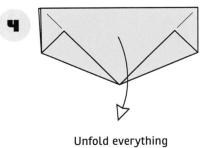

Unfold everything
and rotate model.

**5**

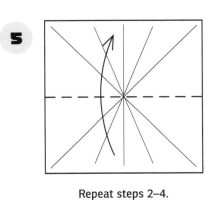

Repeat steps 2–4.

**6**

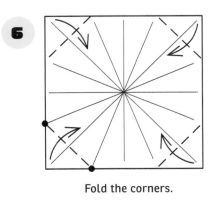

Fold the corners.

**7**

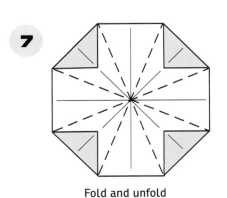

Fold and unfold
along the creases.

**8**

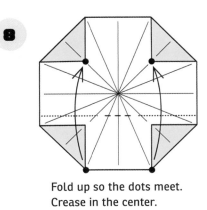

Fold up so the dots meet.
Crease in the center.

**9**

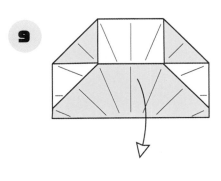

Unfold and rotate model.

**10**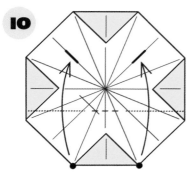

Fold up so the dots meet the bold lines. Crease in the center.

**11**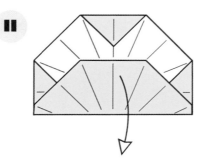

Unfold and rotate model.

**12**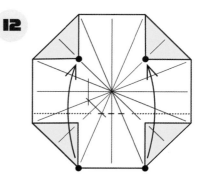

Repeat steps 8–11 three times.

**13**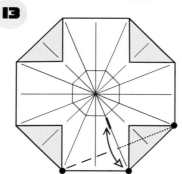

Fold and unfold on the lower half. Rotate model.

**14**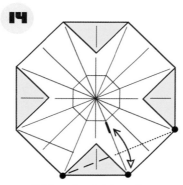

Fold and unfold on the lower half. Rotate model.

**15**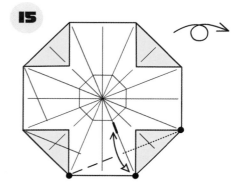

Repeat steps 13–14 three times. Turn over and rotate.

**16**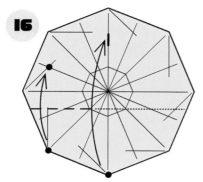

Fold up so the dots meet. Crease on the left.

**17**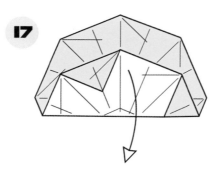

Unfold and rotate model.

**18**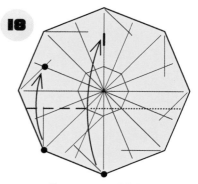

Repeat steps 16–17 seven times.

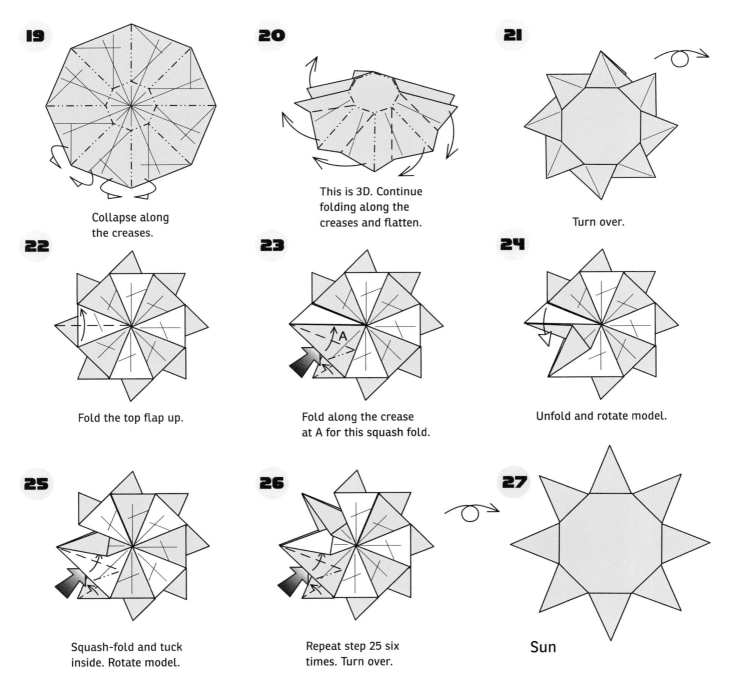

**19**

Collapse along the creases.

**20**

This is 3D. Continue folding along the creases and flatten.

**21**

Turn over.

**22**

Fold the top flap up.

**23**

Fold along the crease at A for this squash fold.

**24**

Unfold and rotate model.

**25**

Squash-fold and tuck inside. Rotate model.

**26**

Repeat step 25 six times. Turn over.

**27**

Sun

# FORTRESS OF SOLITUDE KEY

Hidden in the Arctic's wasteland, Superman's Fortress of Solitude serves as a headquarters, a laboratory, and a museum of wonders from across the universe. But getting inside the Man of Steel's fortress is no small feat. The citadel's gigantic door can be opened only with a colossal golden key, which only Superman can lift. Whenever the key is not being used, it stands disguised as a directional marker for airplanes flying over the frigid polar region.

**LEVEL: ★★★**

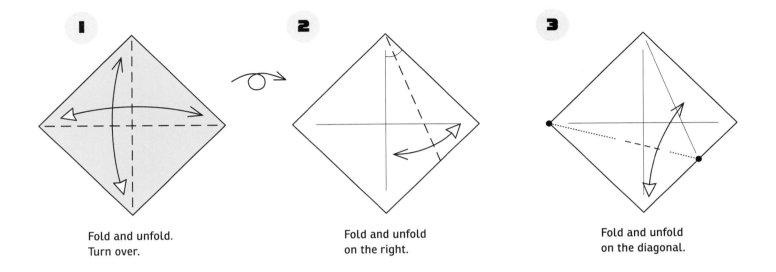

**1** Fold and unfold.
Turn over.

**2** Fold and unfold
on the right.

**3** Fold and unfold
on the diagonal.

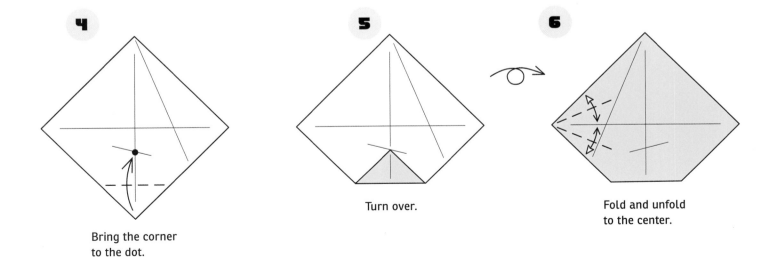

**4** Bring the corner
to the dot.

**5** Turn over.

**6** Fold and unfold
to the center.

**7**

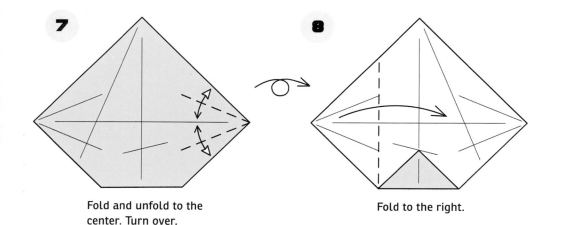

Fold and unfold to the center. Turn over.

**8**

Fold to the right.

**9**

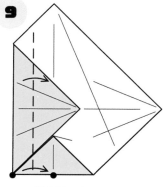

Fold to the center.

**10**

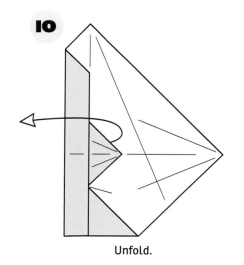

Unfold.

**11**

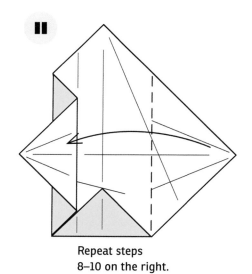

Repeat steps 8–10 on the right.

**12**

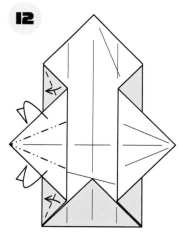

Fold inside along the creases.

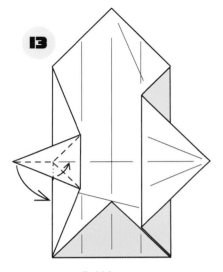

**13**

Rabbit-ear.

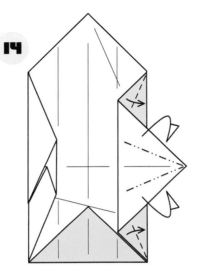

**14**

Repeat steps
12–13 on the right.

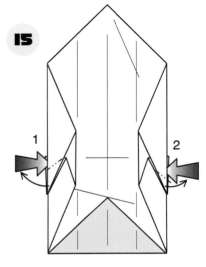

**15**

1. Reverse-fold.
2. Make a smaller reverse fold.

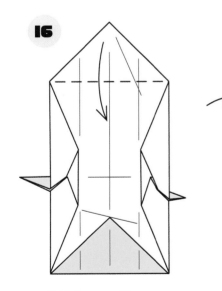

**16**

Fold down and turn over.

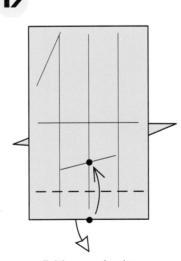

**17**

Fold up so the dots
meet and swing out
from behind.

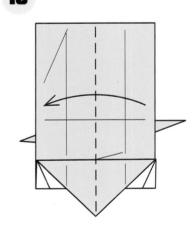

**18**

Fold in half and
rotate model.

**19**

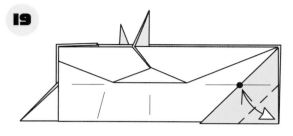

Fold and unfold all the layers.

**20**

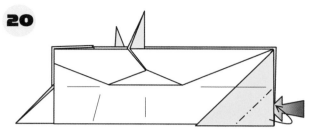

Reverse-fold.

**21**

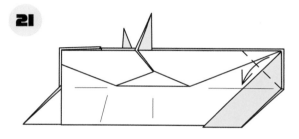

Fold the top flap. Do
not repeat behind.

**22**

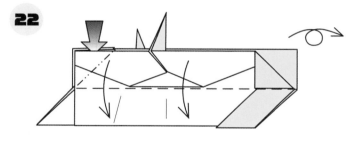

Squash-fold, repeat
behind. Turn over.

**23**

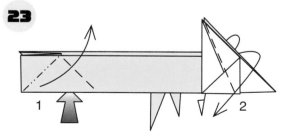

1. Squash-fold.
2. Outside-reverse-fold.

**24**

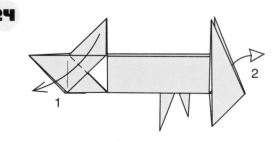

1. Fold down.
2. Pull out.

**25**

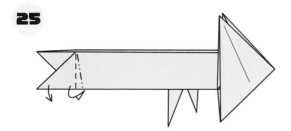

Pleat-fold. Valley-fold
along the vertical line.

**26**

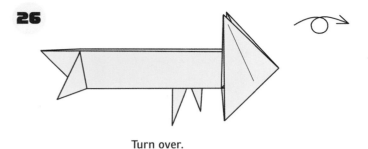

Turn over.

**27**

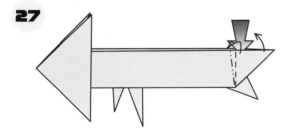

Push inside. Valley-fold
along the vertical line.

**28**

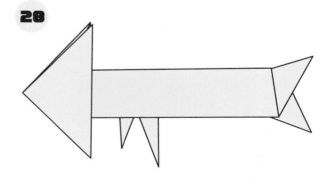

Fortress of Solitude Key

# S-SHIELD

On the planet Krypton, members of the House of El, including Jor-El and his wife, Lara, wore the S-shield as a symbol of hope. However, soon after their son, Kal-El, was born, nearly all hope was lost when Krypton exploded. Luckily, Kal-El escaped to planet Earth and grew into the super hero known as Superman. Soon, the S-shield became a symbol of hope on Earth as the Man of Steel used his newfound powers to fight for truth and justice.

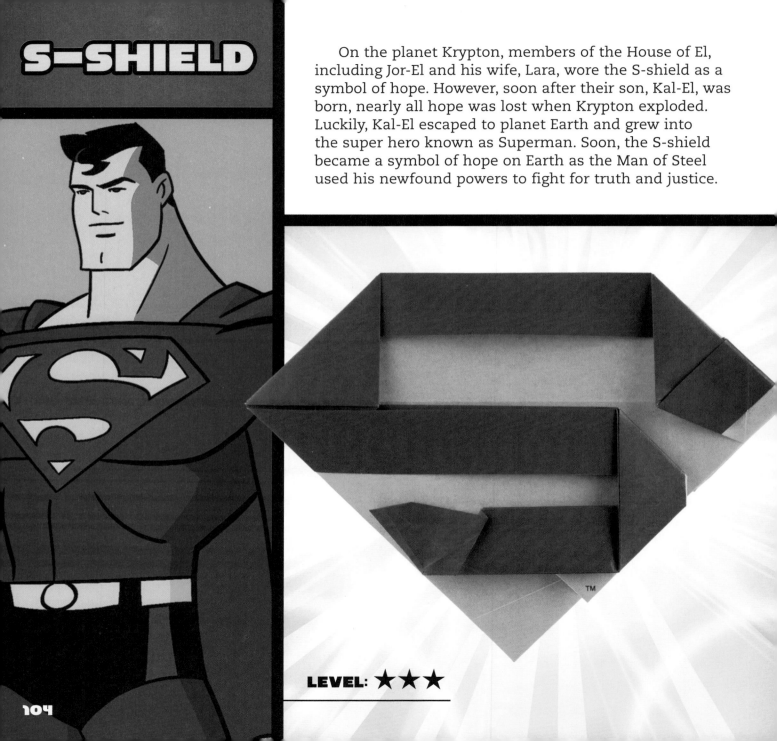

™

**LEVEL: ★★★**

**1**

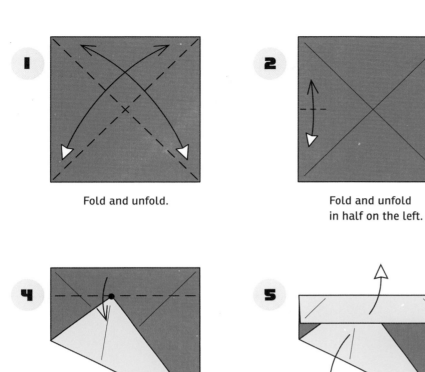

Fold and unfold.

**2**

Fold and unfold
in half on the left.

**3**

Fold up.

**4**

Fold down
at the dot.

**5**

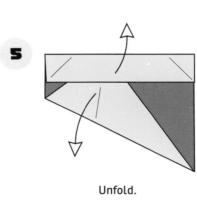

Unfold.

**6**

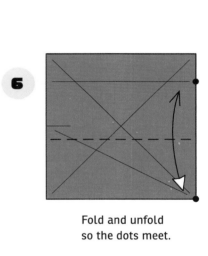

Fold and unfold
so the dots meet.

**7**

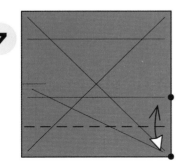

Fold and unfold.

**8**

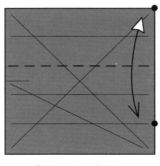

Fold and unfold.
Rotate model 180°.

**9**

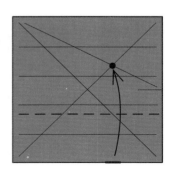

Fold the edge
to the dot.

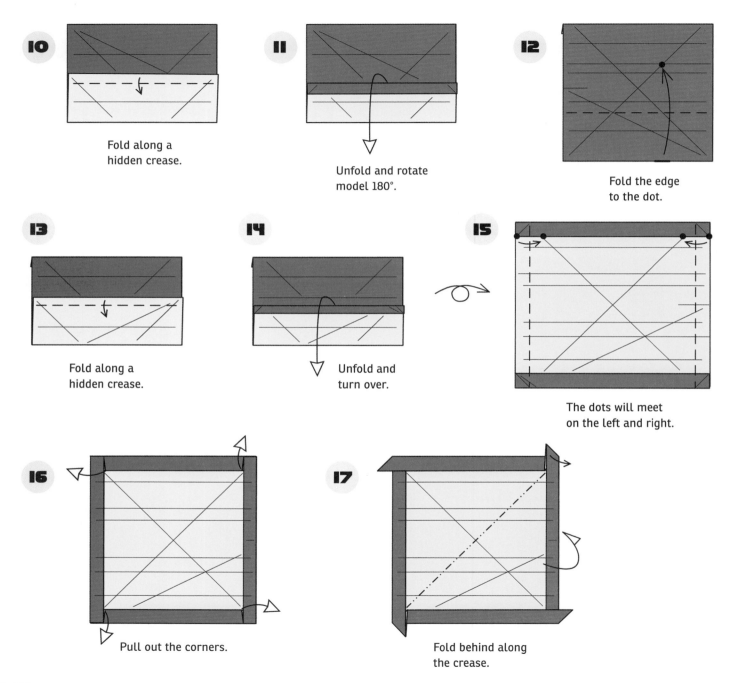

**10** Fold along a hidden crease.

**11** Unfold and rotate model 180°.

**12** Fold the edge to the dot.

**13** Fold along a hidden crease.

**14** Unfold and turn over.

**15** The dots will meet on the left and right.

**16** Pull out the corners.

**17** Fold behind along the crease.

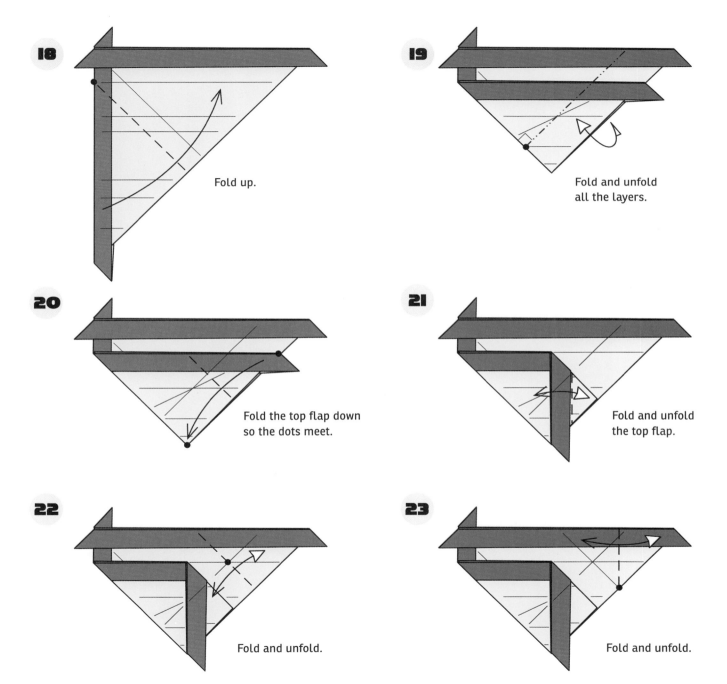

**18** Fold up.

**19** Fold and unfold all the layers.

**20** Fold the top flap down so the dots meet.

**21** Fold and unfold the top flap.

**22** Fold and unfold.

**23** Fold and unfold.

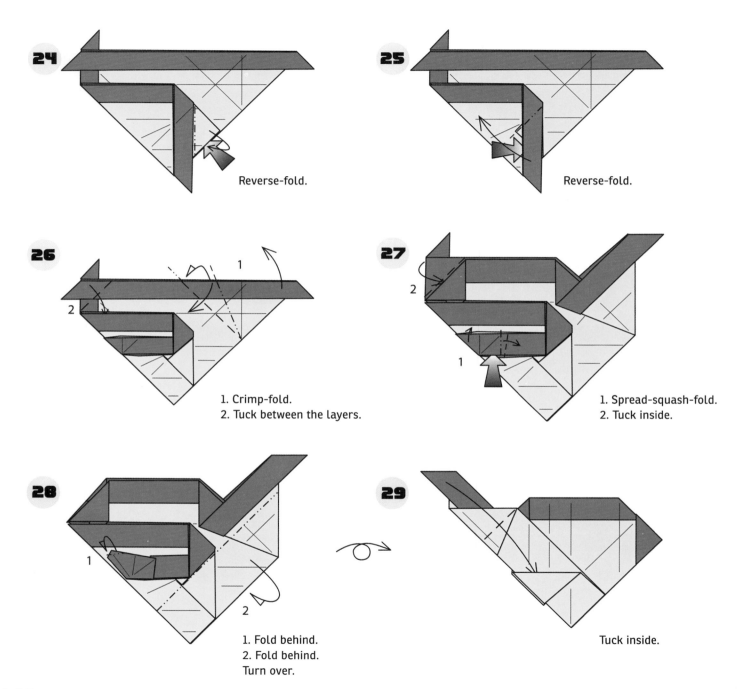

**24**

Reverse-fold.

**25**

Reverse-fold.

**26**

1. Crimp-fold.
2. Tuck between the layers.

**27**

1. Spread-squash-fold.
2. Tuck inside.

**28**

1. Fold behind.
2. Fold behind.
Turn over.

**29**

Tuck inside.

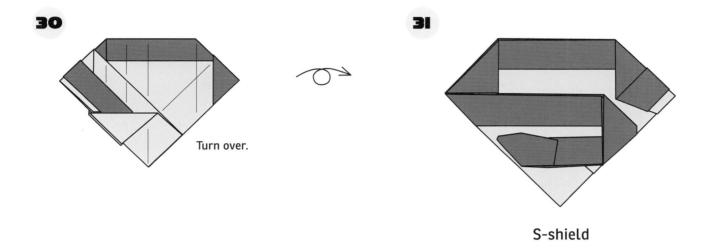

**30**

Turn over.

**31**

S-shield

To fold the Bizarro S-shield, begin
with step 16 of the S-shield.

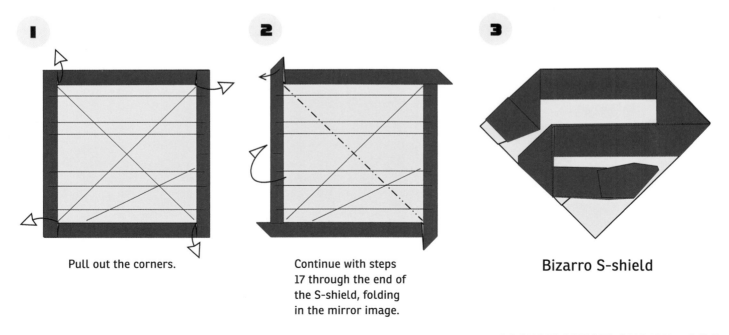

**1**

Pull out the corners.

**2**

Continue with steps
17 through the end of
the S-shield, folding
in the mirror image.

**3**

Bizarro S-shield

# KRYPTO

As a young pup, Krypto grew up on the planet Krypton, Superman's home world. Just weeks before Krypton exploded, the Super-Dog escaped aboard an experimental rocket ship. On Earth, the yellow Sun gave Krypto the same superpowers as his master, the Man of Steel. With these powers, Krypto the Super-Dog leads the Space Canine Patrol Agents, a group of powerful pooches who protect the universe from evil. But, first and foremost, he's the Man of Steel's best friend.

**LEVEL:** ★★★

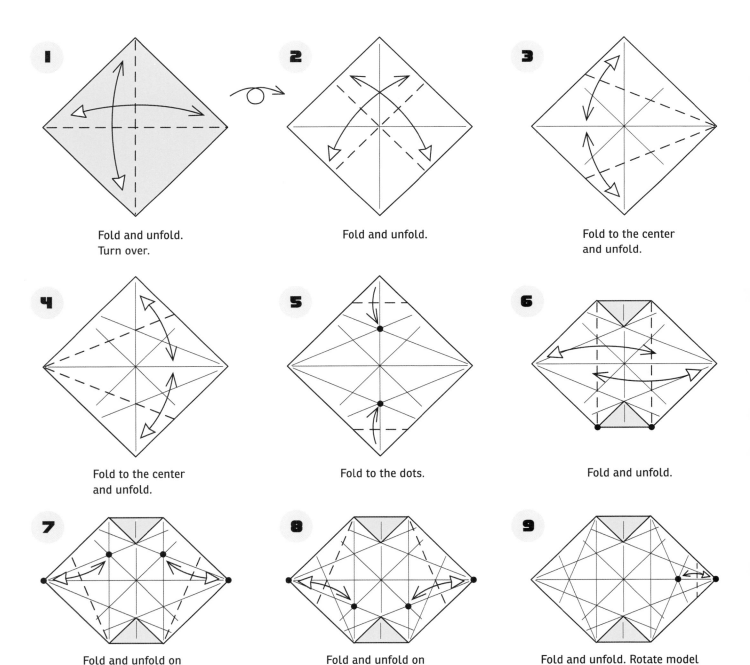

**1** Fold and unfold.
Turn over.

**2** Fold and unfold.

**3** Fold to the center
and unfold.

**4** Fold to the center
and unfold.

**5** Fold to the dots.

**6** Fold and unfold.

**7** Fold and unfold on
the left and right.

**8** Fold and unfold on
the left and right.

**9** Fold and unfold. Rotate model
so the dots are at the top.

**10**

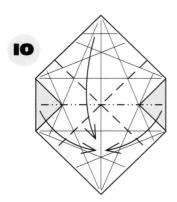

Fold along the
creases. This is similar
to the preliminary fold.

**11**

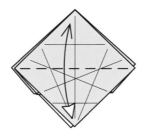

Fold and unfold
the top layer.

**12**

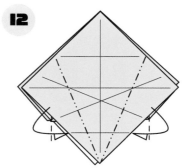

Make reverse folds
along the creases.

**13**

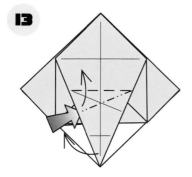

Squash-fold.

**14**

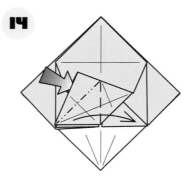

Squash-fold.

**15**

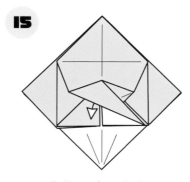

Pull out from inside.

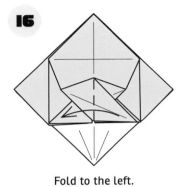

**16**

Fold to the left.

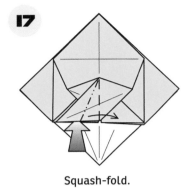

**17**

Squash-fold.

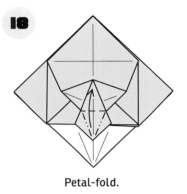

**18**

Petal-fold.

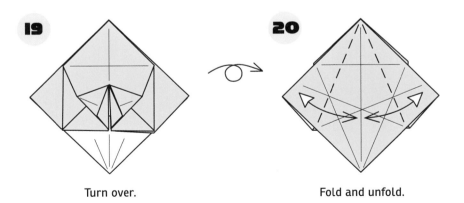

**19**

Turn over.

**20**

Fold and unfold.

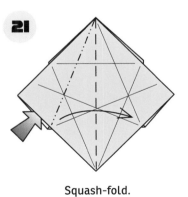

**21**

Squash-fold.

**22**

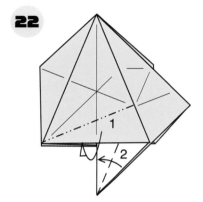

Fold behind at 1 while folding in half at 2.

**23**

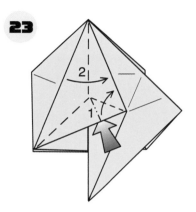

Lift up at 1 while folding to the right at 2.

**24**

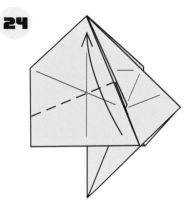

Fold along the crease.

**25**

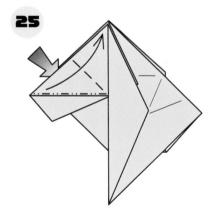

Squash-fold.

**26**

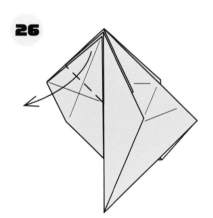

Fold the top flap.

**27**

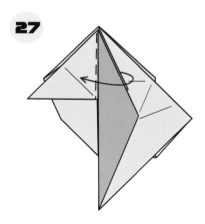

Fold the long, dark triangle to the left.

**28**

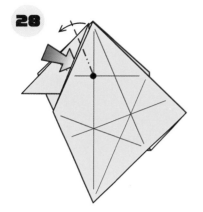

Reverse-fold the leg.

**29**

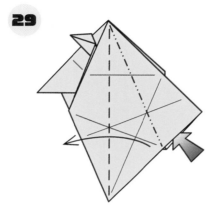

Repeat steps 21–28 on the right.

**30**

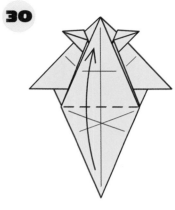

Fold up.

**31**

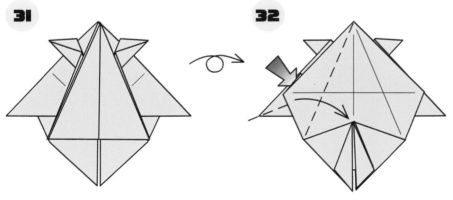

Turn over.

**32**

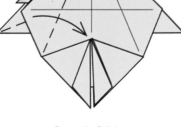

Squash-fold.

**33**

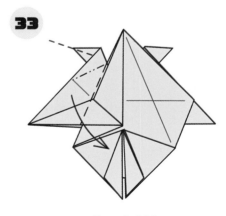

Squash-fold.

**34**

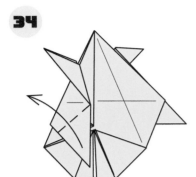

Fold the leg.

**35**

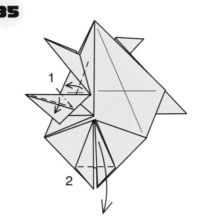

1. Squash-fold.
2. Fold down.

**36**

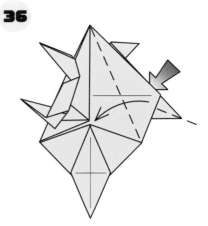

Repeat steps 32–35 on
the right for the legs.

**37**

Fold in half and
rotate model.

**38**

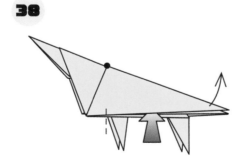

Pivot at the dot to
slide the cape.

**39**

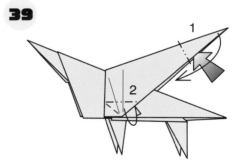

1. Reverse-fold.
2. Fold inside, repeat behind.

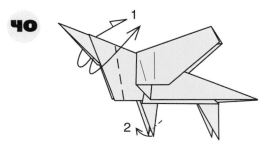

**40**

1. Outside-reverse-fold.
2. Reverse-fold, repeat behind.

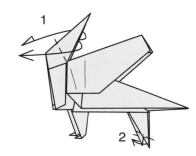

**41**

1. Outside-reverse-fold.
2. Crimp-fold, repeat behind.

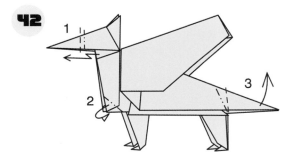

**42**

1. Crimp-fold.
2. Fold inside, repeat behind.
3. Crimp-fold.

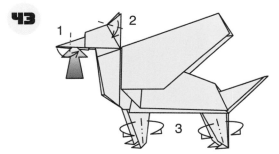

**43**

1. Reverse-fold.
2. Fold the ear down, repeat behind.
3. Thin and shape the legs, repeat behind.

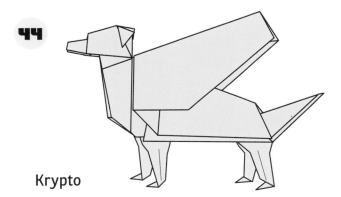

**44**

Krypto

# LEX LUTHOR

Lex Luthor is one of the richest and most powerful people in all of Metropolis. To most he's simply a successful businessman. But Superman knows Luthor's dirty little secret—behind the scenes he is actually a criminal mastermind! Superman has stopped many of Luthor's sinister schemes, but Lex is careful to avoid getting caught red-handed. While Lex wants to control Superman to strengthen his grip on Metropolis, the Man of Steel is immune to Luthor's influence.

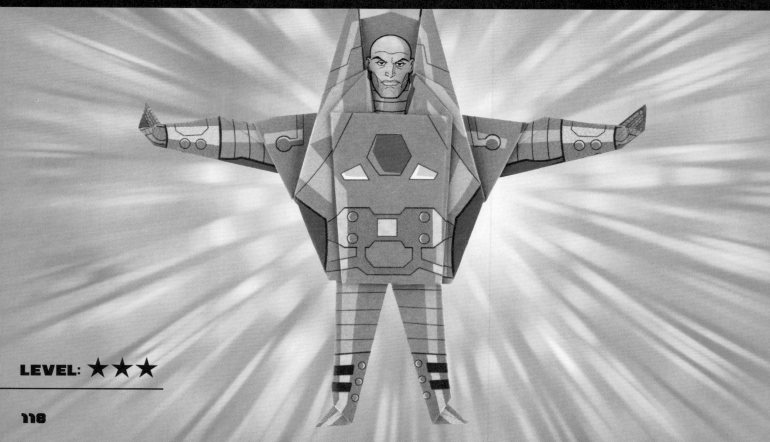

**LEVEL: ★★★**

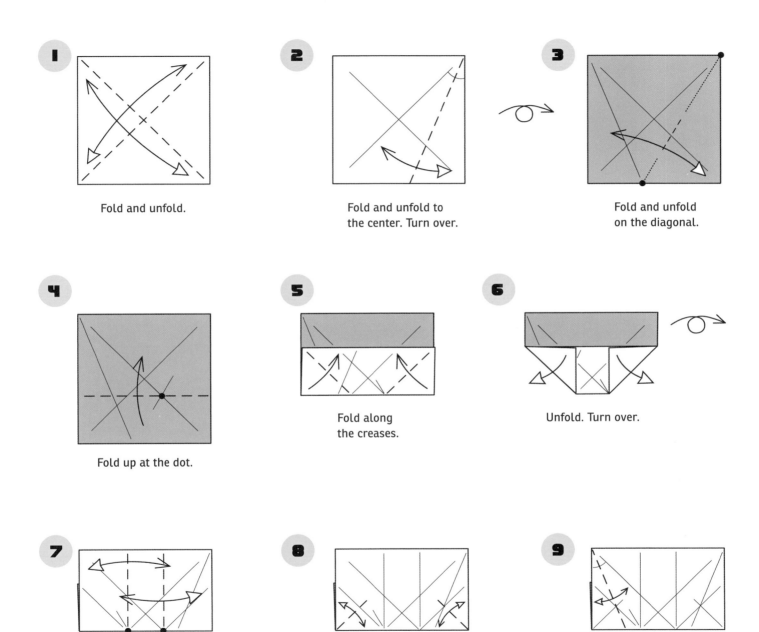

**1** Fold and unfold.

**2** Fold and unfold to the center. Turn over.

**3** Fold and unfold on the diagonal.

**4** Fold up at the dot.

**5** Fold along the creases.

**6** Unfold. Turn over.

**7** Fold and unfold.

**8** Fold and unfold the top layer.

**9** Fold and unfold on the left.

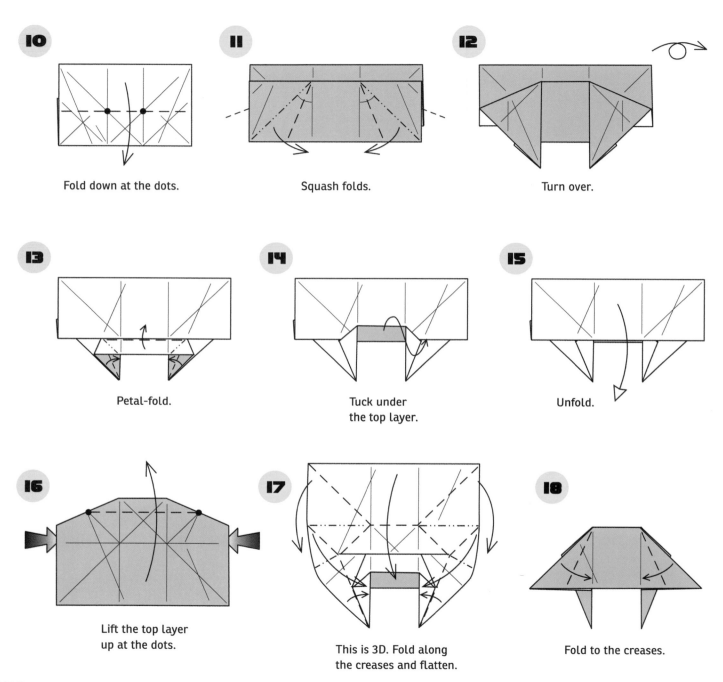

**10** Fold down at the dots.

**11** Squash folds.

**12** Turn over.

**13** Petal-fold.

**14** Tuck under the top layer.

**15** Unfold.

**16** Lift the top layer up at the dots.

**17** This is 3D. Fold along the creases and flatten.

**18** Fold to the creases.

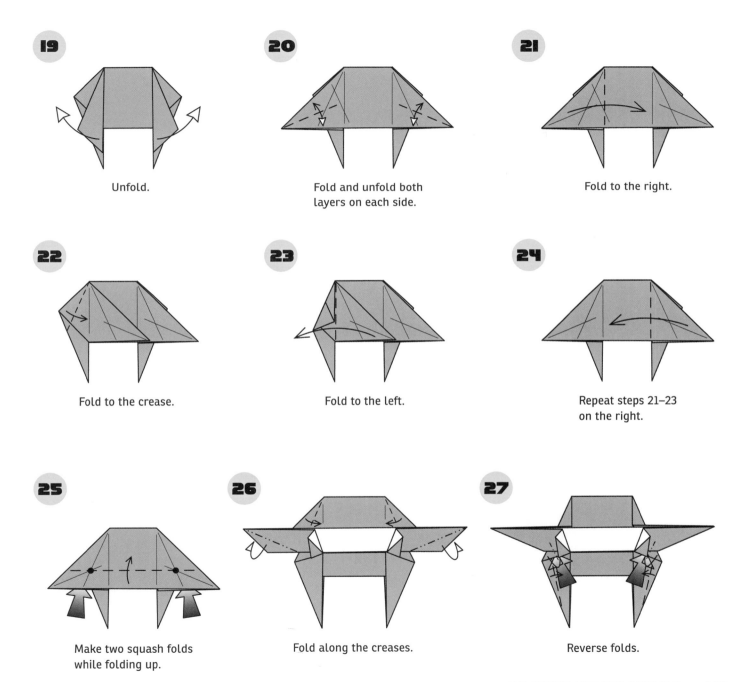

**19**

Unfold.

**20**

Fold and unfold both layers on each side.

**21**

Fold to the right.

**22**

Fold to the crease.

**23**

Fold to the left.

**24**

Repeat steps 21–23 on the right.

**25**

Make two squash folds while folding up.

**26**

Fold along the creases.

**27**

Reverse folds.

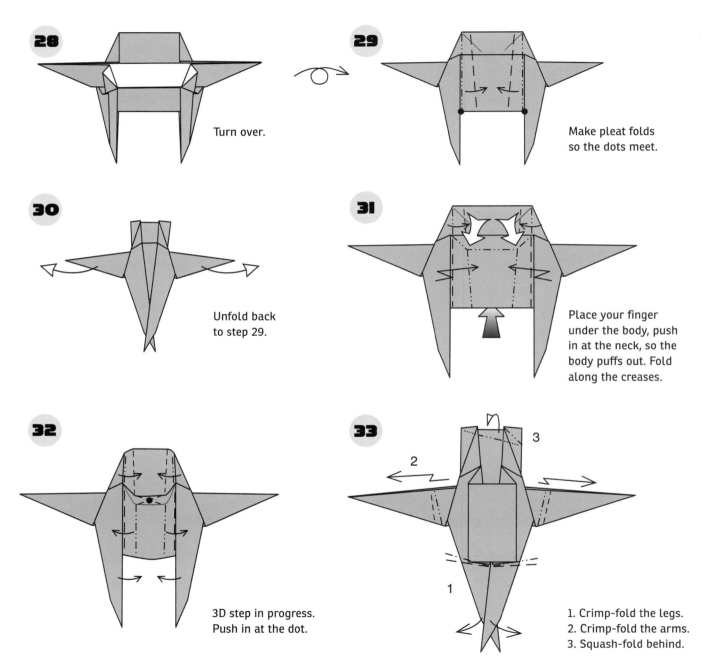

**28** Turn over.

**29** Make pleat folds so the dots meet.

**30** Unfold back to step 29.

**31** Place your finger under the body, push in at the neck, so the body puffs out. Fold along the creases.

**32** 3D step in progress. Push in at the dot.

**33**
1. Crimp-fold the legs.
2. Crimp-fold the arms.
3. Squash-fold behind.

**34**

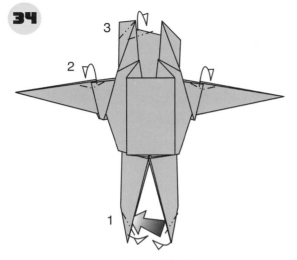

3

2

1

1. Squash-fold behind.
2. Fold inside, repeat behind.
3. Squash-fold behind.

**35**

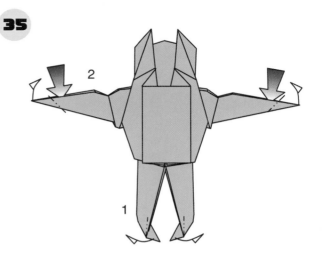

2

1

1. Fold the feet.
2. Squash-fold the
   hands from behind.

**36**

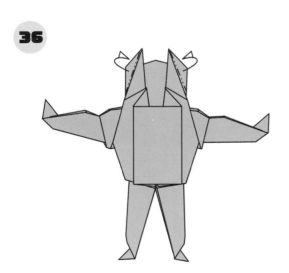

Fold behind.

**37**

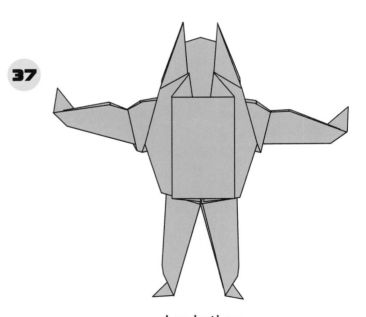

Lex Luthor

# SUPERMAN

An infant from an exploding planet. An orphan with amazing abilities above and beyond his peers. An alien teenager who kept an out-of-this-world secret. A bespectacled newspaper reporter who always scooped the biggest stories. Epic at any age, Superman is the World's Greatest Super Hero. He survived a doomed world to make our planet his new home. His powers and courageous heart are always on call to vanquish the evil, subdue the oppressors, defend the helpless, and protect the innocent. While others may strive to follow his lead or imitate his greatness, Superman is the ultimate hero.

**LEVEL:** ★ ★ ★

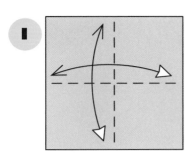

1

Fold and unfold.

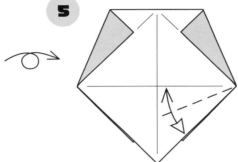

2

Fold to the center.

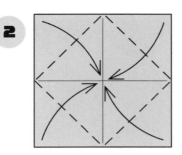

3

Fold to the edge.

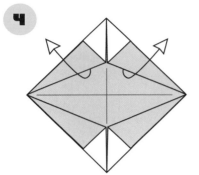

4

Unfold and turn over.

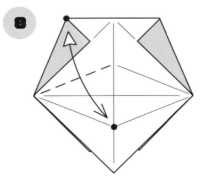

5

Fold to the crease
and unfold. Crease
on the right.

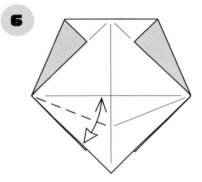

6

Fold to the crease
and unfold. Crease
on the left.

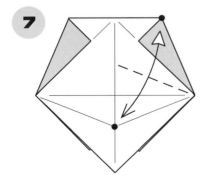

7

Fold and unfold so the dots
meet. Crease on the right.

8

Fold and unfold so the dots
meet. Crease on the left.

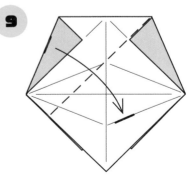

9

Bring the left edge
to the crease.

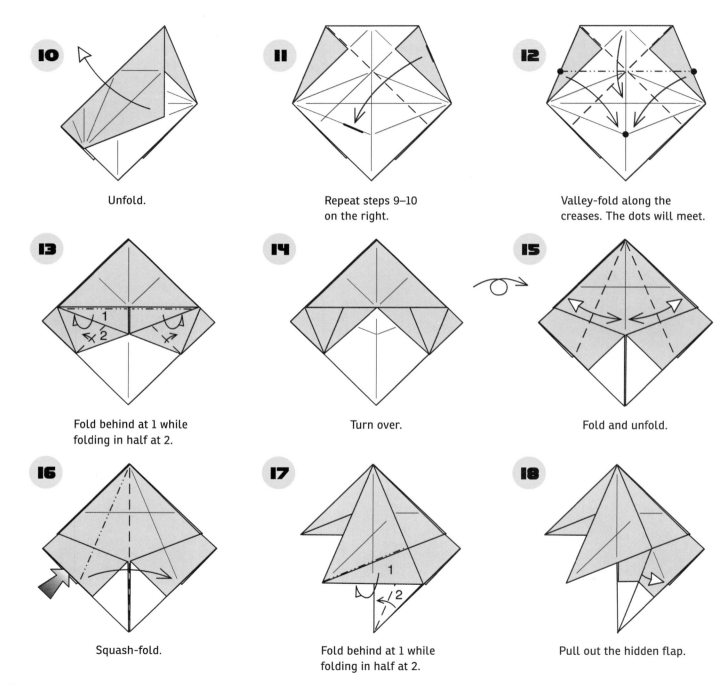

**10** Unfold.

**11** Repeat steps 9–10 on the right.

**12** Valley-fold along the creases. The dots will meet.

**13** Fold behind at 1 while folding in half at 2.

**14** Turn over.

**15** Fold and unfold.

**16** Squash-fold.

**17** Fold behind at 1 while folding in half at 2.

**18** Pull out the hidden flap.

**19**

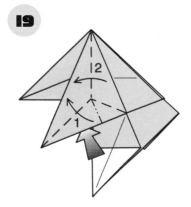

Lift up at 1 while folding to the left at 2.

**20**

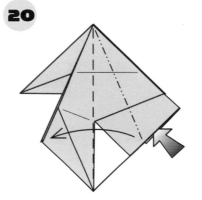

Repeat steps 16–19 on the right.

**21**

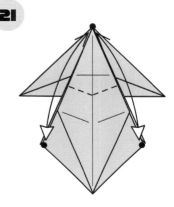

Fold and unfold on the left and right so the dots meet at the top.

**22**

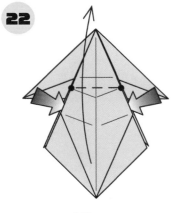

Lift up.

**23**

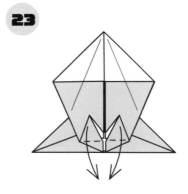

This is 3D. Fold down and flatten.

**24**

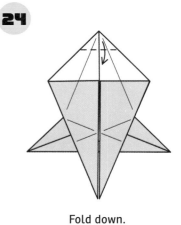

Fold down.

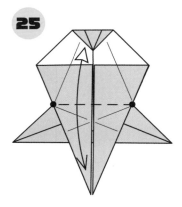

**25**

Fold and unfold.

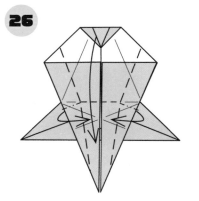

**26**

Thin the legs and cape while folding the cape down.

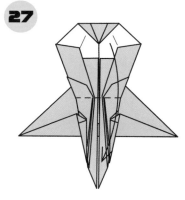

**27**

3D step in progress. Fold the cape down.

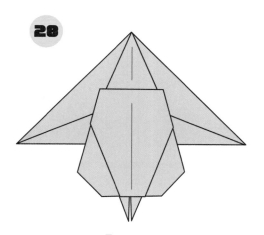

**28**

Turn over.

**29**

Rabbit-ear the arms. Bring the edges of the arms to the edges of the cape.

**30**

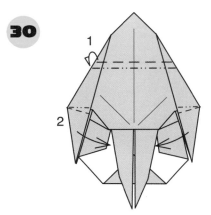

1. Pleat-fold between the body and cape.
2. Crimp-fold the arms.

**31**

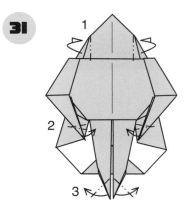

1. Fold behind and make small hidden squash folds at the neck.
2. Squash folds.
3. Reverse-fold and spread the feet.

**32**

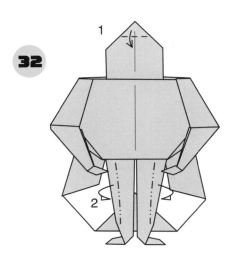

1. Fold down.
2. Thin and shape the legs.

**33**

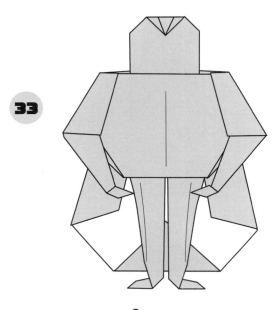

Superman

# SUPERMAN FLYING

Look! Up in the sky! It's a bird! It's a plane! It's Superman! The Man of Steel came to Earth as an infant, rocketing to safety before his planet of Krypton exploded. His father, the scientist Jor-El, knew that Earth's lower gravity and yellow Sun would grant his son, Kal-El, abilities far beyond those of mortal humans. His most striking ability is the power to fly. Superman can circle the globe in seconds. His uniform, made of Kryptonian materials from that early rocket ship, resists the friction of Earth's atmosphere and never burns up. The hero's familiar red and blue blur is a welcome sight as he arcs across the sky on a never-ending fight for truth and justice.

**LEVEL: ★ ★ ★**

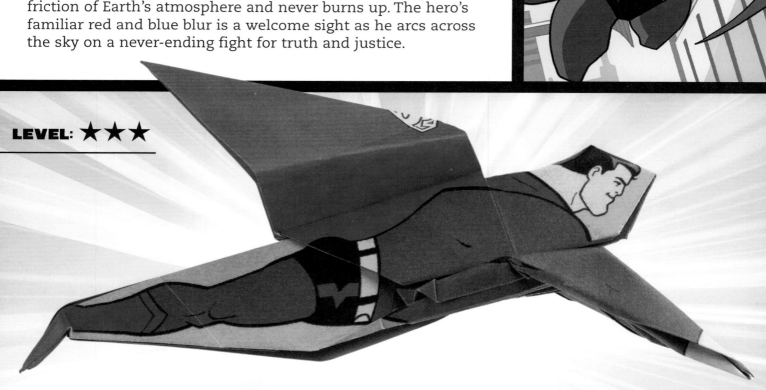

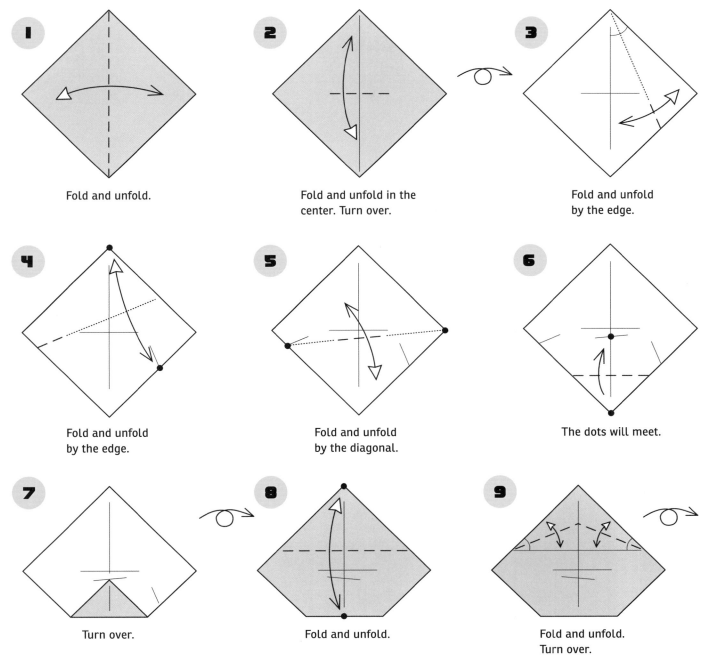

**1** Fold and unfold.

**2** Fold and unfold in the center. Turn over.

**3** Fold and unfold by the edge.

**4** Fold and unfold by the edge.

**5** Fold and unfold by the diagonal.

**6** The dots will meet.

**7** Turn over.

**8** Fold and unfold.

**9** Fold and unfold. Turn over.

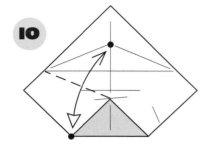

**10**

Fold and unfold.

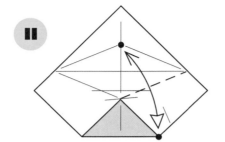

**11**

Fold and unfold.

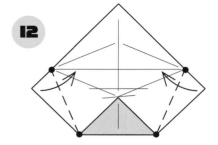

**12**

Fold by the dots.

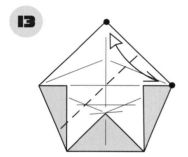

**13**

Fold and unfold.

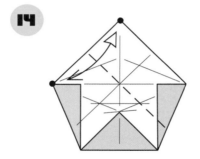

**14**

Fold and unfold.

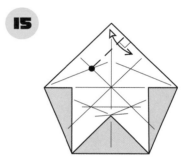

**15**

Fold and unfold
at the top.

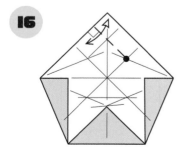

**16**

Fold and unfold
at the top.

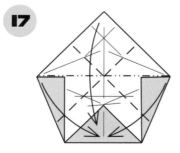

**17**

This is similar to the
preliminary fold.

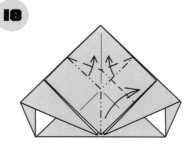

**18**

Fold along the
creases and flatten.

**19**

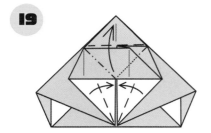

Petal-fold.

**20**

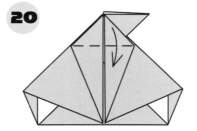

Fold down.

**21**

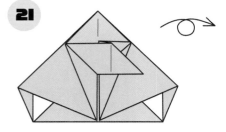

Turn over.

**22**

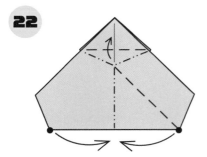

Fold along the creases.
The dots will meet.

**23**

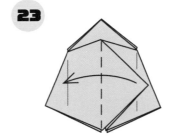

Fold to the left.

**24**

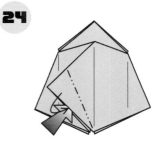

Reverse-fold.

**25**

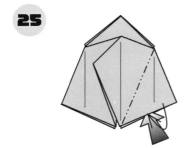

Reverse-fold.

**26**

Reverse-fold
hidden layers.

**27**

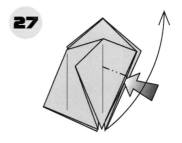

Reverse-fold.

**28**

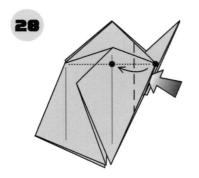

Fold to the center and
make a small squash fold.

**29**

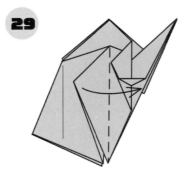

Fold to the right.

**30**

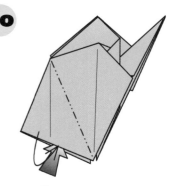

Repeat steps
25–28 on the left.

**31**

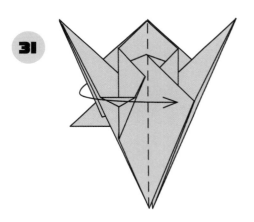

Fold in half and
rotate model.

**32**

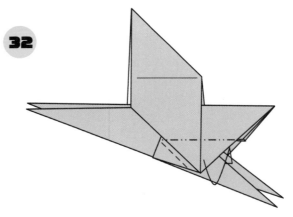

Fold inside and
repeat behind.

**33**

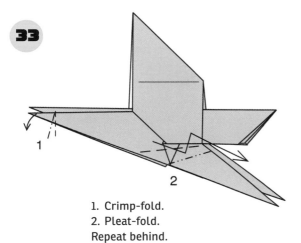

1. Crimp-fold.
2. Pleat-fold.
Repeat behind.

**34**

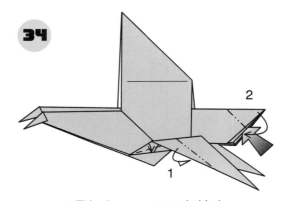

1. Thin the arm, repeat behind.
2. Reverse-fold.

**35**

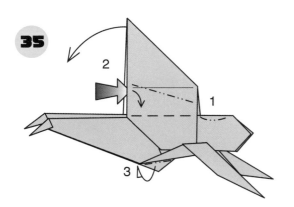

1. Shape the head.
2. Shape the cape.
3. Fold inside.

**36**

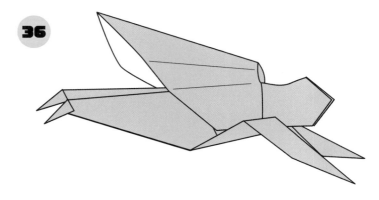

Superman Flying

# THE WONDER WOMAN COLLECTION

# WONDER WOMAN'S TIARA

Princess Diana, known to the world as Wonder Woman, is a true sovereign. Her mother, Hippolyta, is Queen of the Amazons, a race of warrior women who inhabit the hidden island of Themyscira. To declare her royal blood, Wonder Woman wears a golden tiara—which also serves as a weapon! With a flick of the wrist, she flings it through the air like a ninja star. The tiara's sharp, almost unbreakable metal can slice through rock, wire, and steel, giving the hero a crowning edge over her foes.

**LEVEL:** ★☆☆

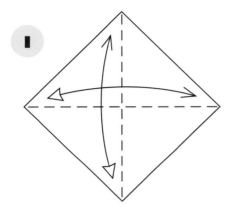

1

Fold and unfold.

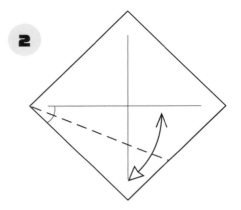

2

Fold and unfold.

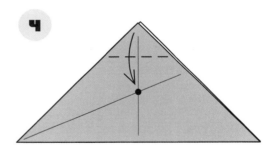

3

Fold in half.

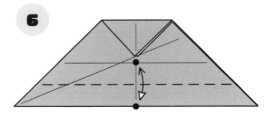

4

Fold both layers
to the dot.

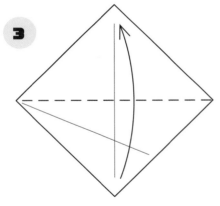

5

Fold and unfold.

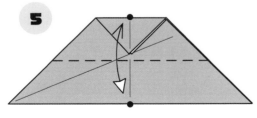

6

Fold and unfold.

**7**

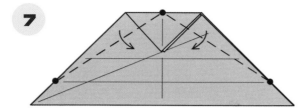

Fold on the left and right.

**8**

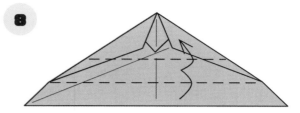

Fold along the creases.

**9**

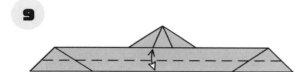

Fold in half and unfold.

**10**

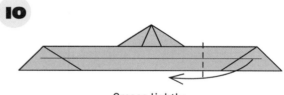

Crease lightly.

**11**

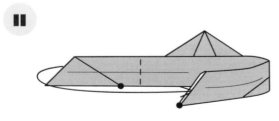

Tuck inside. The
dots will meet.

**12**

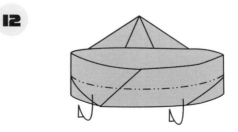

Fold inside and make
the band round.

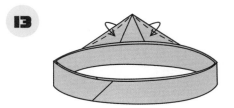

**13**

Fold the edges to
shape the tiara.

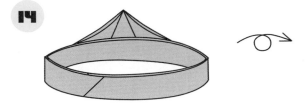

**14**

Turn over.

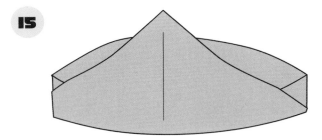

**15**

Wonder Woman's Tiara

# SILVER BRACELET

Wonder Woman frequently faces foes with fearsome weapons. Yet she wears no armor, and she carries no shield. Her gear is built for speed and freedom of movement, not for protection. But the Amazonian warrior does, it turns out, have a secret defense: her silver bracelets. The jewelry serves her better than a bulletproof vest. Combined with dazzling acrobatics, swiftness, and strength, the bracelets deflect arrows, axes, spears, swords—and even bullets. Trust the Princess of the Amazons to turn a little silver bling into a buffer zone.

LEVEL: ★☆☆

**1**

Fold and unfold.

**2**

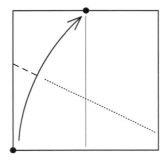

Fold up so the dots meet.
Crease on the left.

**3**

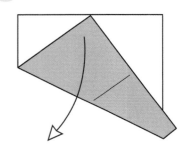

Unfold. Rotate
model 180°.

**4**

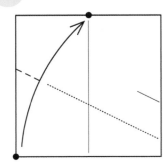

Repeat steps 2–3.

**5**

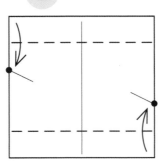

Fold to the dots.

**6**

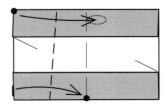

Bring the left edge to the dot
at the bottom and the upper
left corner into the top strip.

**7**

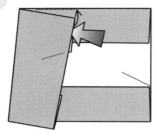

Slide the paper up to the edge at the dotted line.

**8**

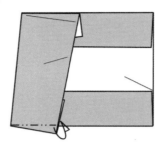

Tuck inside.

**9**

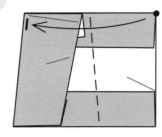

Bring the dot close to the left edge. Fold at an angle similar to that in step 6.

**10**

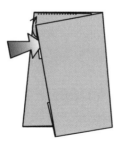

Slide the paper up to the edge at the dotted line.

**11**

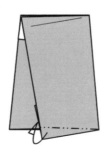

Fold behind.

**12**

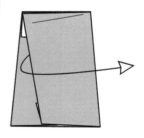

Unfold.

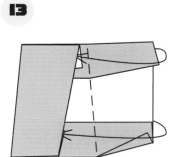

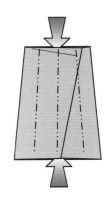

The model is 3D on the right. Tuck inside the pockets.

Shape the bracelet with soft folds to make it round. Repeat behind.

Silver Bracelet

# WONDER WOMAN'S BOOT

The Princess of the Amazons doesn't stand for mundane footwear. As a warrior she needs the best possible gear. Since she can fly on the slightest of breezes, swim with the strength of a shark, and grapple with gods, normal boots would not be up to the task. Her red and white Amazonian "kicks" give her incredible traction. They also provide her with an aerodynamic advantage as she glides over major cities, endless oceans, or the outskirts of Olympus to confront the agents of chaos and dread.

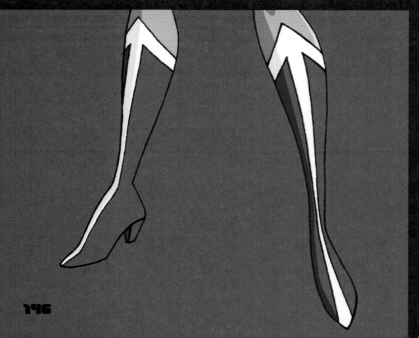

**LEVEL:** ★ ★ ☆

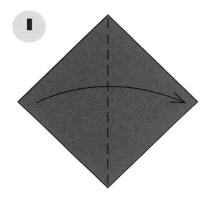

**1**

Fold in half.

**2**

The dots will meet.

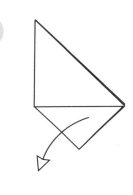

**3**

Unfold.

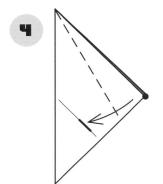

**4**

Bring the dot to the crease, repeat behind.

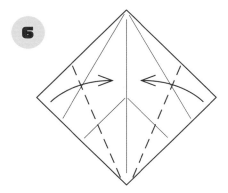

**5**

Unfold everything.

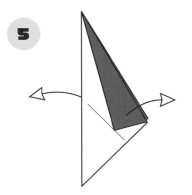

**6**

Fold close to the center.

**7**

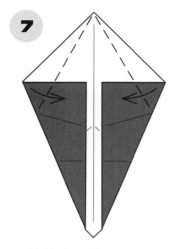

Fold along the creases.

**8**

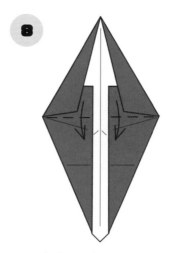

Pull out the corners.

**9**

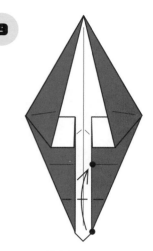

Fold up so the dots meet.

**10**

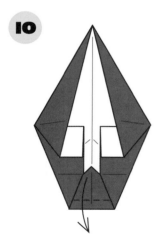

Fold down.

**11**

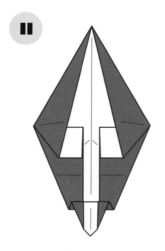

Turn over.

**12**

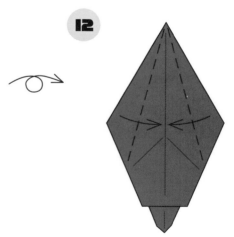

Fold to the center.

**13**

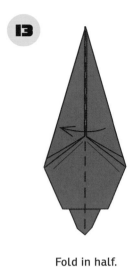

Fold in half.

**14**

Slide the paper.

**15**

Reverse-fold so the edge meets the dot.

**16**

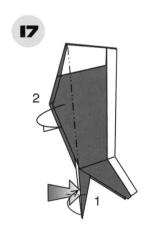

1. Fold inside, repeat behind.
2. Reverse-fold.

**17**

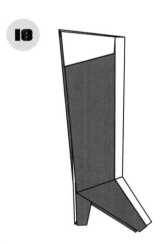

1. Reverse-fold.
2. Wrap around the inner layers, repeat behind.

**18**

Wonder
Woman's
Boot

# STAR

When Wonder Woman rushes toward bad guys in a ferocious fury of justice, the shining star on her golden tiara is the first thing they see. The red, white, and blue of America, as well as the stars on its flag, inspired Princess Diana to create a uniform suitable for a freedom-loving warrior. The blazing symbol on her crown represents the powers of truth and light. It shines as a beacon of hope in a world threatened by darkness. Among all the crime-fighting champions of peace, Wonder Woman is truly a star.

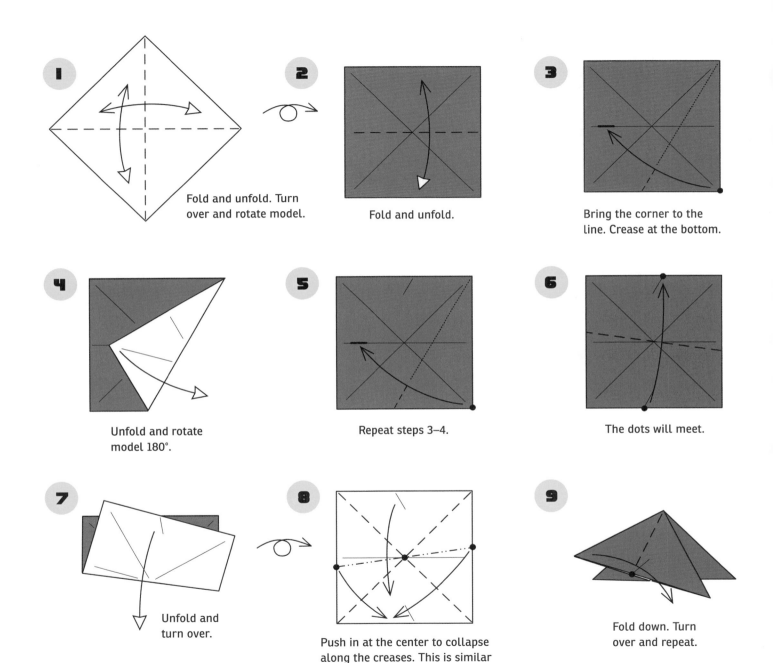

**1** Fold and unfold. Turn over and rotate model.

**2** Fold and unfold.

**3** Bring the corner to the line. Crease at the bottom.

**4** Unfold and rotate model 180°.

**5** Repeat steps 3–4.

**6** The dots will meet.

**7** Unfold and turn over.

**8** Push in at the center to collapse along the creases. This is similar to the waterbomb base.

**9** Fold down. Turn over and repeat.

**10**

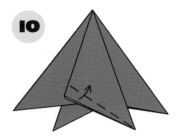

Fold the thin strip up as high as possible. Turn over and repeat.

**11**

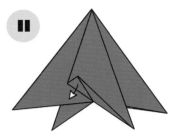

Unfold. Turn over and repeat.

**12**

Sink by tucking between the white layers. Turn over and repeat.

**13**

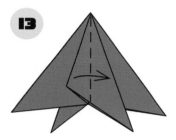

Fold to the right. Turn over and repeat.

**14**

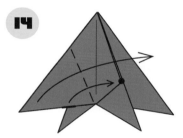

The edge will meet the dot. Turn over and repeat.

**15**

Imagine the line between A and B. Squash-fold along that line. Turn over and repeat.

**16**

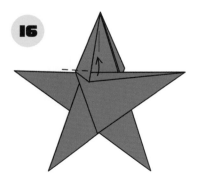

Fold up. Turn over and repeat.

**17**

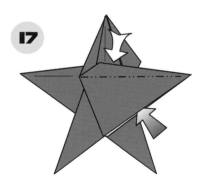

Sink. Turn over and repeat.

**18**

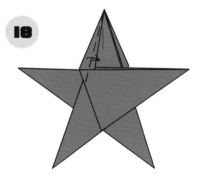

Fold a thin strip. Turn over and repeat.

**19**

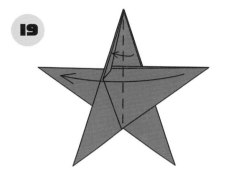

Fold two layers together.
Turn over and repeat.

**20**

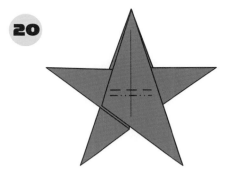

Lightly fold and unfold, without making any crease, in both directions to keep the model together.

**21**

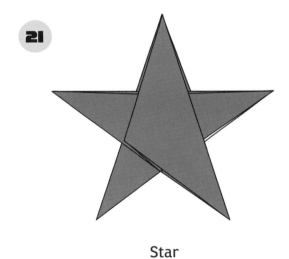

Star

# WONDER WOMAN'S ARROW

To become Wonder Woman, Diana endured numerous trials and contests. Even though her mother was the queen of Themyscira, the Amazonian princess had to compete against her sisters—all of them warriors from the day they were born. Hand-to-hand combat, sword fighting, marathon racing, and javelin throwing were among the tests. Diana also had to show prowess with the bow and arrow. As a young princess she delighted in developing her hand-eye coordination, perfect posture, and steady breath to loose arrows that always flew straight and true. Now Wonder Woman is a gifted athlete, a confident wielder of traditional weaponry, and an overpowering opponent in any showdown.

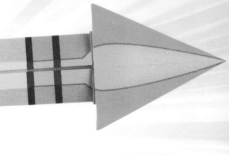

**LEVEL:** ★★☆

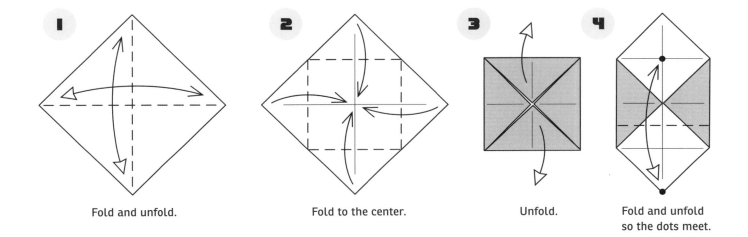

**1** Fold and unfold.

**2** Fold to the center.

**3** Unfold.

**4** Fold and unfold so the dots meet.

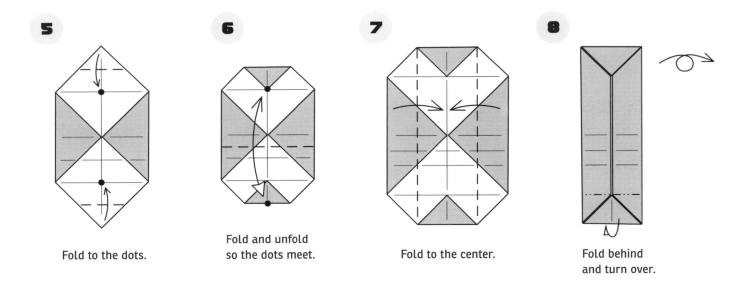

**5** Fold to the dots.

**6** Fold and unfold so the dots meet.

**7** Fold to the center.

**8** Fold behind and turn over.

**9**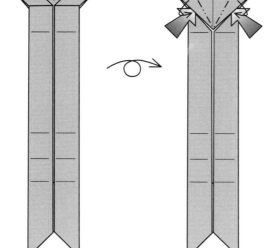

Squash-fold.

**10**

Squash-fold.

**11**

Fold to
the center.

**12**

Squash folds.
(This is similar
to steps 9–10.)

**13**

Turn over.

**14**

Reverse folds.

**15**

Turn over.

**16**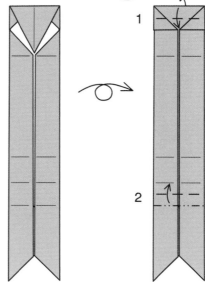

1

2

1. Fold down and
   swing out from behind.
2. Pleat-fold to the
   crease. Mountain-fold
   along the crease.

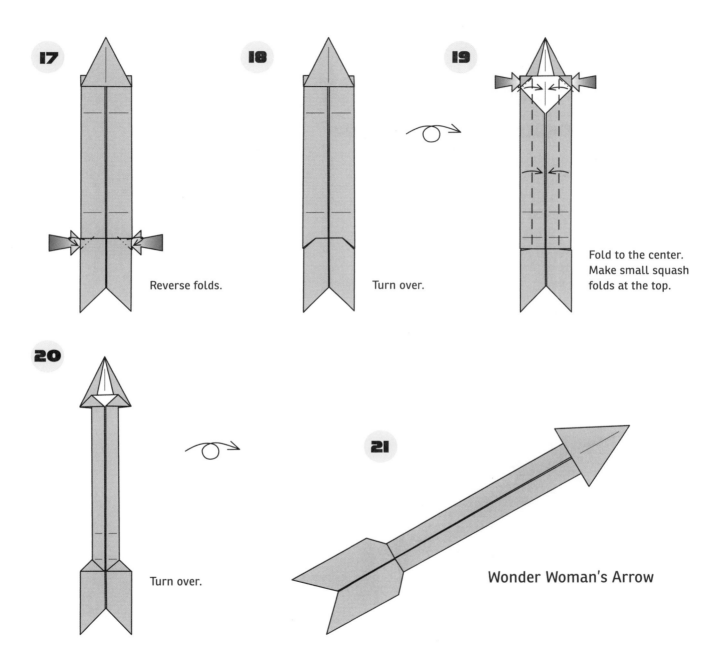

**17** Reverse folds.

**18** Turn over.

**19** Fold to the center. Make small squash folds at the top.

**20** Turn over.

**21** Wonder Woman's Arrow

# WONDER WOMAN'S SWORD

Before she became Wonder Woman, Princess Diana had to prove she was worthy to be the first Amazon to enter the world of mortals. She competed against her sister-warriors to see who was the fastest, the strongest, and the best at wielding the weapons of war. Among her amazing arsenal was a magnificent sword. Forged by Vulcan, the weapons maker of the gods, Wonder Woman's sword is powerful enough to duel with other immortals, including Ares, the god of war. So mighty is her blade, the Amazonian princess only wields it in the gravest of situations.

LEVEL: ★ ★ ☆

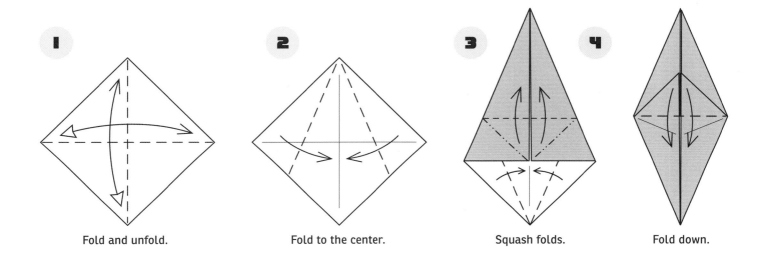

**1** Fold and unfold.

**2** Fold to the center.

**3** Squash folds.

**4** Fold down.

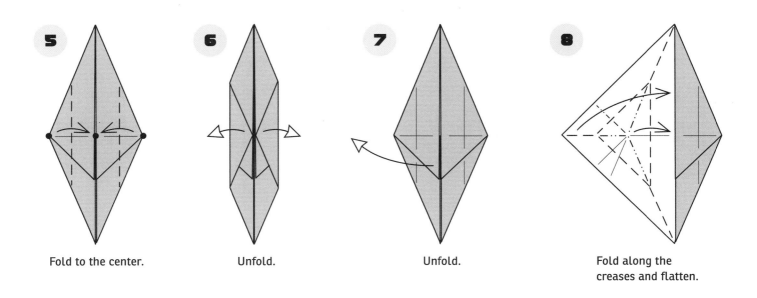

**5** Fold to the center.

**6** Unfold.

**7** Unfold.

**8** Fold along the creases and flatten.

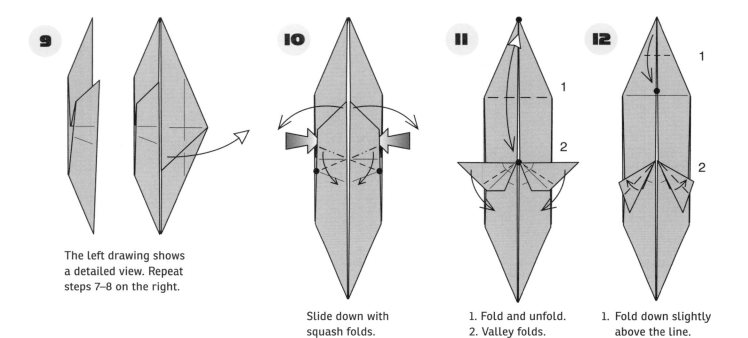

**9**

The left drawing shows a detailed view. Repeat steps 7–8 on the right.

**10**

Slide down with squash folds.

**11**

1. Fold and unfold.
2. Valley folds.

**12**

1. Fold down slightly above the line.
2. Valley folds.

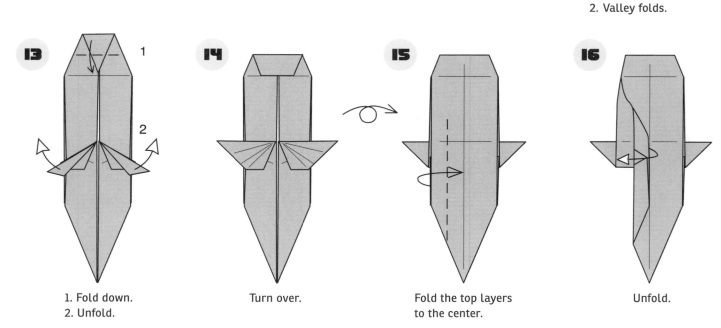

**13**

1. Fold down.
2. Unfold.

**14**

Turn over.

**15**

Fold the top layers to the center.

**16**

Unfold.

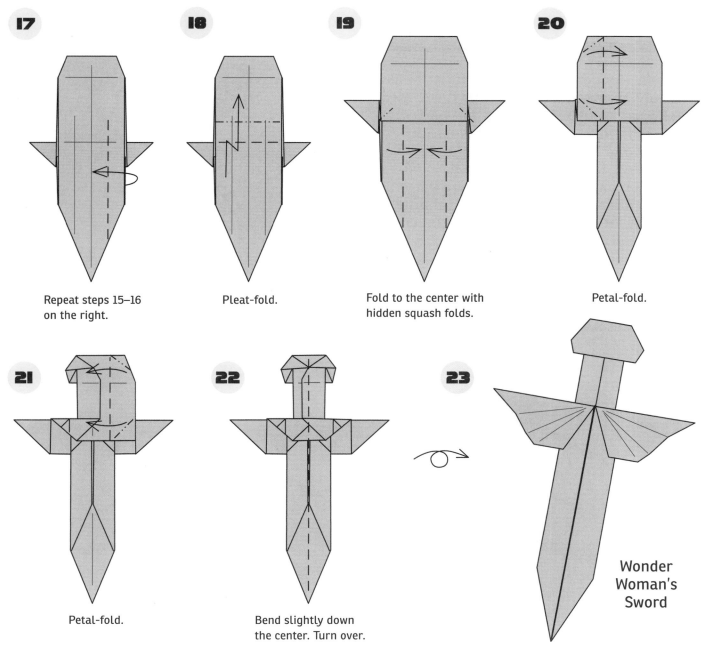

**17**

Repeat steps 15–16 on the right.

**18**

Pleat-fold.

**19**

Fold to the center with hidden squash folds.

**20**

Petal-fold.

**21**

Petal-fold.

**22**

Bend slightly down the center. Turn over.

**23**

Wonder Woman's Sword

# EAGLE

When Wonder Woman first left her hidden home of Themyscira, she came to the United States eager to fight for liberty and justice among all humans. By adopting America as her second home, she also adopted the country's iconic colors and traditional symbols—including the eagle. Diana knew the eagle has symbolized royalty, authority, and power for dozens of countries, kingdoms, empires, and religions around the globe. For Wonder Woman, the radiant raptor makes a fitting emblem for a proud princess who strives to bring harmony to the entire planet.

LEVEL: ★★★

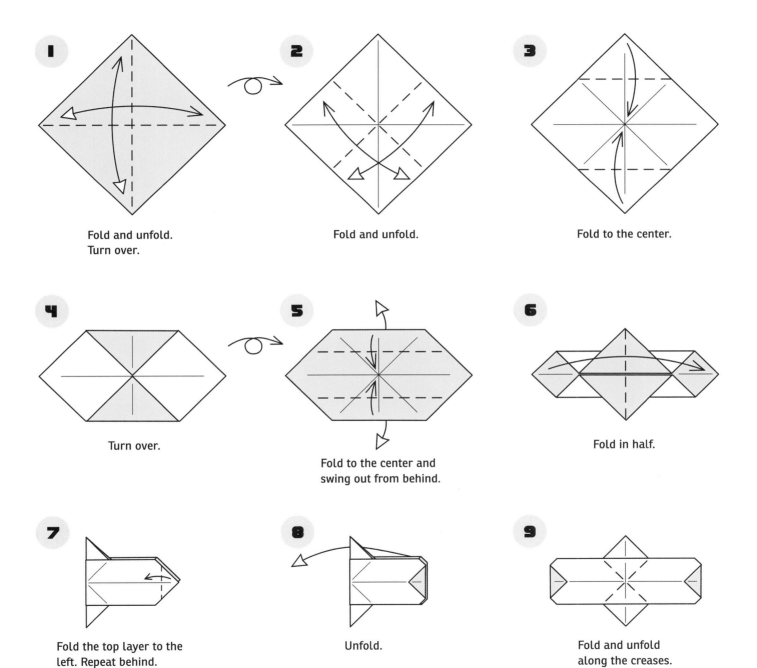

**1** Fold and unfold. Turn over.

**2** Fold and unfold.

**3** Fold to the center.

**4** Turn over.

**5** Fold to the center and swing out from behind.

**6** Fold in half.

**7** Fold the top layer to the left. Repeat behind.

**8** Unfold.

**9** Fold and unfold along the creases.

**10**

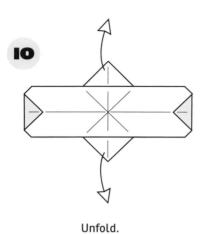

Unfold.

**11**

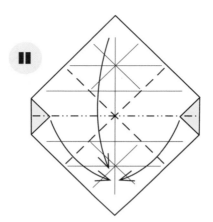

This is similar to the preliminary fold.

**12**

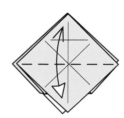

Fold and unfold the top layer. Repeat behind.

**13**

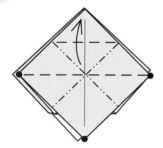

Fold along the creases. The three dots will meet. Repeat behind.

**14**

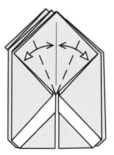

Fold and unfold. Repeat behind.

**15**

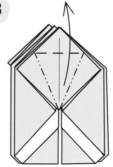

Petal-fold. Repeat behind.

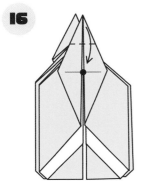

**16**

Fold the top flap
down to the dot.

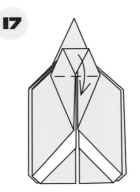

**17**

Fold down.

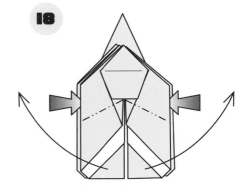

**18**

Reverse folds.
Rotate model 180°.

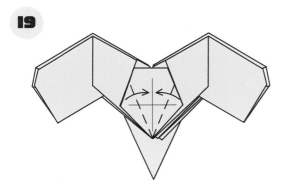

**19**

Fold to the center.

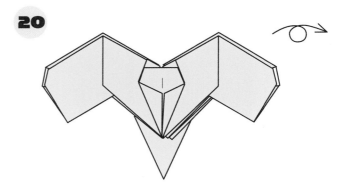

**20**

Turn over.

**21**

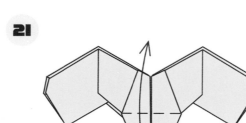

Fold up.

**22**

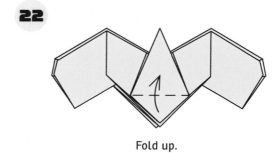

Fold up.

**23**

Fold up.

**24**

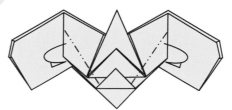

Fold behind.

**25**

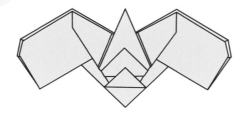

Turn over.

**26**

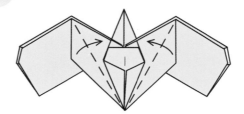

Fold toward the center.

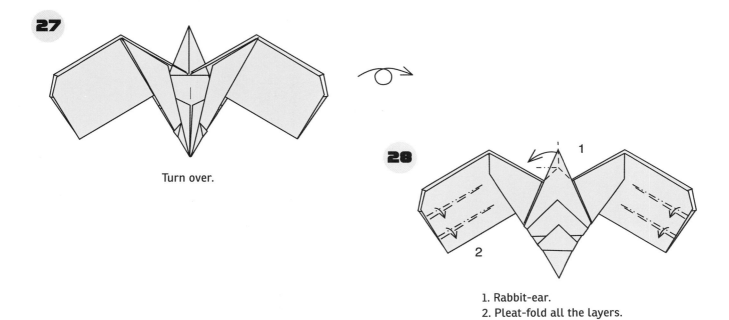

**27**

Turn over.

**28**

1
2

1. Rabbit-ear.
2. Pleat-fold all the layers.

**29**

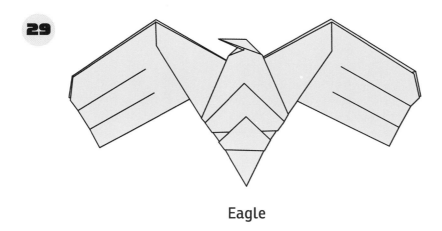

Eagle

# WONDER WOMAN SYMBOL

The iconic shape of the Princess of the Amazons' symbol perfectly suits its awe-inspiring hero. First and foremost, the golden double Ws stand for her alter ego as Wonder Woman. The solid interlocking letters also resemble bars of iron or steel, reminding evildoers of the hero's incredible strength and stamina. Finally, the design looks like a stylized eagle—Wonder Woman's alternate trademark—and has served as the chestplate of the champion's famous star-spangled uniform.

**LEVEL: ★★★**

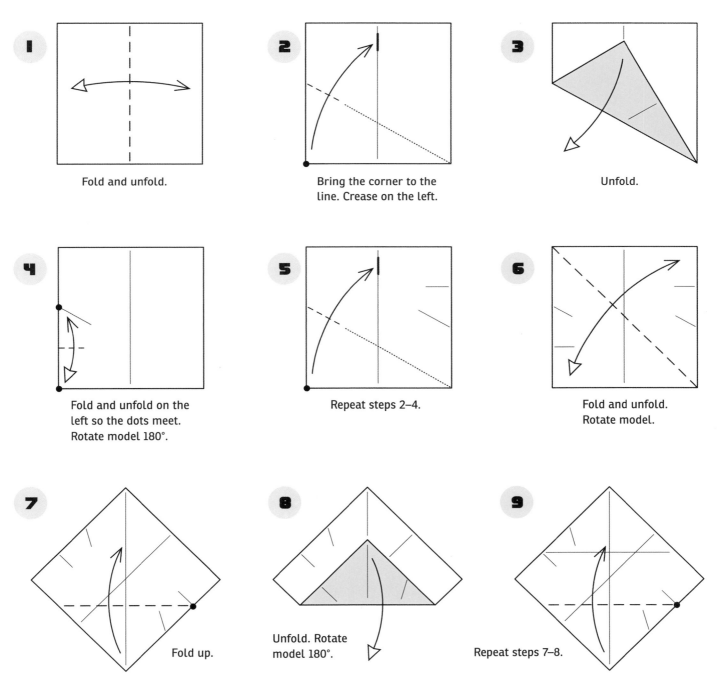

**1** Fold and unfold.

**2** Bring the corner to the line. Crease on the left.

**3** Unfold.

**4** Fold and unfold on the left so the dots meet. Rotate model 180°.

**5** Repeat steps 2–4.

**6** Fold and unfold. Rotate model.

**7** Fold up.

**8** Unfold. Rotate model 180°.

**9** Repeat steps 7–8.

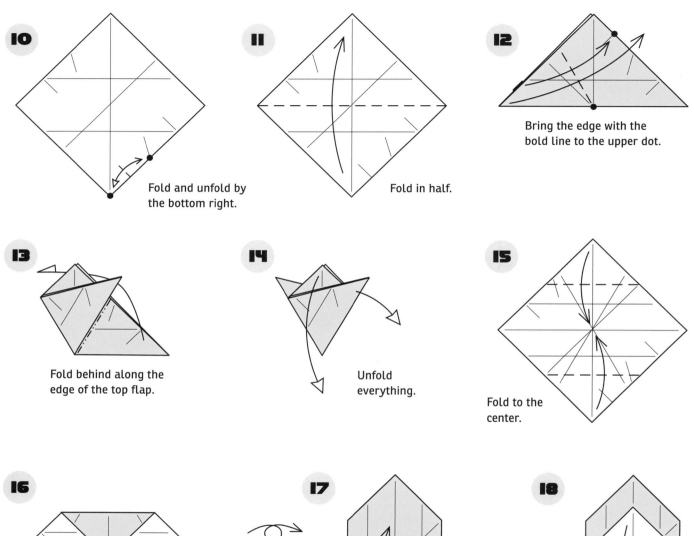

**10** Fold and unfold by the bottom right.

**11** Fold in half.

**12** Bring the edge with the bold line to the upper dot.

**13** Fold behind along the edge of the top flap.

**14** Unfold everything.

**15** Fold to the center.

**16** Turn over and rotate model 90°.

**17** Fold up by the intersections.

**18** Fold down along a hidden crease.

**19**

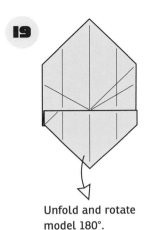

Unfold and rotate
model 180°.

**20**

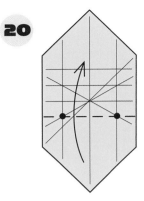

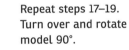

Repeat steps 17–19.
Turn over and rotate
model 90°.

**21**

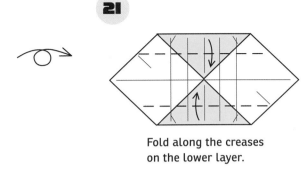

Fold along the creases
on the lower layer.

**22**

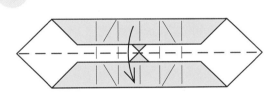

Fold in half.

**23**

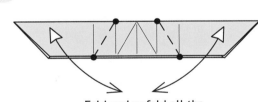

Fold and unfold all the
layers by the dots.

**24**

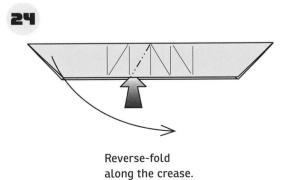

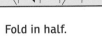

Reverse-fold
along the crease.

**25**

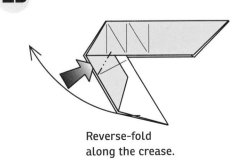

Reverse-fold
along the crease.

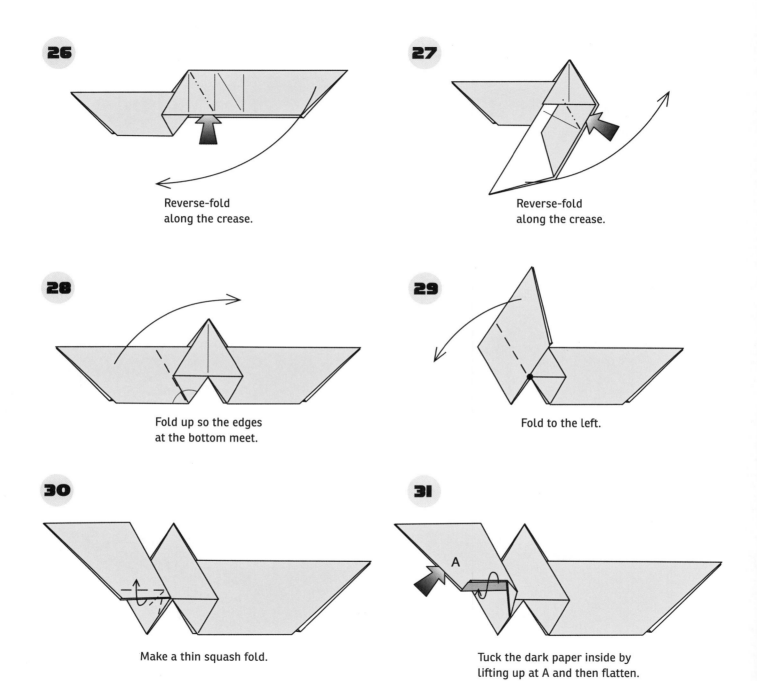

**26** Reverse-fold along the crease.

**27** Reverse-fold along the crease.

**28** Fold up so the edges at the bottom meet.

**29** Fold to the left.

**30** Make a thin squash fold.

**31** Tuck the dark paper inside by lifting up at A and then flatten.

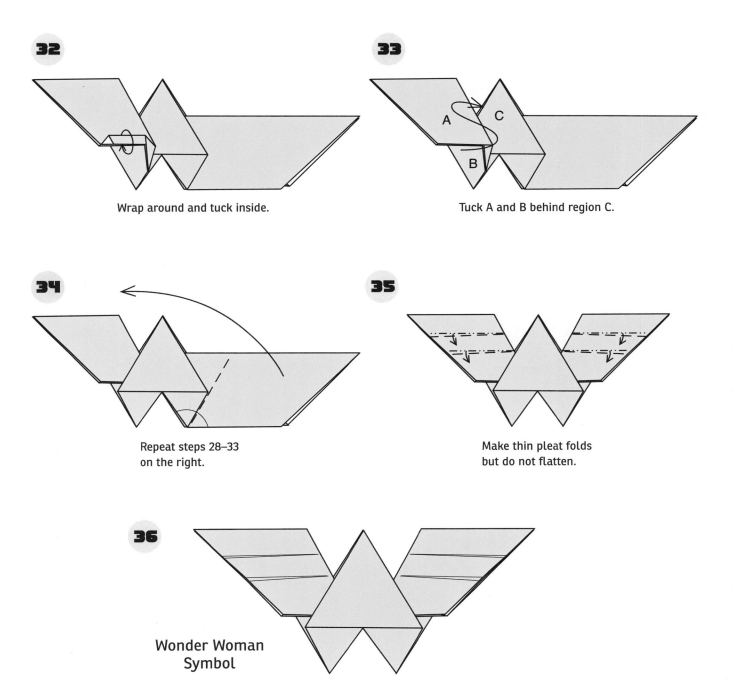

**32**

Wrap around and tuck inside.

**33**

A    C

B

Tuck A and B behind region C.

**34**

Repeat steps 28–33
on the right.

**35**

Make thin pleat folds
but do not flatten.

**36**

Wonder Woman
Symbol

# INVISIBLE JET

On the secret island of Themyscira, Wonder Woman learned to fly on air currents like a human paraglider. But when she needs speed, the Princess of the Amazons jumps into her supersonic turbojet. This high-tech, aerodynamic aircraft was built by the immortal Amazonian engineers of Queen Hippolyta. Best of all, it's invisible! Villains never know the plane has invaded their airspace until Wonder Woman is already on the scene.

**LEVEL: ★★★**

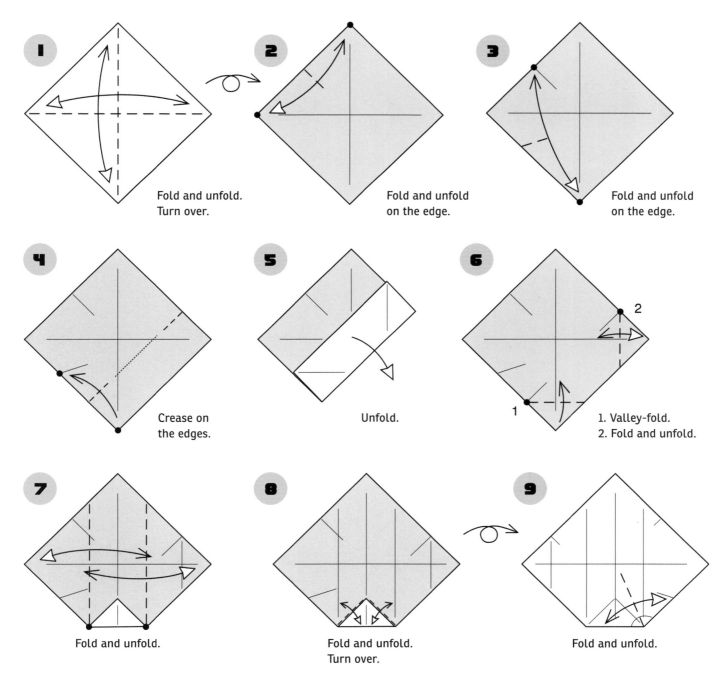

**1** Fold and unfold. Turn over.

**2** Fold and unfold on the edge.

**3** Fold and unfold on the edge.

**4** Crease on the edges.

**5** Unfold.

**6**
1. Valley-fold.
2. Fold and unfold.

**7** Fold and unfold.

**8** Fold and unfold. Turn over.

**9** Fold and unfold.

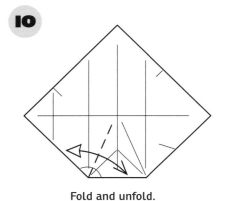

**10**

Fold and unfold.

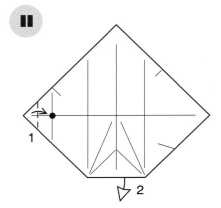

**11**

1. Fold to the dot.
2. Unfold.

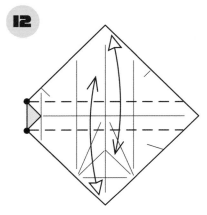

**12**

Fold and unfold.

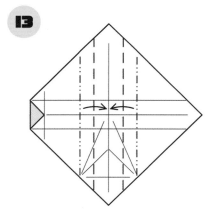

**13**

Pleat folds. Mountain-fold along the creases.

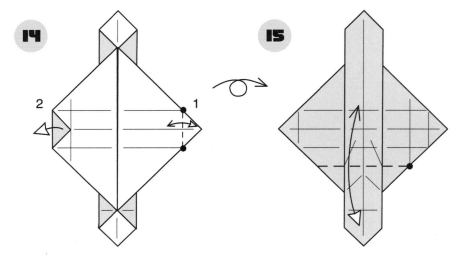

**14**

1. Fold and unfold.
2. Unfold.
Turn over.

**15**

Fold and unfold.

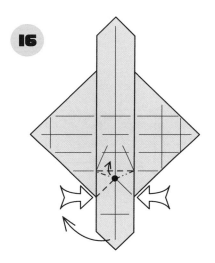

**16**

Lift up at the dot, push in on the sides, and fold along the creases.

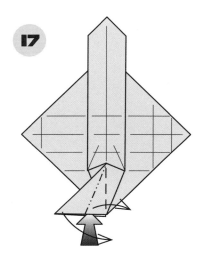

**17**

Squash-fold.

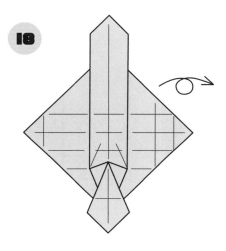

**18**

Turn over.

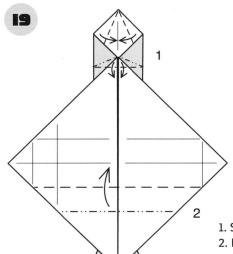

**19**

1. Squash folds.
2. Pleat-fold along the creases

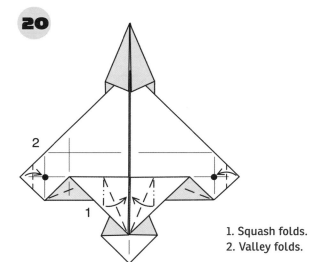

**20**

1. Squash folds.
2. Valley folds.

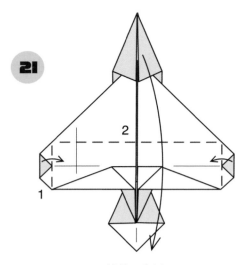

**21**

Valley folds.

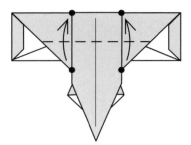

**22**

Fold up so the
dots meet.

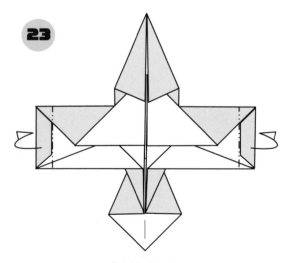

**23**

Fold behind.

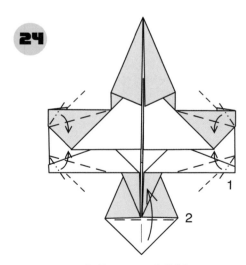

**24**

1. Four squash folds.
2. Valley-fold.

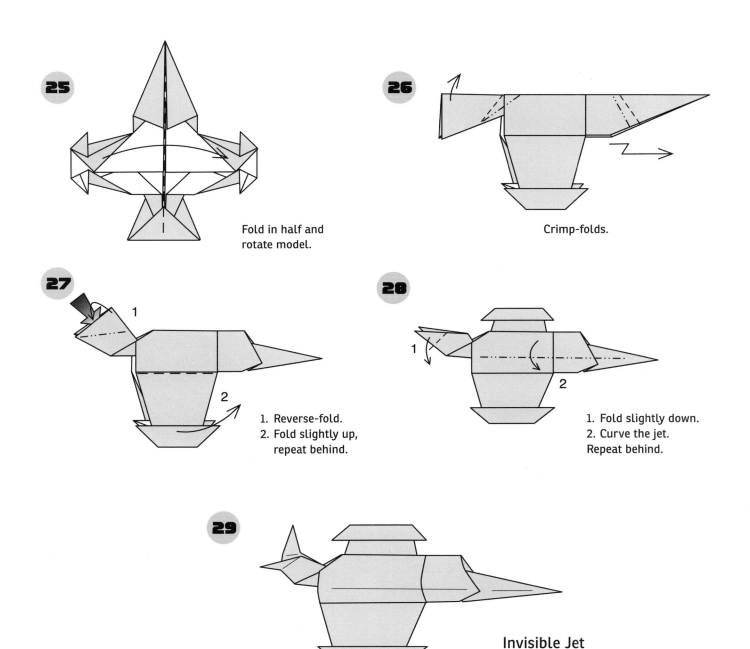

**25** Fold in half and rotate model.

**26** Crimp-folds.

**27**
1. Reverse-fold.
2. Fold slightly up, repeat behind.

**28**
1. Fold slightly down.
2. Curve the jet.
Repeat behind.

**29** Invisible Jet

# JUMPA THE KANGA

Kangas are found only on the secret island of Themyscira. Like kangaroos, they can leap long distances, but they're also lightning fast. These speedy steeds are the royal rides of the island's warrior race, the Amazons. Jumpa is Wonder Woman's loyal Super-Pet. This crime-kicking kanga carries royal weapons in her pouch, including a tiara, silver bracelets, and a Lasso of Truth.

**LEVEL:** ★★★

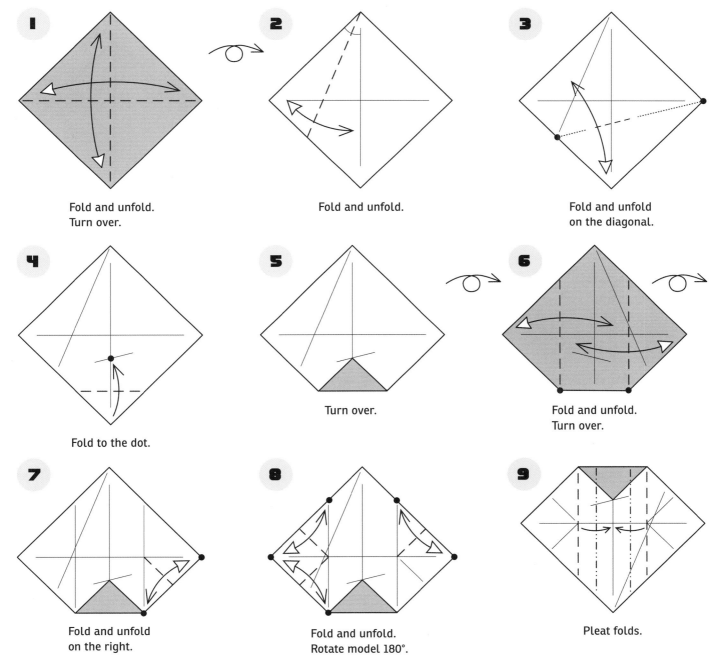

**1** Fold and unfold. Turn over.

**2** Fold and unfold.

**3** Fold and unfold on the diagonal.

**4** Fold to the dot.

**5** Turn over.

**6** Fold and unfold. Turn over.

**7** Fold and unfold on the right.

**8** Fold and unfold. Rotate model 180°.

**9** Pleat folds.

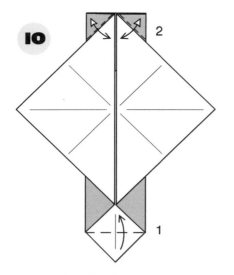

**10**

1. Valley-fold.
2. Fold and unfold.

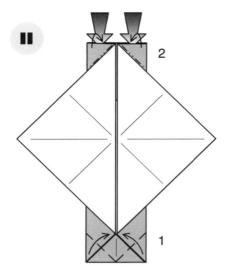

**11**

1. Valley folds.
2. Reverse folds.

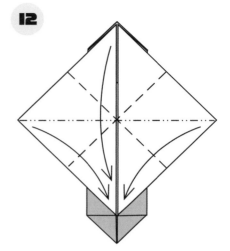

**12**

This is similar to the preliminary fold.

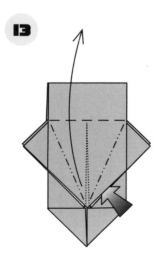

**13**

Petal-fold. Mountain-fold along hidden creases.

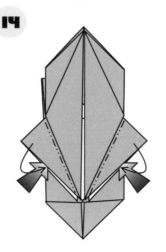

**14**

Reverse folds.

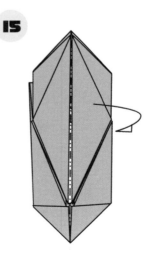

**15**

Fold in half.

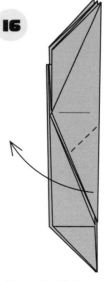

**16**

Repeat behind.

**17**

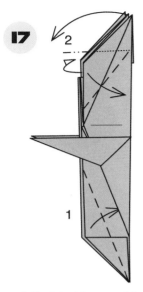

1. Tuck inside, repeat behind.
2. Crimp-fold.

**18**

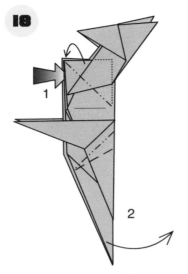

1. Reverse-fold.
2. Crimp-fold.
Rotate model.

**19**

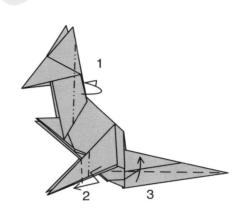

1. Fold behind.
2. Crimp-fold.
3. Valley-fold.
Repeat behind.

**20**

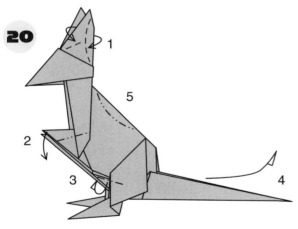

1. Shape the ear.
2. Reverse-fold.
3. Fold inside.
4. Curl the tail.
5. Shape the back.
Repeat behind.

**21**

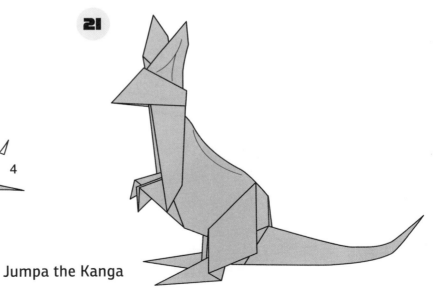

Jumpa the Kanga

# WONDER WOMAN

A world at war. Countries in chaos. Humanity without harmony. The planet cried out for a hero, but would that cry be heard? In Earth's darkest hour, the Amazons on the secret island of Themyscira held a trial to find their strongest and bravest champion. From that contest one warrior triumphed over all: Wonder Woman. With an Invisible Jet and invincible weapons, the Princess of the Amazons boldly entered the world of mortals. Her mission to bring peace, defend justice, and restore harmony across the globe has only just begun.

**LEVEL:** ★ ★ ★

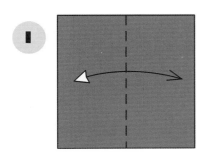

**1** Fold and unfold. Turn over.

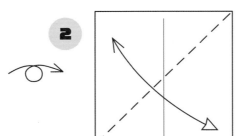

**2** Fold and unfold.

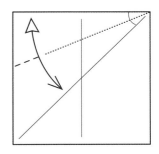

**3** Fold to the crease and unfold. Crease on the left.

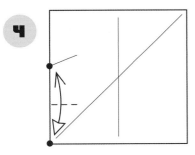

**4** Fold and unfold on the left so the dots meet.

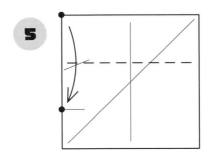

**5** Fold down so the dots meet.

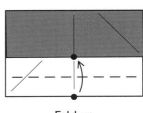

**6** Fold up.

**7** Fold and unfold.

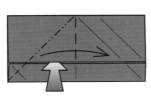

**8** Squash-fold.

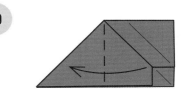

**9** Fold the top flap.

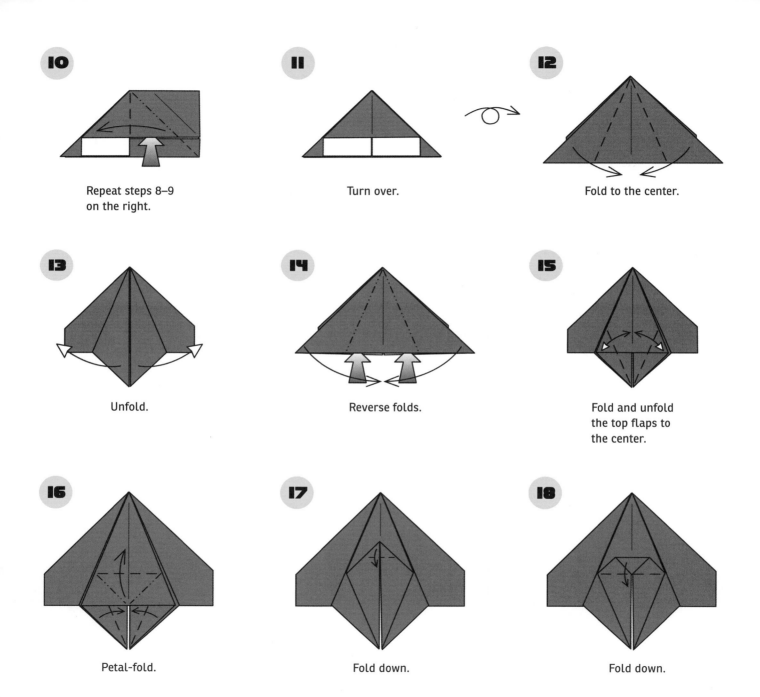

**10** Repeat steps 8–9 on the right.

**11** Turn over.

**12** Fold to the center.

**13** Unfold.

**14** Reverse folds.

**15** Fold and unfold the top flaps to the center.

**16** Petal-fold.

**17** Fold down.

**18** Fold down.

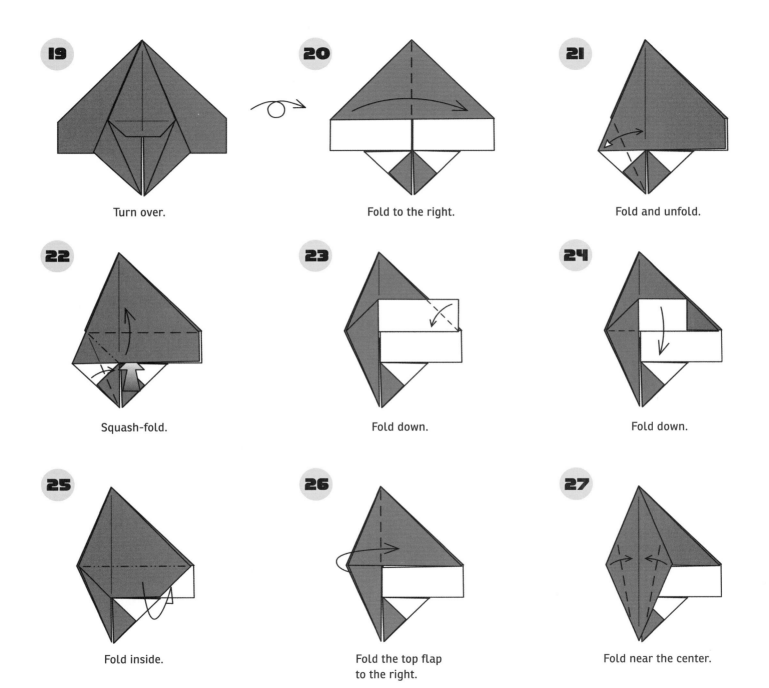

**19** Turn over.

**20** Fold to the right.

**21** Fold and unfold.

**22** Squash-fold.

**23** Fold down.

**24** Fold down.

**25** Fold inside.

**26** Fold the top flap to the right.

**27** Fold near the center.

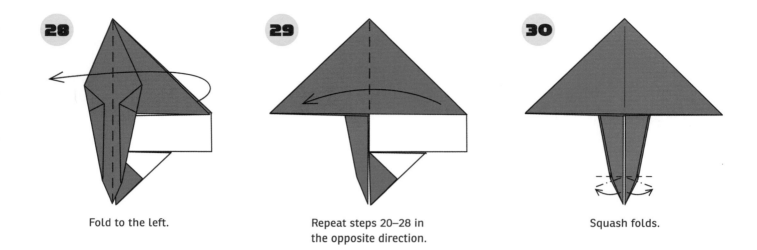

**28** Fold to the left.

**29** Repeat steps 20–28 in the opposite direction.

**30** Squash folds.

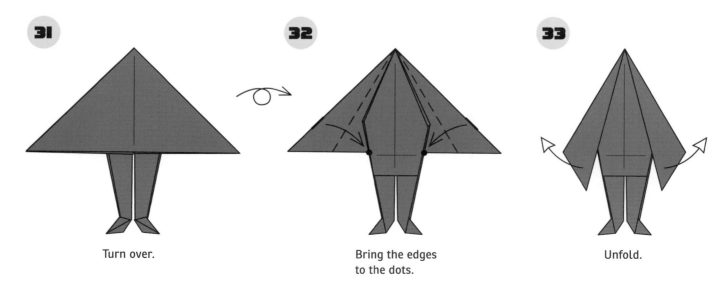

**31** Turn over.

**32** Bring the edges to the dots.

**33** Unfold.

**34**

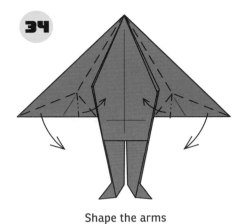

Shape the arms
with rabbit ears.

**35**

Pleat-fold.

**36**

1. Spread at the head.
2. Squash-fold the hands.

**37**

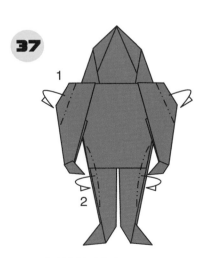

1. Fold behind.
2. Shape the body and legs.

**38**

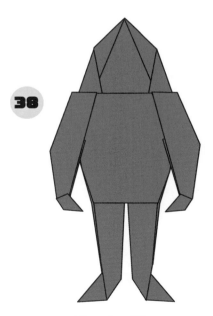

Wonder Woman

# SECTION FOUR:
# THE JUSTICE LEAGUE COLLECTION

# MARTIAN MANHUNTER SYMBOL

J'onn J'onnz, the green-skinned hero from Mars, possesses the powers of his pal Superman and the detecting dexterity of Batman. To fight crime across his adopted planet, Earth, the Martian Manhunter unleashes his unearthly strength and super-breath. He also possesses abilities such as flight, invisibility, and shape-shifting—frequently assuming the human identity of police detective John Jones. Whenever he morphs into his true form, the Manhunter's blazing scarlet harness reminds bad guys that the Martian is an X-pert at crossing paths with criminals.

LEVEL: ★☆☆

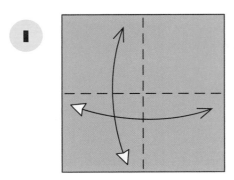

1

Fold and unfold.

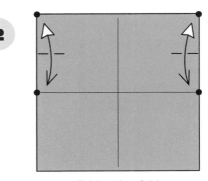

2

Fold and unfold
on the edges.

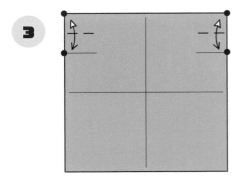

3

Fold and unfold
on the edges.

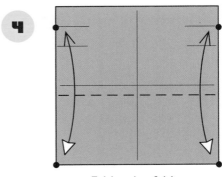

4

Fold and unfold.

5

Fold in half.

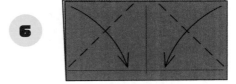

6

Fold the top layer
down to the crease.

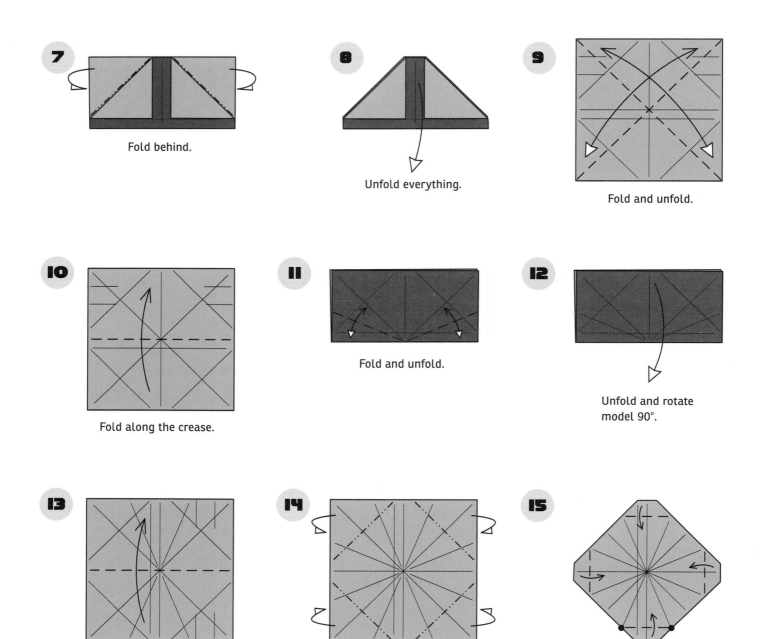

**7** Fold behind.

**8** Unfold everything.

**9** Fold and unfold.

**10** Fold along the crease.

**11** Fold and unfold.

**12** Unfold and rotate model 90°.

**13** Repeat steps 10–12.

**14** Fold along the creases.

**15** Fold four sides.

**16**

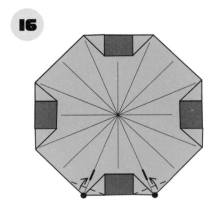

Fold the corners up
and rotate model 90°.

**17**

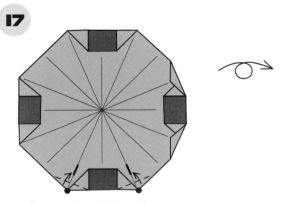

Repeat step 16 three times.
Rotate model and turn over.

**18**

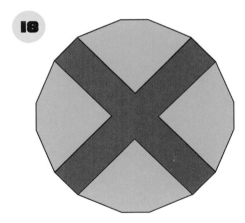

Martian Manhunter Symbol

# SHAZAM! SYMBOL

When young Billy Batson stumbled into a long-lost lair of ancient magic, he was granted six amazing talents: the wisdom of Solomon, the strength of Hercules, the stamina of Atlas, the power of Zeus, the courage of Achilles, and the speed of Mercury. By shouting the mystical word made from the first letters of their names—SHAZAM!—Billy warps into one of the world's most powerful super heroes. The blazing symbol on his chest stands for the thunderbolt that accompanies each and every transformation. In the lightning split-second it takes to utter the six-letter secret sound, Billy changes from a mere mortal into the mighty Shazam!

LEVEL: ★ ★ ☆

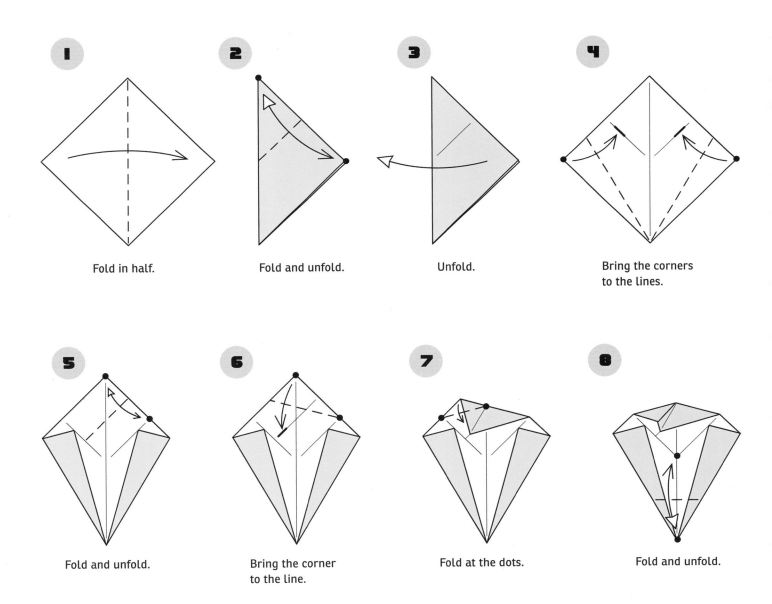

**1** Fold in half.

**2** Fold and unfold.

**3** Unfold.

**4** Bring the corners to the lines.

**5** Fold and unfold.

**6** Bring the corner to the line.

**7** Fold at the dots.

**8** Fold and unfold.

**9**

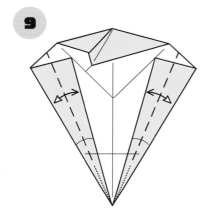

Fold and unfold to bisect the angles. Do not crease at the bottom.

**10**

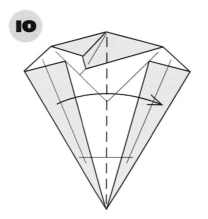

Fold in half.

**11**

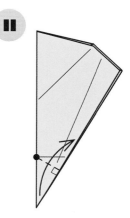

Fold up at a right angle.

**12**

Fold down at a right angle.

**13**

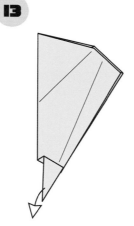

Unfold.

**14**

Crimp-fold.

**15**

Mountain-fold along the crease. Repeat behind.

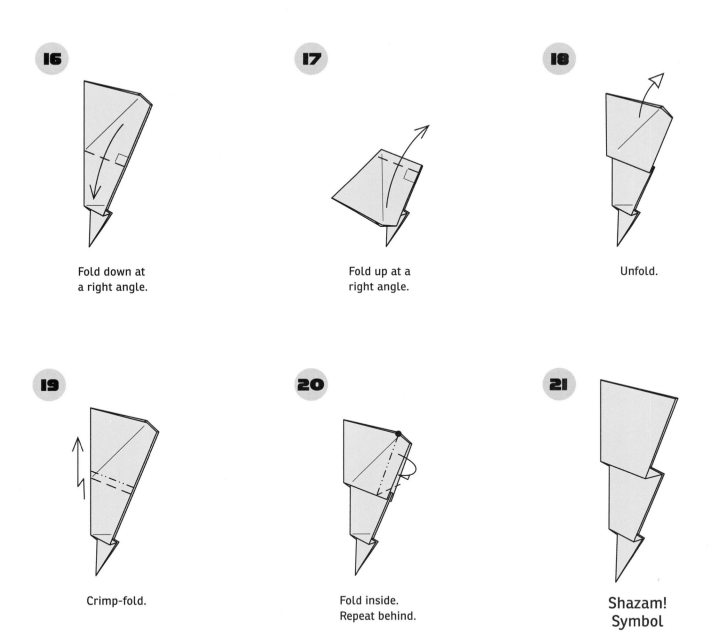

**16**

Fold down at
a right angle.

**17**

Fold up at a
right angle.

**18**

Unfold.

**19**

Crimp-fold.

**20**

Fold inside.
Repeat behind.

**21**

Shazam!
Symbol

# THE FLASH SYMBOL

Emblazoned on The Flash's red-and-yellow uniform, the lightning bolt represents this super hero's amazing speed and incredible origin story. One stormy night, a bolt of lightning illuminated the laboratory of Barry Allen. It struck a case of dangerous chemicals, spilling them onto the police scientist and transforming him into the Scarlet Speedster. As the Fastest Man Alive, The Flash quickly handles Central City's worst criminals, known as the Rogues.

LEVEL: ★ ★ ☆

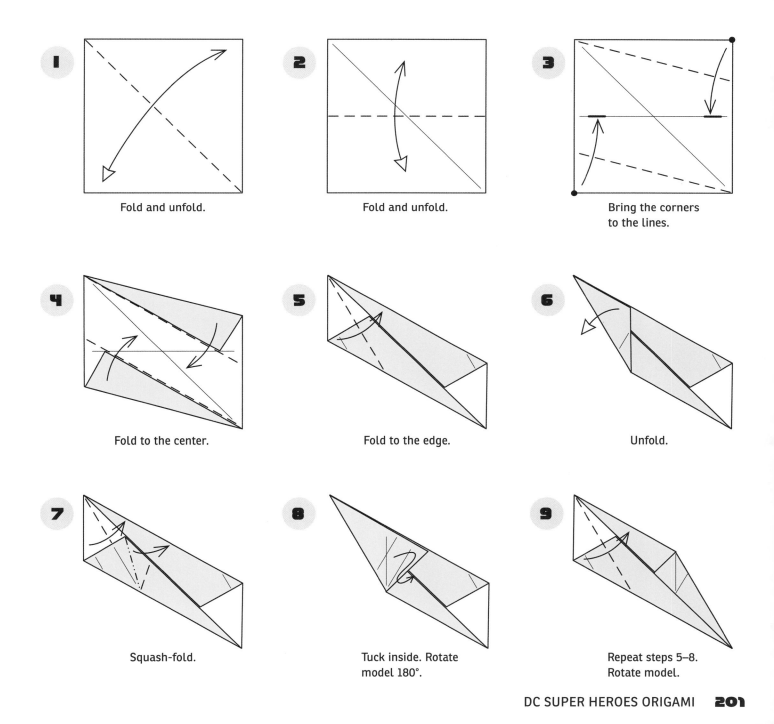

**1** Fold and unfold.

**2** Fold and unfold.

**3** Bring the corners to the lines.

**4** Fold to the center.

**5** Fold to the edge.

**6** Unfold.

**7** Squash-fold.

**8** Tuck inside. Rotate model 180°.

**9** Repeat steps 5–8. Rotate model.

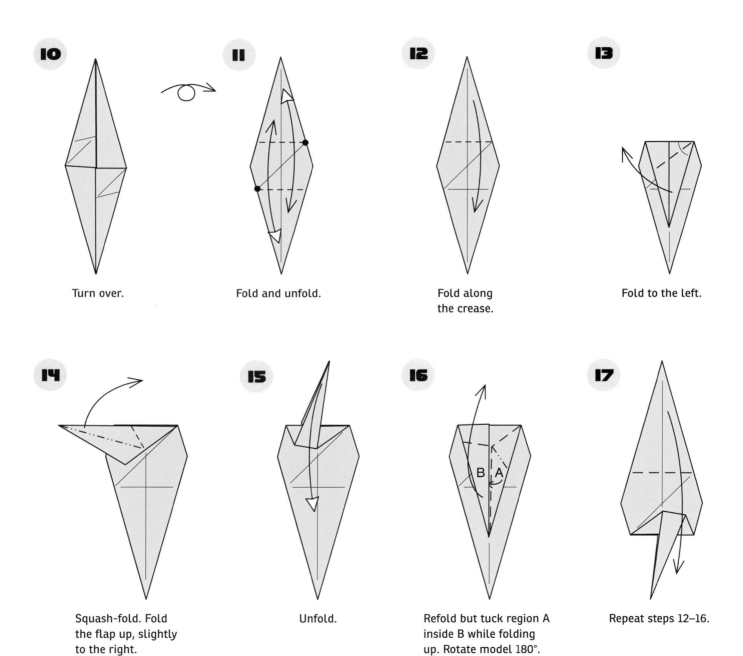

**10** Turn over.

**11** Fold and unfold.

**12** Fold along the crease.

**13** Fold to the left.

**14** Squash-fold. Fold the flap up, slightly to the right.

**15** Unfold.

**16** Refold but tuck region A inside B while folding up. Rotate model 180°.

**17** Repeat steps 12–16.

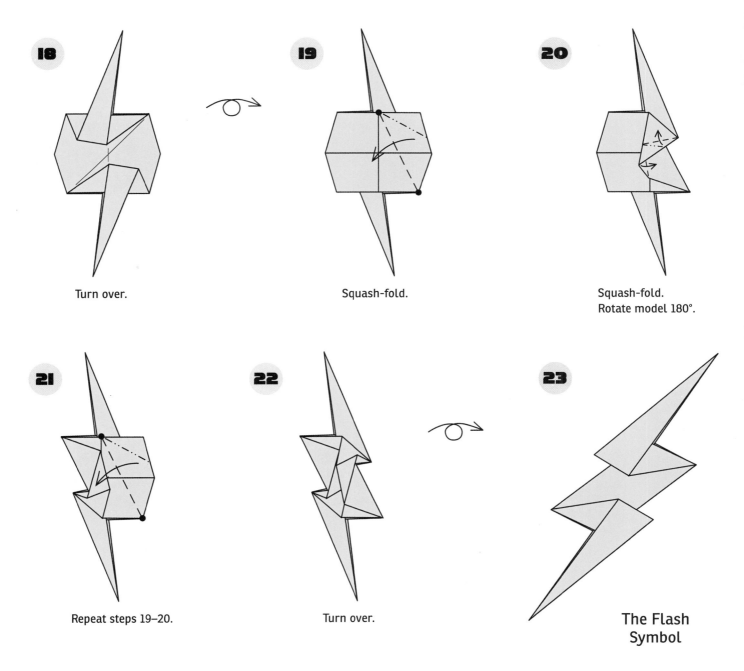

**18**

Turn over.

**19**

Squash-fold.

**20**

Squash-fold.
Rotate model 180°.

**21**

Repeat steps 19–20.

**22**

Turn over.

**23**

The Flash
Symbol

# GREEN ARROW'S HAT

After a spike in crime in Star City, billionaire Oliver Queen dedicated his life to becoming a thorn in the side of lawbreakers. He became the ace archer, Green Arrow. From his high-tech quiver he draws weapons that bristle with electricity, capture crooks with expanding nets, or puncture tires on speeding getaway cars. In addition to protecting his identity with a mask, the Emerald Archer wears a hat similar to Robin Hood's. With his evergreen uniform, his bow and arrows, and an eagle-eyed aim, Queen instills fear in the hearts of his primary targets: evildoers.

**LEVEL:** ★★☆

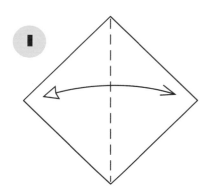

1

Fold and unfold.

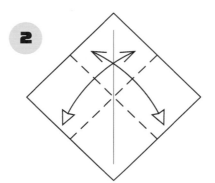

2

Fold and unfold.

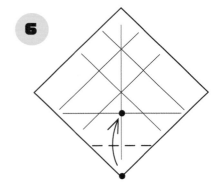

3

Fold to the center
and unfold.

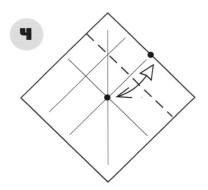

4

Fold to the center
and unfold.

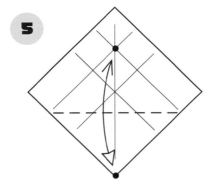

5

Fold and unfold
so the dots meet.

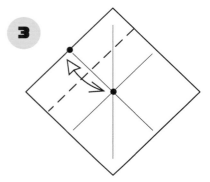

6

Fold up so the
dots meet.

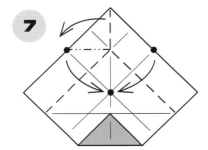

7

Fold along the creases.

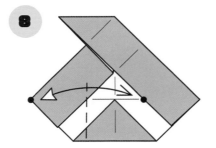

8

Fold and unfold
on the lower half.

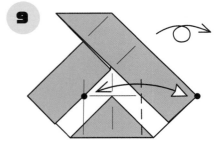

9

Fold and unfold on the
lower half. Turn over.

**10**

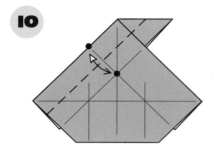

Fold and unfold.

**11**

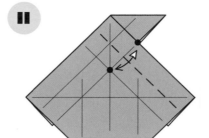

Fold and unfold.

**12**

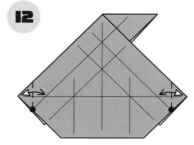

Fold and unfold.

**13**

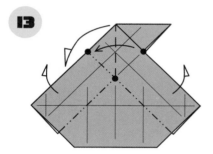

Puff out at the central dot.
The upper dots will meet.

**14**

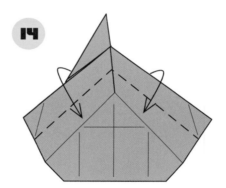

This is 3D. Wrap around
along the creases.

**15**

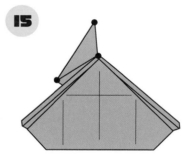

Rotate the model
to view the left
side with the dots.

**16**

Fold the top layer
so the dots meet.

**17**

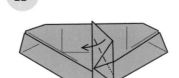

Fold the feather from
inside at the bottom.

**18**

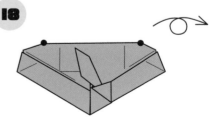

Turn over and rotate
the model so the dots
are at the front.

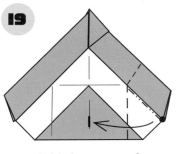

**19**

Fold along some of the creases. Bring the dot to the center.

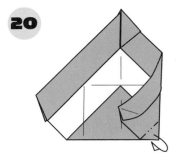

**20**

Fold behind.

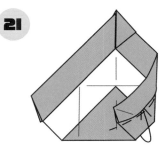

**21**

Fold up and tuck inside.

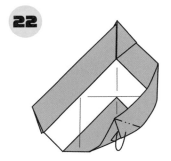

**22**

Fold along the crease to wrap around the hidden layers.

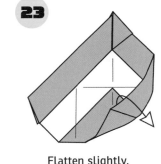

**23**

Flatten slightly.

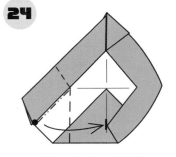

**24**

Repeat steps 19–23 on the left.

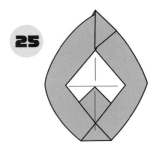

**25**

Turn over.

**26**

Green Arrow's Hat

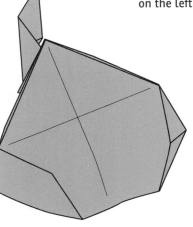

# GREEN LANTERN SYMBOL

Long ago, an alien race known as the Guardians of the Universe divided space into 3,600 sectors. To protect each of these sectors, they created the Green Lantern Corps. This intergalactic police force's symbol and its color represent willpower. With special power rings, Green Lanterns harness willpower to create anything imaginable and guard the galaxy against evil. Thousands of Green Lanterns protect the many sectors of space, but one sacred oath unites them: "In brightest day, in blackest night, no evil shall escape my sight. Let those who worship evil's might, beware my power ... Green Lantern's light!"

**LEVEL:** ★ ☆ ☆

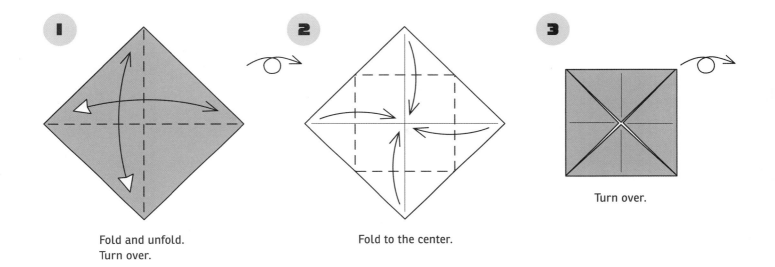

**1** Fold and unfold.
Turn over.

**2** Fold to the center.

**3** Turn over.

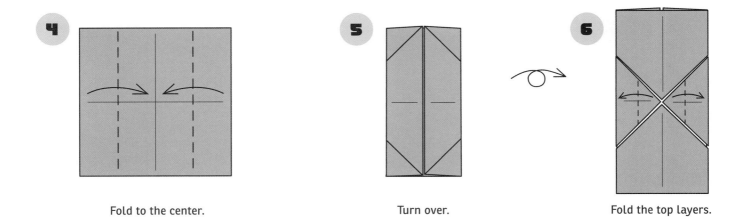

**4** Fold to the center.

**5** Turn over.

**6** Fold the top layers.

**7**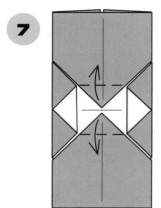

Fold the top layers.

**8**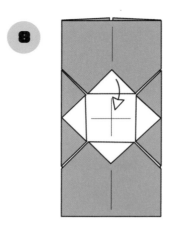

Unfold.

**9**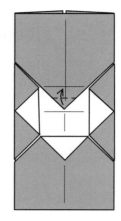

Fold the top layer.

**10**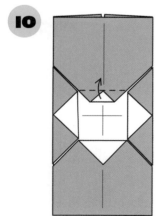

Fold along
the crease.

**11**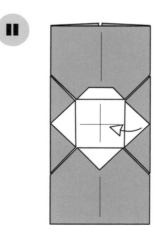

Repeat steps
8–10 three times.

**12**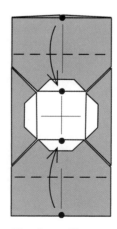

The dots will meet.

**13**

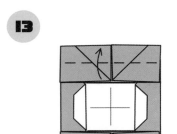

Fold to the top
and bottom.

**14**

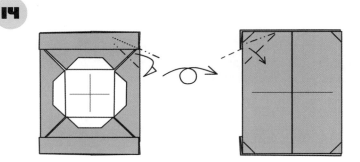

Squash-fold. Turn over
to view the back.

**15**

Squash-fold.

**16**

Repeat steps 14–15
three times. Turn over.

**17**

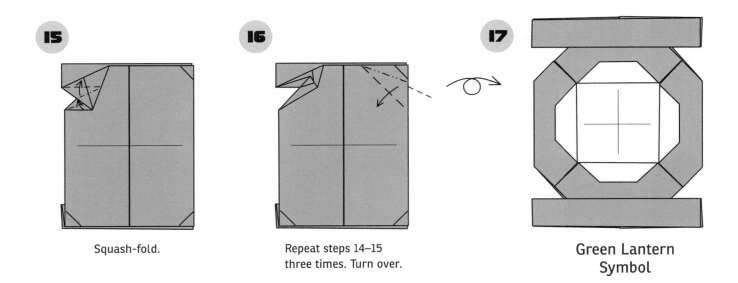

**Green Lantern
Symbol**

# GREEN LANTERN B'DG

Members of the Green Lantern Corps come in all shapes, sizes, and species—including space squirrels! B'dg (pronounced like "badge") may look small, but he is a full-fledged Green Lantern. He guards Space Sector 1014, which includes his home planet, H'lven. Like all Green Lanterns, B'dg wears a power ring, which is fueled by his own willpower. With the ring, B'dg can fly, create anything imaginable, and protect his sector of space.

LEVEL: ★ ★ ☆

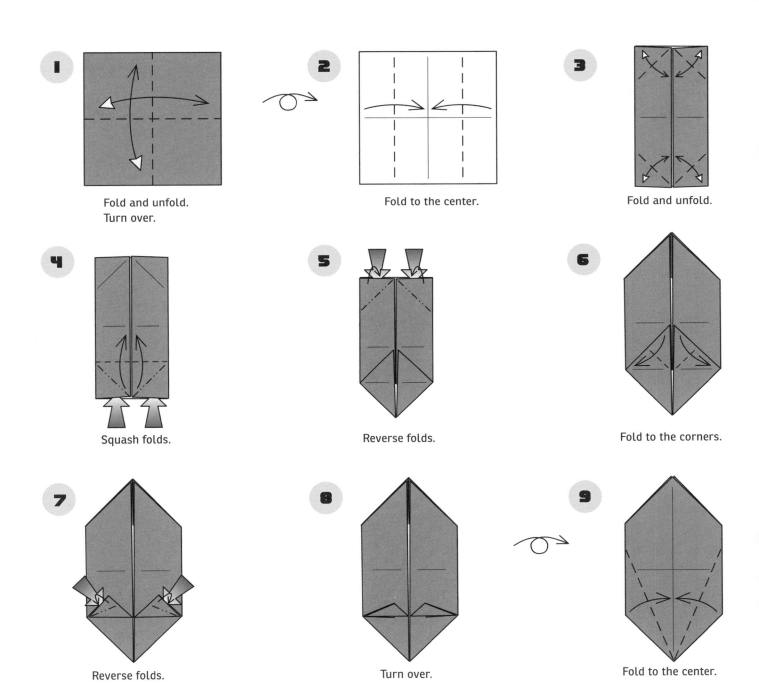

**1** Fold and unfold.
Turn over.

**2** Fold to the center.

**3** Fold and unfold.

**4** Squash folds.

**5** Reverse folds.

**6** Fold to the corners.

**7** Reverse folds.

**8** Turn over.

**9** Fold to the center.

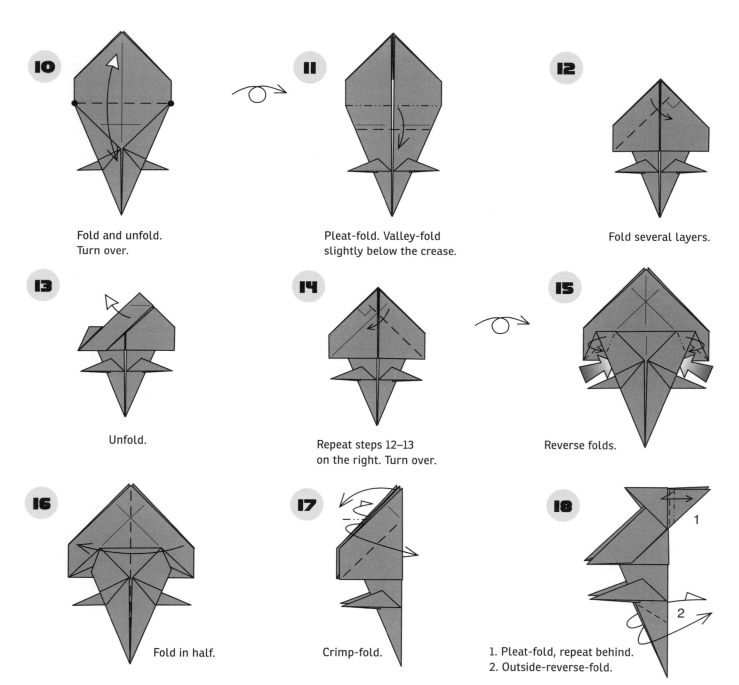

**10** Fold and unfold. Turn over.

**11** Pleat-fold. Valley-fold slightly below the crease.

**12** Fold several layers.

**13** Unfold.

**14** Repeat steps 12–13 on the right. Turn over.

**15** Reverse folds.

**16** Fold in half.

**17** Crimp-fold.

**18** 1. Pleat-fold, repeat behind.
2. Outside-reverse-fold.

**19**

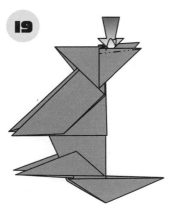

Make a small reverse fold on the left side of the ear. Repeat behind and rotate model.

**20**

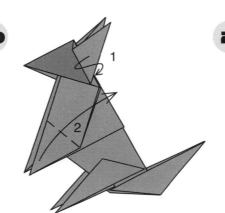

1. Tuck the ear under the darker paper.
2. Fold the arm. Repeat behind.

**21**

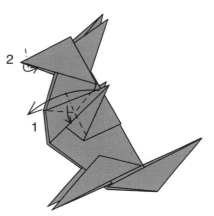

1. Rabbit-ear, repeat behind.
2. Reverse-fold.

**22**

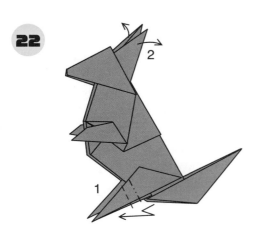

1. Crimp-fold, repeat behind.
2. Spread the ears.

**23**

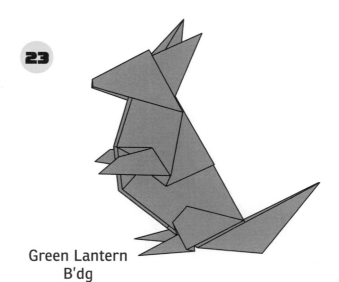

Green Lantern
B'dg

# GREEN LANTERN HAL JORDAN

Hal Jordan was a brash and reckless test pilot for Ferris Aircraft. One day he discovered the severely injured alien Abin Sur in a crashed spaceship. Before he died Abin Sur gave Hal his Green Lantern power ring. Now Hal guards Space Sector 2814, which includes the planet Earth. As a former test pilot, he is no stranger to overcoming fear, an essential trait of any member of the Green Lantern Corps. On Hal's finger, the Green Lantern power ring becomes an unmatched weapon—a powerful force to shield his home planet against evil.

LEVEL: ★★★

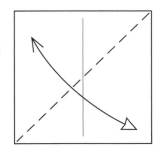

1. Fold and unfold.
Turn over.

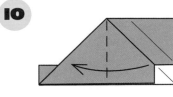

2. Fold and unfold.

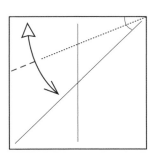

3. Fold to the crease and unfold. Crease on the left.

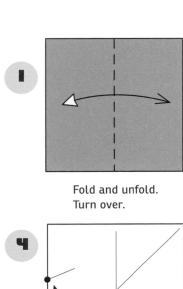

4. Fold and unfold on the left so the dots meet.

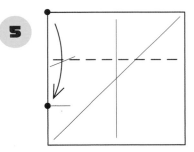

5. Fold down so the dots meet.

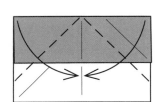

6. Fold to the center.

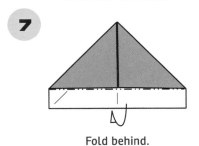

7. Fold behind.

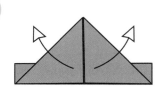

8. Unfold.

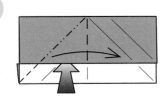

9. Squash-fold.

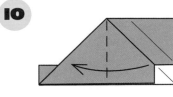

10. Fold the top flap.

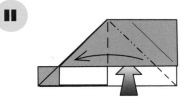

11. Repeat steps 9–10 on the right.

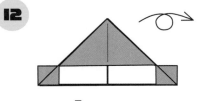

12. Turn over.

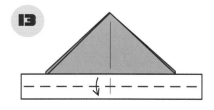

**13**

Fold down.

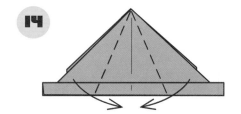

**14**

Fold to the center.

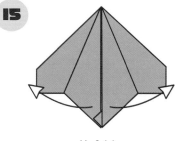

**15**

Unfold.

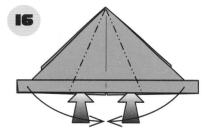

**16**

Reverse folds.

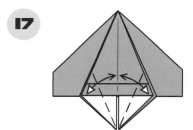

**17**

Fold and unfold the top flaps to the center.

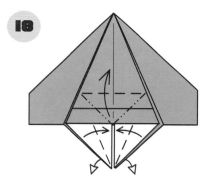

**18**

Petal-fold. Spread at the bottom.

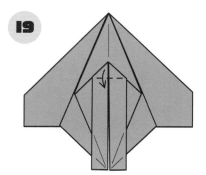

**19**

Fold down.

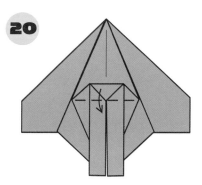

**20**

Fold down.

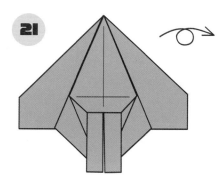

**21**

Turn over.

**22**

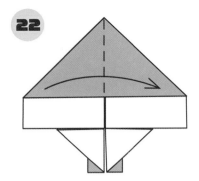

Fold to the right.

**23**

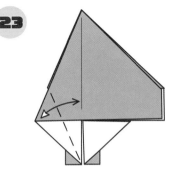

Fold and unfold.

**24**

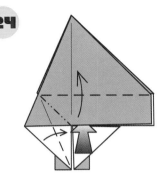

Squash-fold.

**25**

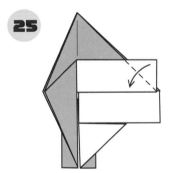

Fold down.

**26**

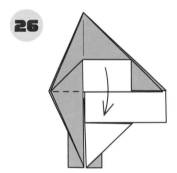

Fold down.

**27**

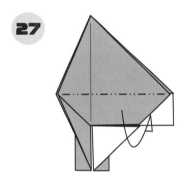

Fold inside.

**28**

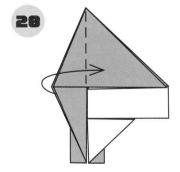

Fold the top flap
to the right.

**29**

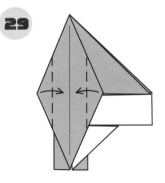

Fold near the center.

**30**

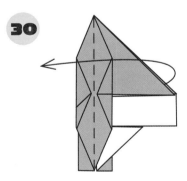

Fold to the left.

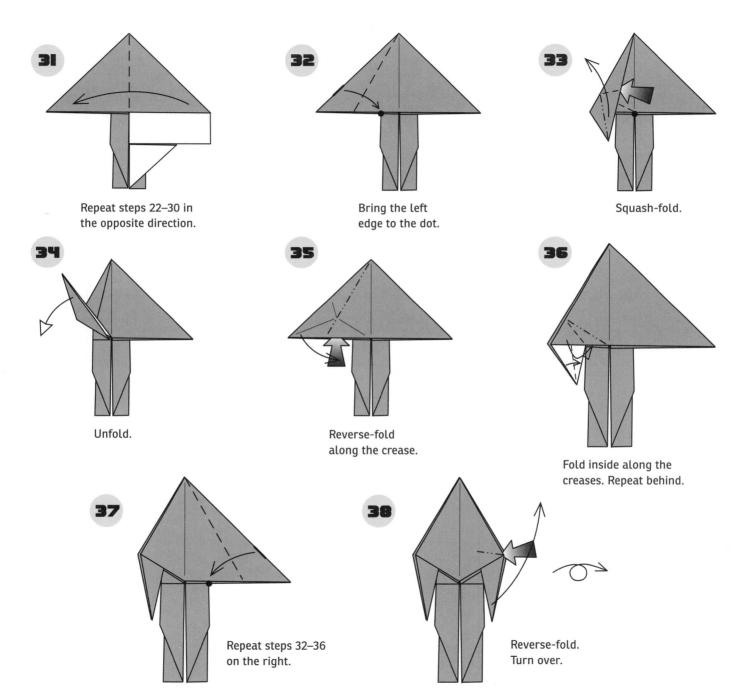

**31**

Repeat steps 22–30 in the opposite direction.

**32**

Bring the left edge to the dot.

**33**

Squash-fold.

**34**

Unfold.

**35**

Reverse-fold along the crease.

**36**

Fold inside along the creases. Repeat behind.

**37**

Repeat steps 32–36 on the right.

**38**

Reverse-fold. Turn over.

**39**

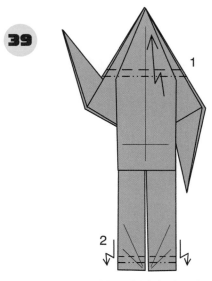

1. Pleat-fold the head.
2. Pleat-fold the feet.

**40**

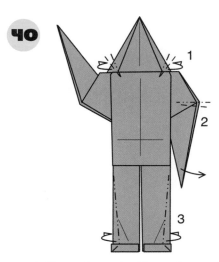

1. Shape the neck with small squash folds.
2. Crimp-fold the arm.
3. Squash-fold to shape the feet and legs.

**41**

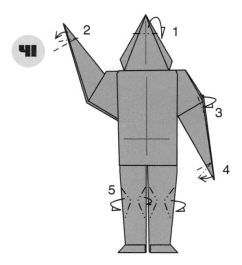

1. Fold behind.
2. Squash-fold.
3. Fold inside, repeat behind.
4. Squash-fold.
5. Shape the legs to make them 3D.

**42**

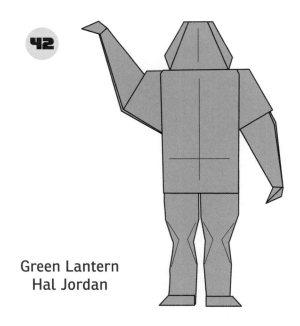

## Green Lantern
## Hal Jordan

# STORM

As Aquaman's mighty steed, Storm helps protect the Seven Seas, including the royal city of Atlantis. With telepathic powers and tsunami-like speed, Storm is no ordinary sea horse. He carries the Sea King into battle against natural disasters and underwater enemies, such as Black Manta and Ocean Master. Together, Aquaman and Storm ensure that Atlantis—and all of the wonders it contains—is never lost again.

LEVEL: ★★☆

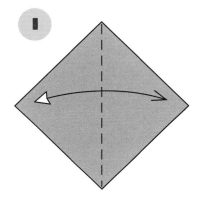

**1**

Fold and unfold.

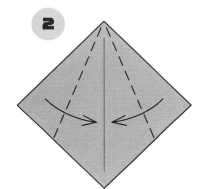

**2**

Fold to the center.

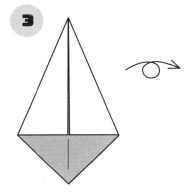

**3**

Turn over.

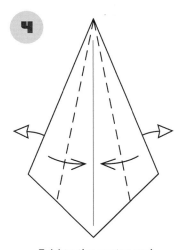

**4**

Fold to the center and swing out from behind.

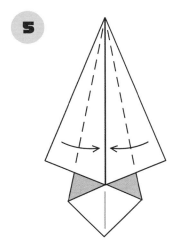

**5**

Fold to the center.

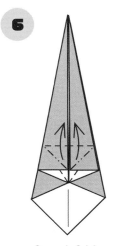

**6**

Squash folds.

**7**

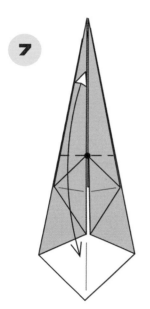

Fold and unfold.

**8**

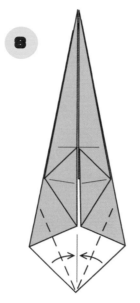

Fold to the center.

**9**

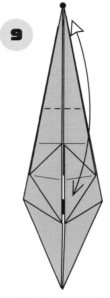

Fold and unfold. Bring the dot to the bold line. There is no exact landmark.

**10**

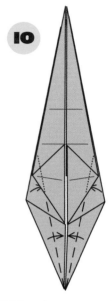

Fold to the center and tuck under the top layer.

**11**

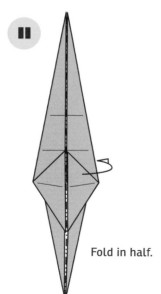

Fold in half.

**12**

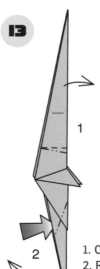

Fold to the crease and repeat behind.

**13**

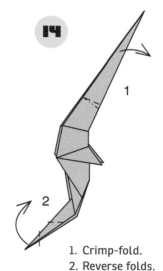

1. Crimp-fold.
2. Reverse-fold.

**14**

1. Crimp-fold.
2. Reverse folds.
Rotate model.

**15**

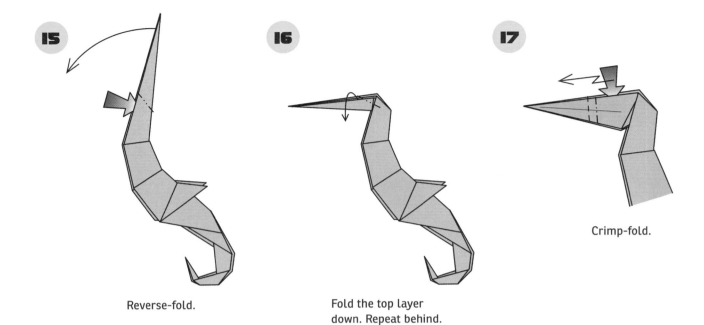

Reverse-fold.

**16**

Fold the top layer
down. Repeat behind.

**17**

Crimp-fold.

**18**

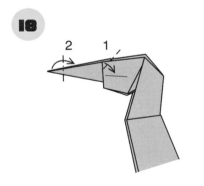

2    1

1. Fold the eye, repeat behind.
2. Reverse-fold.

**19**

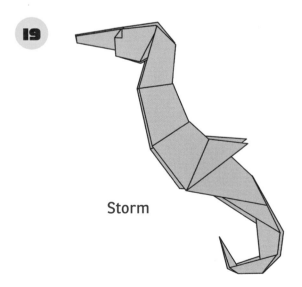

Storm

# AQUAMAN'S TRIDENT

The trident is a centuries-old symbol for Neptune, the ancient Roman god of the sea. The trident was known as "Earthshaker" because Neptune could create shattering earthquakes by striking it into coastlines or seabeds. As the new oceanic ruler, Aquaman now wields the golden trident and uses it to command the seven seas. The mighty three-pronged weapon can defeat his foes by emitting force fields, creating giant columns of water, or generating whirlpools and turbulent tidal waves.

LEVEL: ★ ★ ☆

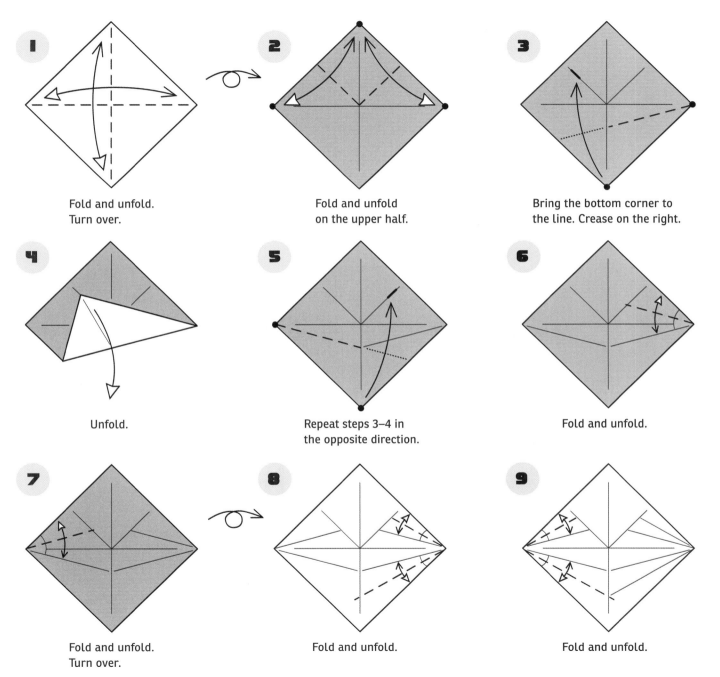

**1** Fold and unfold. Turn over.

**2** Fold and unfold on the upper half.

**3** Bring the bottom corner to the line. Crease on the right.

**4** Unfold.

**5** Repeat steps 3–4 in the opposite direction.

**6** Fold and unfold.

**7** Fold and unfold. Turn over.

**8** Fold and unfold.

**9** Fold and unfold.

**10**

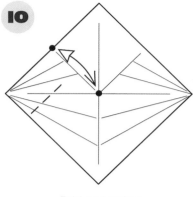

Fold and unfold
on the left.

**11**

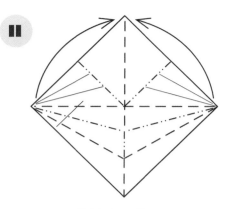

Fold along the
creases and flatten.

**12**

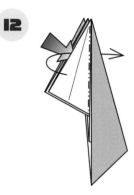

Reverse-fold,
repeat behind.

**13**

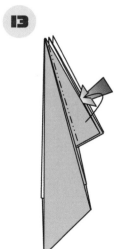

Reverse-fold,
repeat behind.

**14**

Fold in half.

**15**

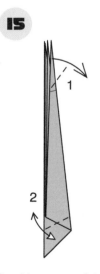

1  Outside-reverse-fold
   slightly above the crease.
2. Fold and unfold.

**16**

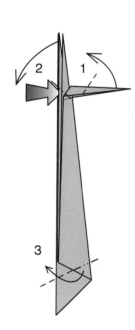

1. Outside-reverse-fold.
2. Reverse-fold.
3. Reverse-fold.

**17**

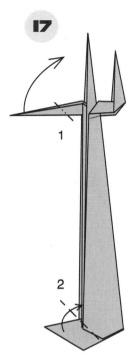

1. Reverse-fold.
2. Fold inside.

**18**

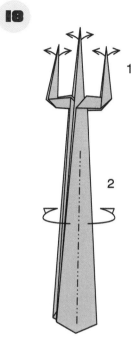

1. Spread the tips.
2. Thin.

**19**

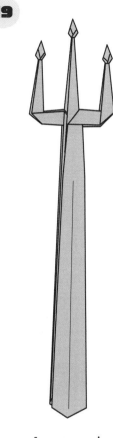

Aquaman's
Trident

# AQUAMAN

As the King of the Seven Seas, Aquaman defends all living things that call the ocean home. His telepathic powers enable him to communicate with all sea creatures, from shrimp and whales to hammerhead sharks and electric eels. Obeying their ruler's commands, these ocean dwellers pursue evildoers who treat the ocean as their private treasure trove, or use it as their hideout. Just as Superman and Batman fight for justice above the waves, Aquaman ensures that the two-thirds of our planet below the waves are washed clean of crime.

**LEVEL:** ★★★

**1**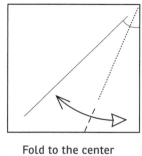

Fold and unfold.

**2**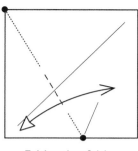

Fold to the center
and unfold. Crease
at the bottom.

**3**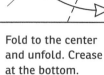

Fold and unfold
on the diagonal.

**4**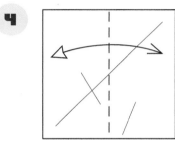

Fold and unfold.
Turn over.

**5**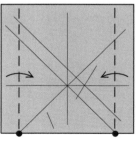

Fold up at the dot.

**6**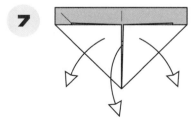

Fold to the center.

**7**

Unfold everything.

**8**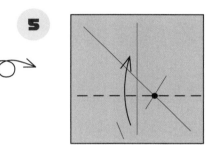

Fold on the
left and right.

**9**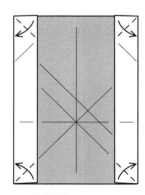

Fold the corners.

**10**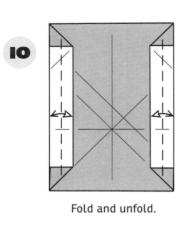

Fold and unfold.

**11**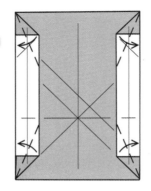

Fold to the edges.

**12**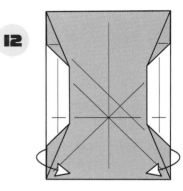

Unfold at the bottom.

**13**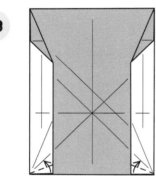

Fold along the creases.

**14**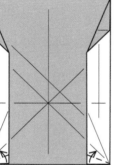

Fold along the creases.

**15**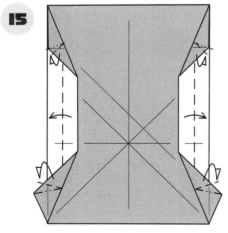

Fold inside at the top and bottom.

**16**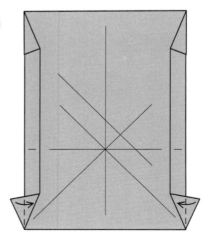

Fold at the bottom.

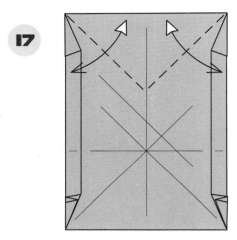

**17**

Fold and unfold.
Turn over.

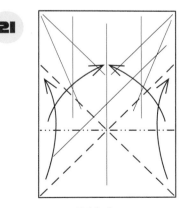

**18**

Fold and unfold.

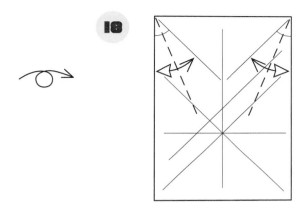

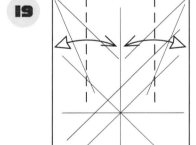

**19**

Fold to the center
and unfold.

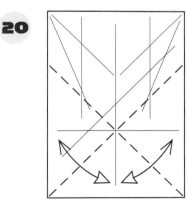

**20**

Fold and unfold
along the creases.

**21**

Fold along
the creases.

**22**

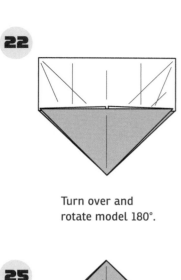

Turn over and
rotate model 180°.

**23**

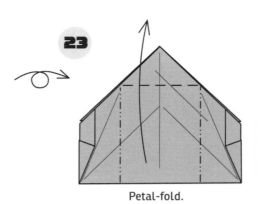

Petal-fold.

**24**

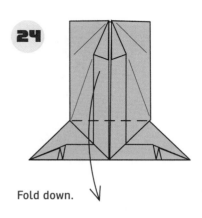

Fold down.

**25**

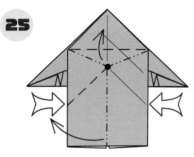

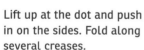

Lift up at the dot and push
in on the sides. Fold along
several creases.

**26**

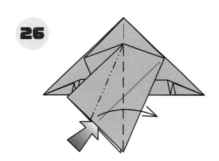

Squash-fold.

**27**

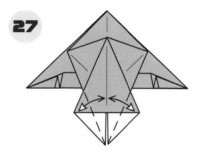

Fold to the center
and unfold.

**28**

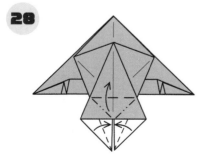

Petal-fold.

**29**

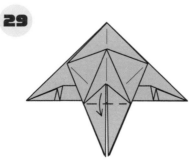

Fold down.

**30**

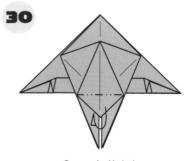

Spread slightly
to tuck inside.

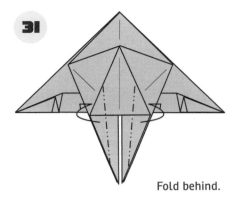

**31**

Fold behind.

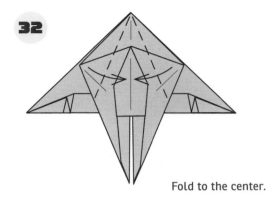

**32**

Fold to the center.

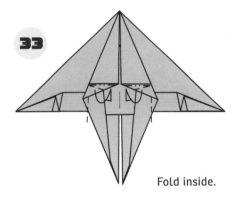

**33**

Fold inside.

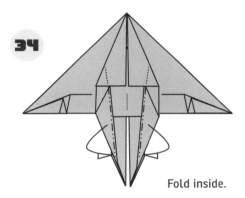

**34**

Fold inside.

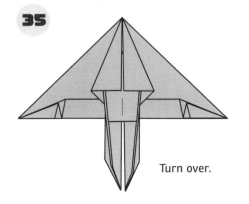

**35**

Turn over.

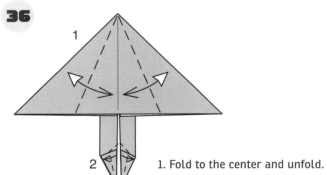

**36**

1. Fold to the center and unfold.
2. Make small squash folds.

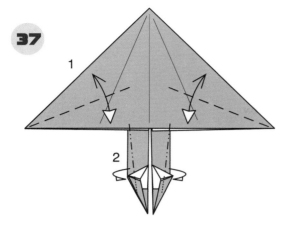

**37**

1. Fold and unfold
   all the layers.
2. Tuck inside.

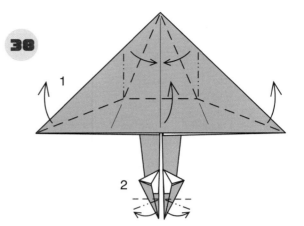

**38**

1. Fold along the creases.
2. Squash folds.

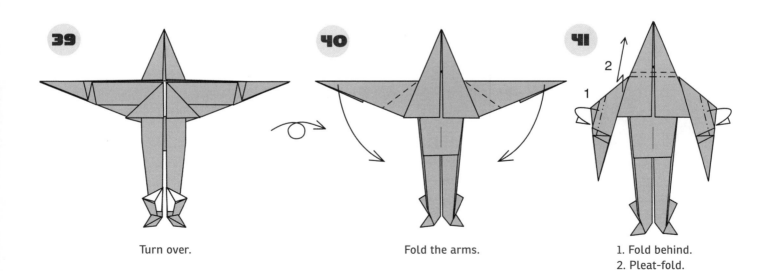

**39**

Turn over.

**40**

Fold the arms.

**41**

1. Fold behind.
2. Pleat-fold.

**42**

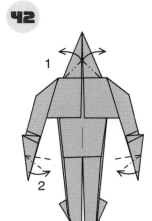

1. Spread.
2. Squash folds.

**43**

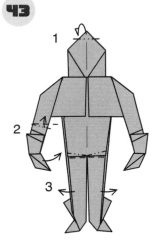

1. Fold behind.
2. Pleat-fold.
3. Pleat folds.

**44**

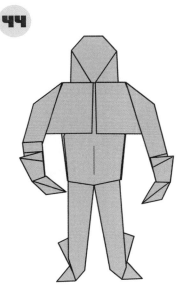

Aquaman

# HAWKGIRL'S MACE

Hawkgirl, an alien crime fighter from the distant planet of Thanagar, came to Earth to study human law enforcement methods. While posing as Shiera Hall, co-director of the Midway City Museum, she takes time to learn about weapons, old and new, that can aid her in the battle against bad guys. Naturally, the museum's collection of rare and ancient spears, crossbows, and swords bring a gleam to this super hero's eagle eye. But Hawkgirl's armament of choice is a wicked metal mace. Combined with her superb strength and mighty wing power, the mace becomes a terrifying tool for smashing robots or pounding the lights out of mindless monsters from outer space.

LEVEL: ★★★

**1**

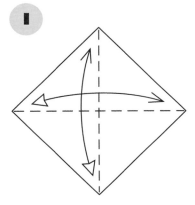

Fold and unfold.

**2**

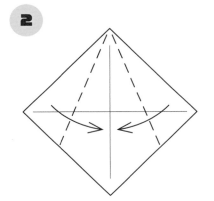

Fold to the center.

**3**

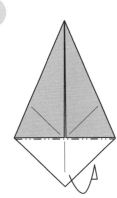

Fold behind.

**4**

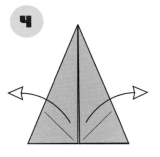

Unfold.

**5**

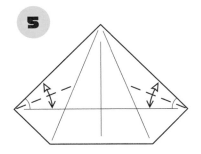

Fold to the crease
and unfold.

**6**

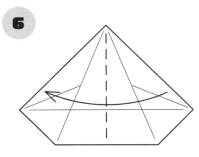

Fold in half.

**7**

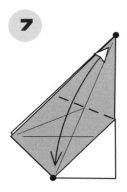

Fold and unfold
so the dots meet.

**8**

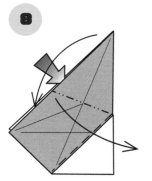

Squash-fold and
rotate model.

**9**

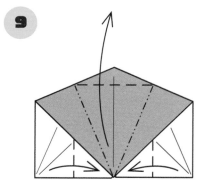

Petal-fold.

**10**

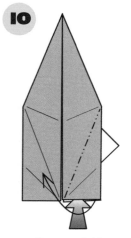

Reverse-fold.

**11**

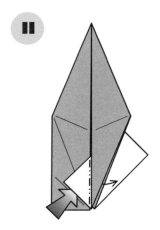

Reverse-fold.

**12**

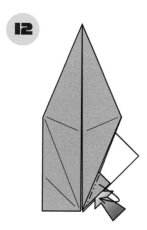

Reverse-fold.

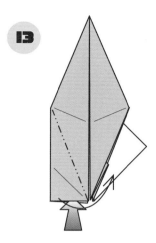

**13**

Repeat steps
10–12 on the left.

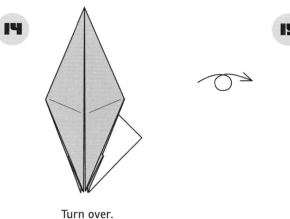

**14**

Turn over.

**15**

Fold to the right.

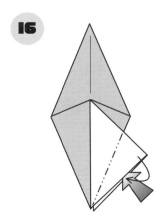

**16**

Reverse-fold.

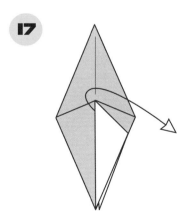

**17**

Spread to pull out
the white corner.

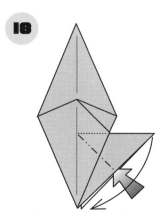

**18**

Reverse-fold.

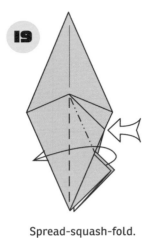

**19**

Spread-squash-fold.

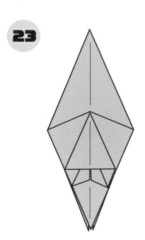

**20**

Fold to the center
and unfold.

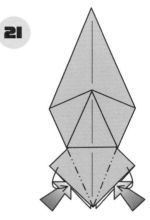

**21**

Reverse folds.

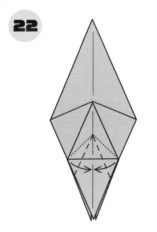

**22**

Fold the partially hidden
flaps to the center.

**23**

Turn over.

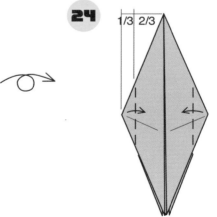

**24**

1/3   2/3

Fold about one-third
of the way toward
the center.

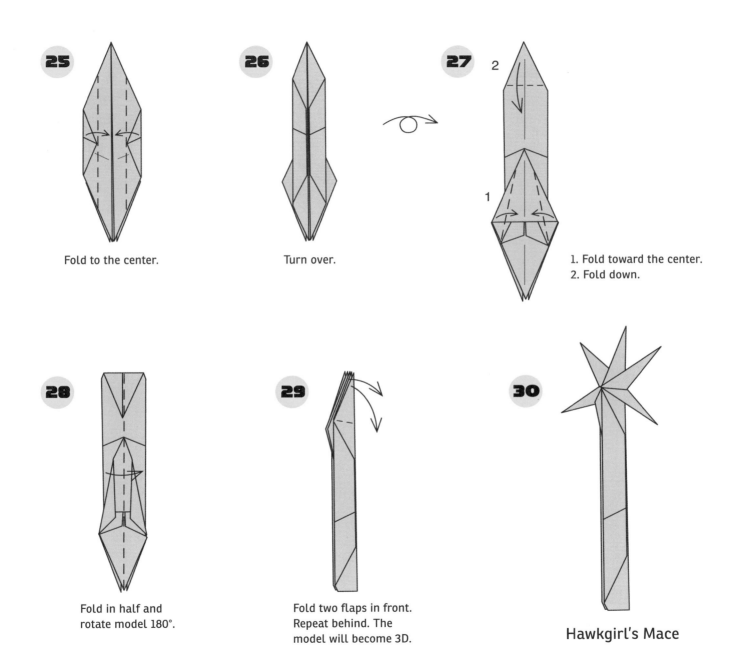

**25**

Fold to the center.

**26**

Turn over.

**27**

2

1

1. Fold toward the center.
2. Fold down.

**28**

Fold in half and rotate model 180°.

**29**

Fold two flaps in front. Repeat behind. The model will become 3D.

**30**

Hawkgirl's Mace

# HAWKGIRL

Hawkgirl swoops down on evildoers in Midway City. As a law enforcer from the distant planet Thanagar, she came to Earth to enhance her crime-fighting skills. By working undercover at the Midway City Museum, Hawkgirl remains ready to soar. When duty calls, she straps on her wing-harness and cowl, snatches an ancient weapon from the museum's collection, and takes flight as a feathered figure of swift justice.

**LEVEL:** ★★★

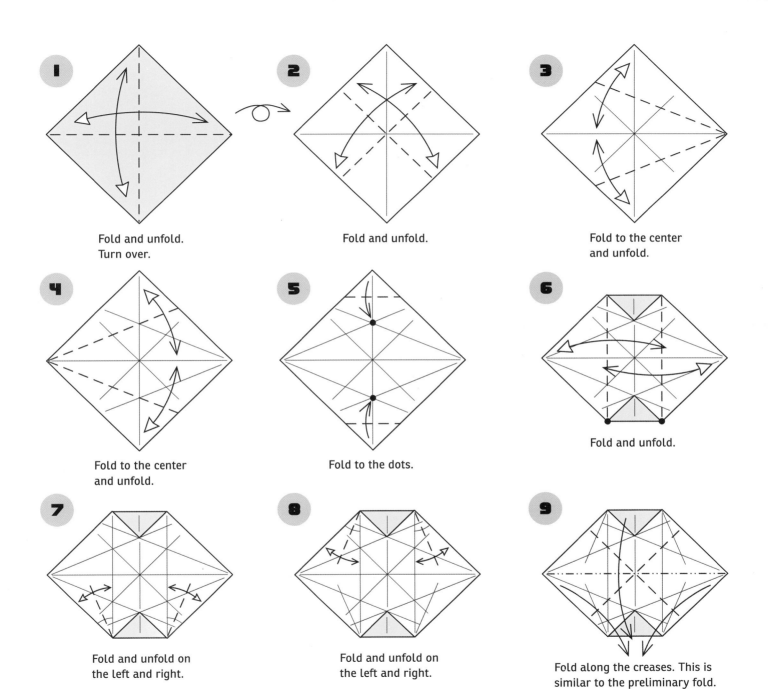

**1** Fold and unfold. Turn over.

**2** Fold and unfold.

**3** Fold to the center and unfold.

**4** Fold to the center and unfold.

**5** Fold to the dots.

**6** Fold and unfold.

**7** Fold and unfold on the left and right.

**8** Fold and unfold on the left and right.

**9** Fold along the creases. This is similar to the preliminary fold.

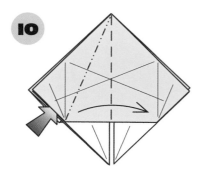

**10**

Squash-fold.

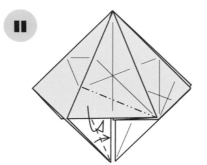

**11**

Tuck inside.

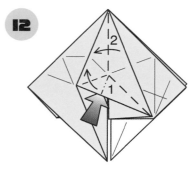

**12**

Lift up at 1 while folding to the left at 2.

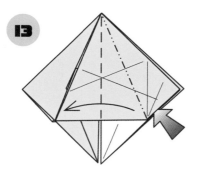

**13**

Repeat steps 10–12 on the right.

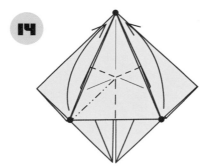

**14**

This is similar to a rabbit-ear. The dots will meet at the top.

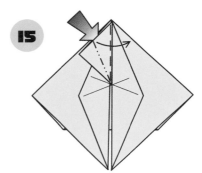

**15**

Squash–fold.

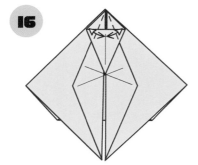

**16**

Fold and unfold.

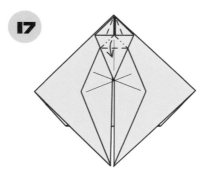

**17**

Petal-fold.

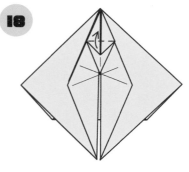

**18**

Fold up.

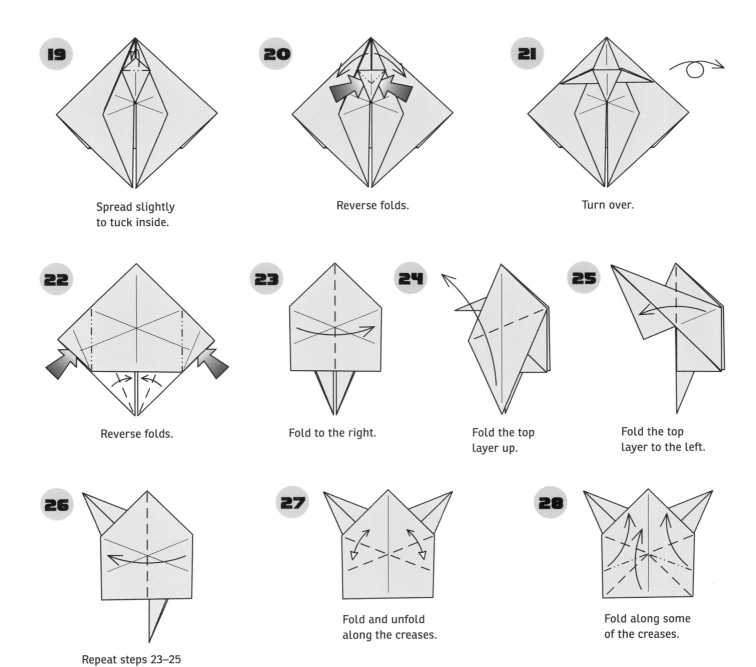

**19** Spread slightly to tuck inside.

**20** Reverse folds.

**21** Turn over.

**22** Reverse folds.

**23** Fold to the right.

**24** Fold the top layer up.

**25** Fold the top layer to the left.

**26** Repeat steps 23–25 in the other direction.

**27** Fold and unfold along the creases.

**28** Fold along some of the creases.

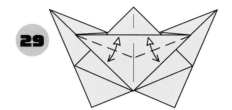

**29** Fold and unfold the top flap.

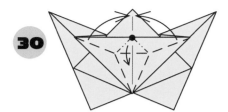

**30** Fold the dot down while bringing the other flaps to the center.

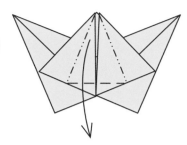

**31** Petal-fold. Mountain-fold along the creases.

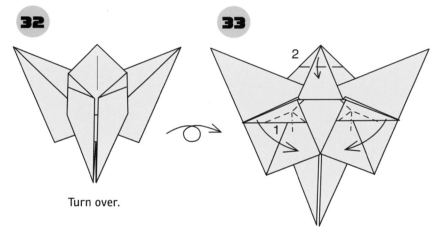

**32** Turn over.

**33**
1. Rabbit-ear the arms.
2. Fold down.

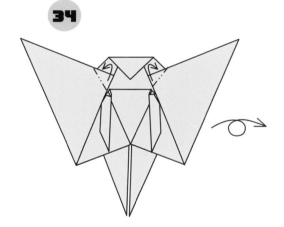

**34** Reverse folds. Turn over.

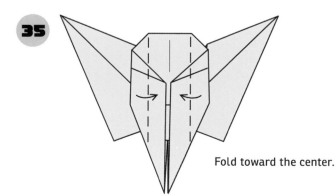

**35** Fold toward the center.

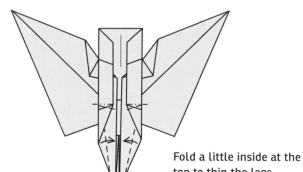

**36** Fold a little inside at the top to thin the legs.

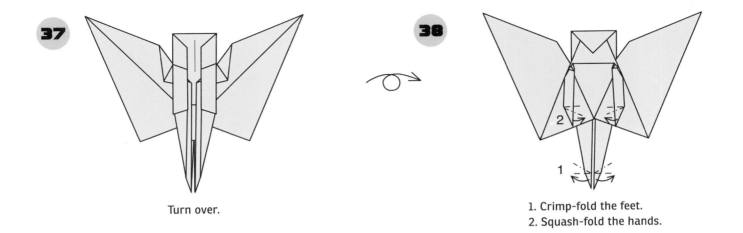

**37**

Turn over.

**38**

1. Crimp-fold the feet.
2. Squash-fold the hands.

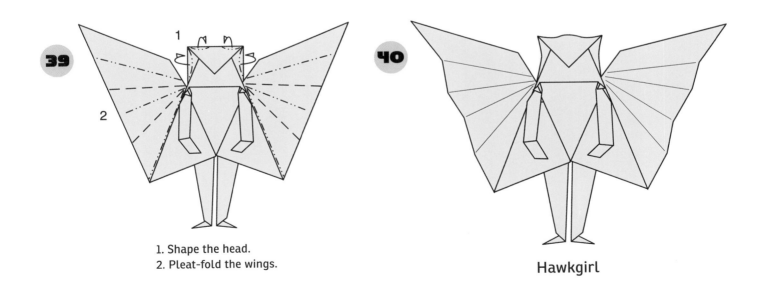

**39**

1. Shape the head.
2. Pleat-fold the wings.

**40**

Hawkgirl

# THE ATOM

Scientist Ray Palmer used the elements from a fallen dwarf star to create a daring device that alters his size from man to microbe. As The Atom he surfs the digital waves between phones, slips through the electrons of locked doors, and hitches rides in criminals' coat collars. Although the Mighty Mite may be a mere six inches tall, he packs a full-size punch by retaining the density and strength of his normal human height. Whether halting a jewel heist or saving the planet from peril, the world's smallest super hero banks on his tiny stature and huge brainpower to cut evil down to size.

LEVEL: ★ ★ ★

**1**

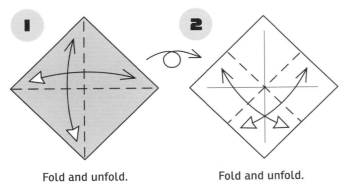

Fold and unfold.
Turn over.

**2**

Fold and unfold.

**3**

Fold to the center
and unfold.

**4**

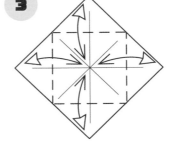

Make the
preliminary fold.

**5**

Squash-fold.
Repeat behind.

**6**

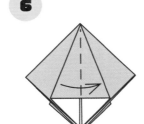

Fold the top layer.
Repeat behind.

**7**

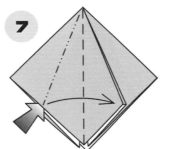

Squash-fold.
Repeat behind.

**8**

Fold to the center.
Repeat behind.

**9**

Unfold. Repeat
behind.

**10**

Petal-fold.
Repeat behind.

**11**

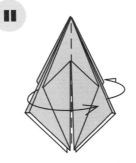

Fold two layers to the
right. Repeat behind.

**12**

Petal-fold.
Repeat behind.

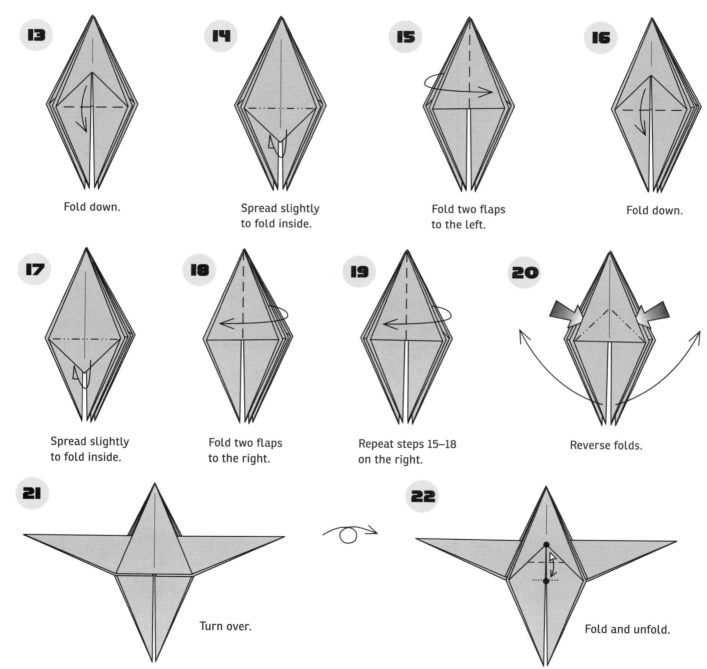

**13** Fold down.

**14** Spread slightly to fold inside.

**15** Fold two flaps to the left.

**16** Fold down.

**17** Spread slightly to fold inside.

**18** Fold two flaps to the right.

**19** Repeat steps 15–18 on the right.

**20** Reverse folds.

**21** Turn over.

**22** Fold and unfold.

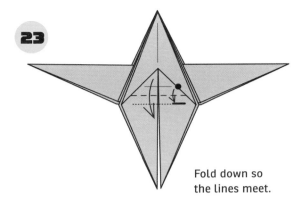

**23**

Fold down so
the lines meet.

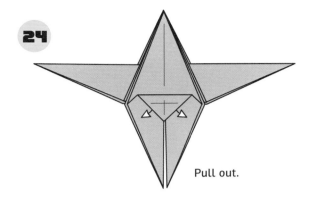

**24**

Pull out.

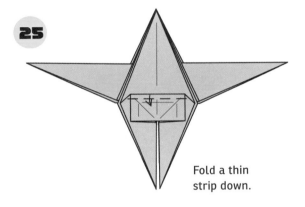

**25**

Fold a thin
strip down.

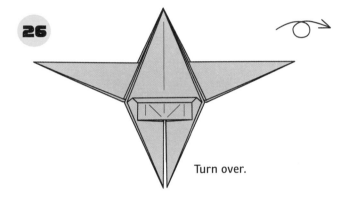

**26**

Turn over.

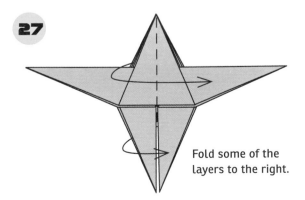

**27**

Fold some of the
layers to the right.

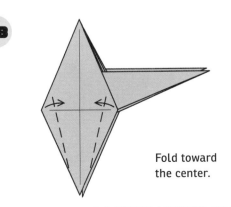

**28**

Fold toward
the center.

DC SUPER HEROES ORIGAMI **253**

**29**

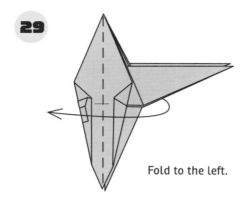

Fold to the left.

**30**

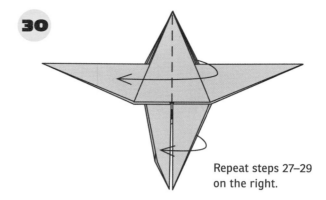

Repeat steps 27–29
on the right.

**31**

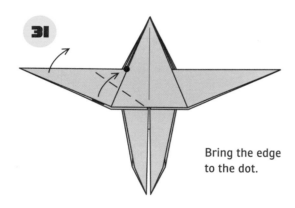

Bring the edge
to the dot.

**32**

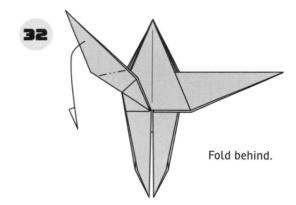

Fold behind.

**33**

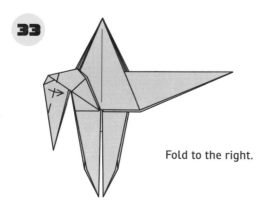

Fold to the right.

**34**

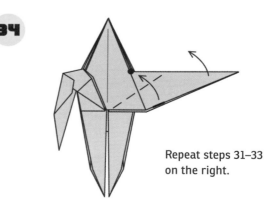

Repeat steps 31–33
on the right.

**35**

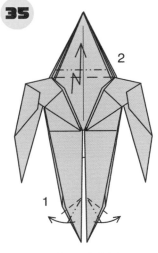

1. Squash folds.
2. Pleat-fold.

**36**

1. Squash folds.
2. Fold down.

**37**

Turn over.

**38**

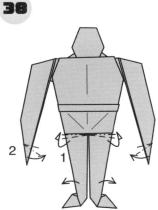

1. Pleat-fold the legs.
2. Squash-fold the hands.

**39**

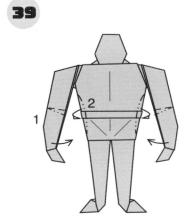

1. Pleat-fold the arms.
2. Shape the body.

**40**

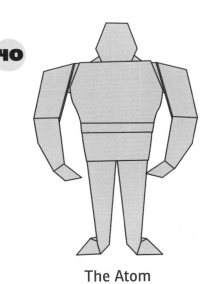

The Atom

# ILLUSTRATED FOLDING PAPER
# USER GUIDE

You've torn out a sheet of illustrated paper and are ready to start folding—but wait! Which side of the paper is the front and which is the back? And how do you know which corner or edge should be at the top in step 1? The answer is simple—just look for this arrow: ↑

Every sheet of illustrated folding paper has an orientation arrow. This arrow is always on the back of the paper, and it always points away from you at the start of the project. Use this arrow to help you determine which side of the paper should be face-up and which direction the paper should be oriented for the first step of every project.

Tip: Maximize your illustrated folding papers! Practice new models with traditional origami paper first. This paper is easy to find in many sizes at craft stores. When you feel confident folding a model, use the illustrated folding papers to create your mini masterpieces!

© DC (515)

©DC (\$15)

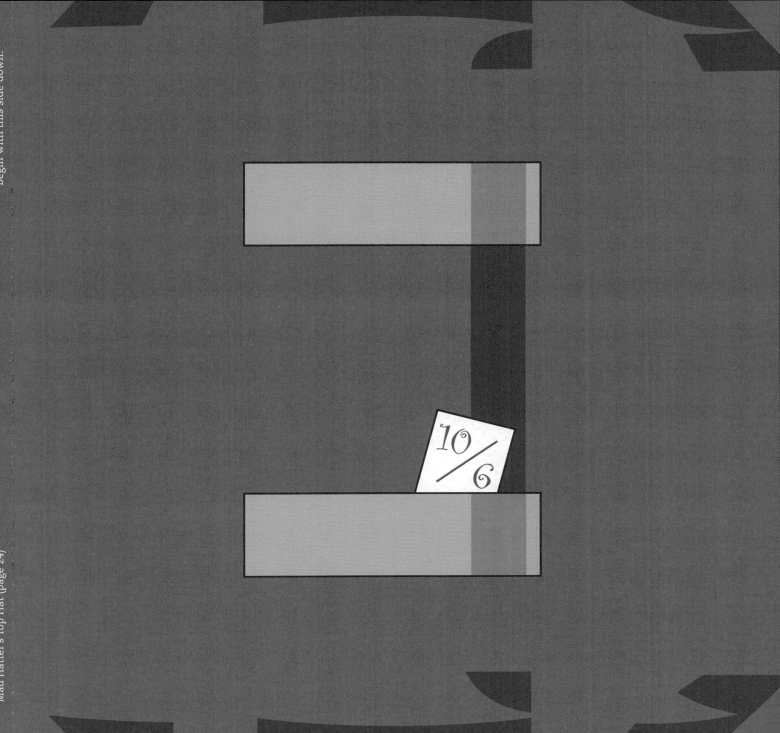

Mad Hatter's Top Hat (page 24)

Begin with this side down.

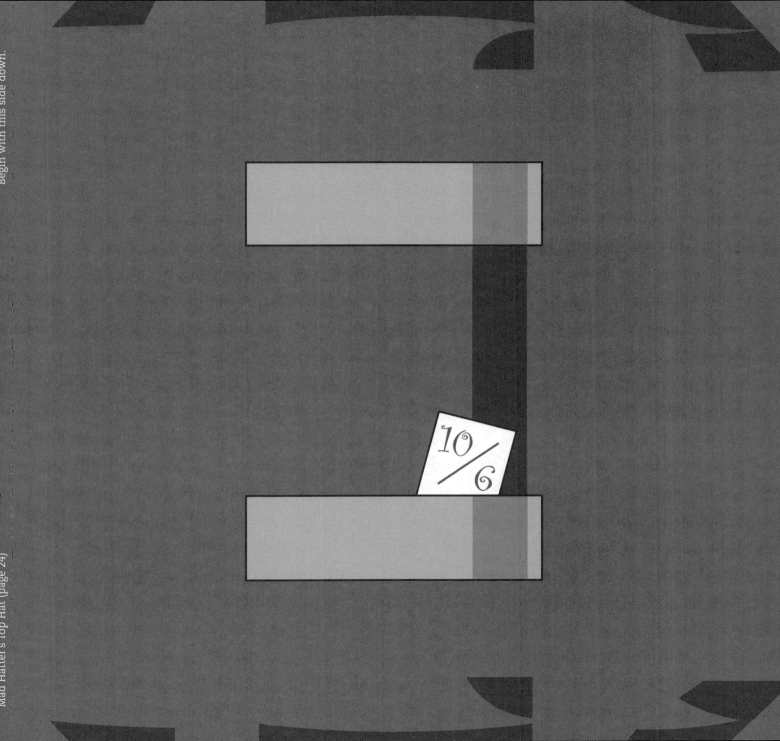

↓ © DC (616)

Mad Hatter's Top Hat (page 24)

Begin with this side up

™

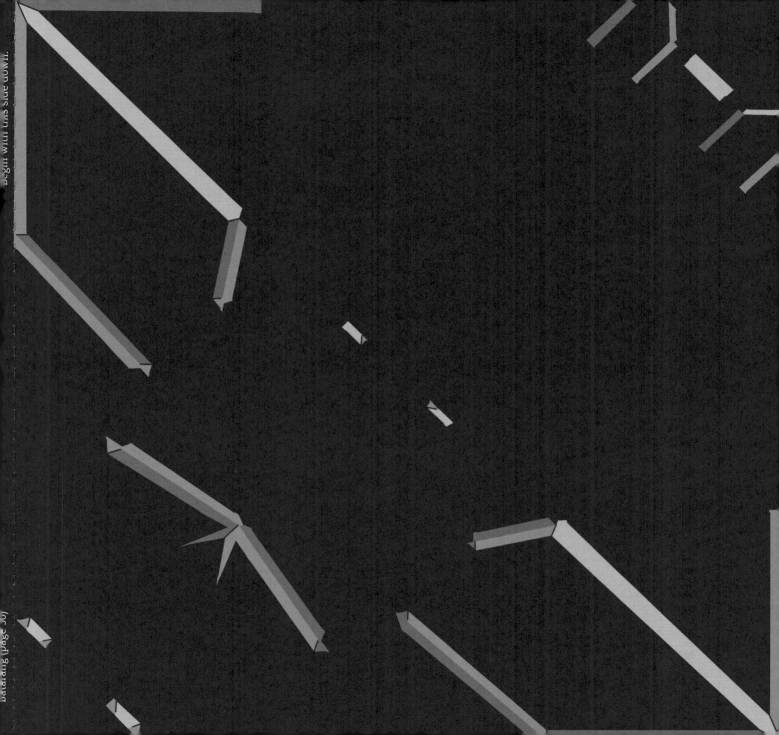

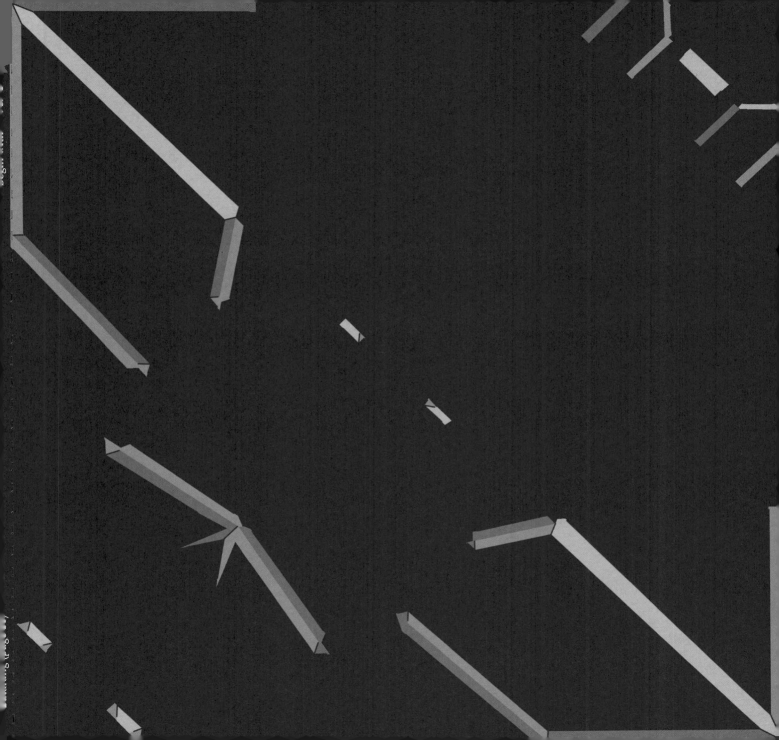

Begin with this side up

Nightwing Symbol (page 40)

© DC (s15)

Begin with this side up

Nightwing Symbol (page 40)

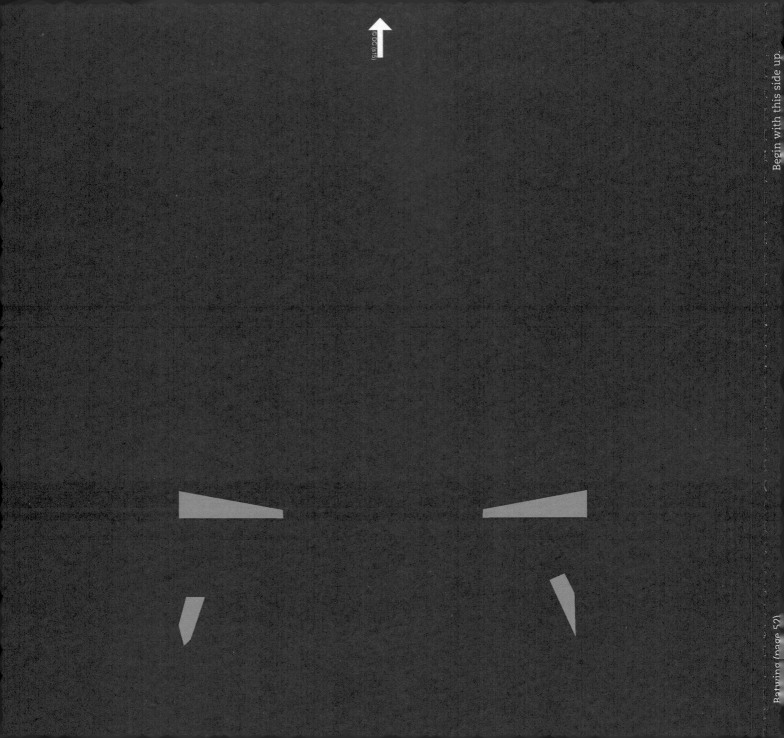

Begin with this side up.

Batwing (page 52)

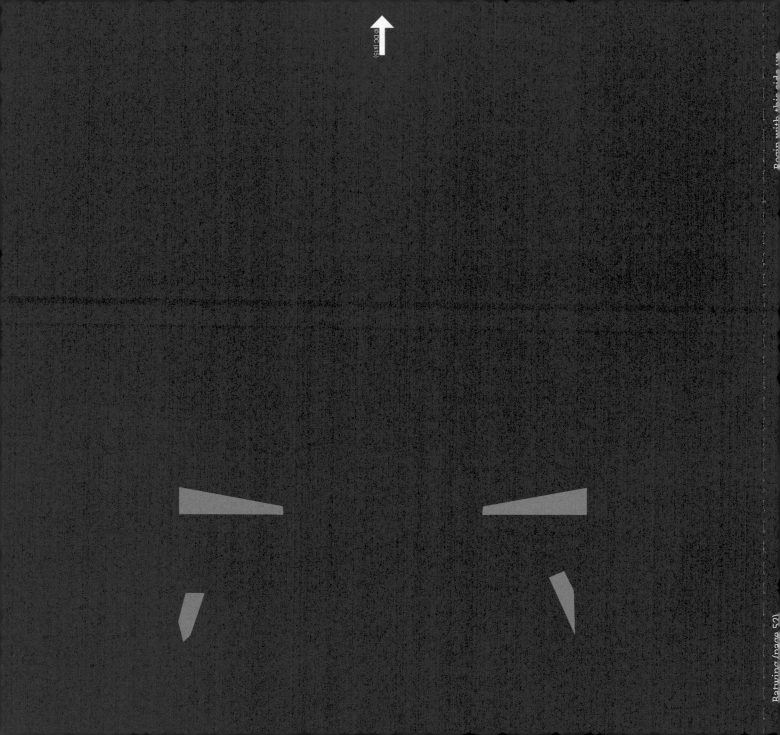

Begin with this side up

Batwing (page 52)

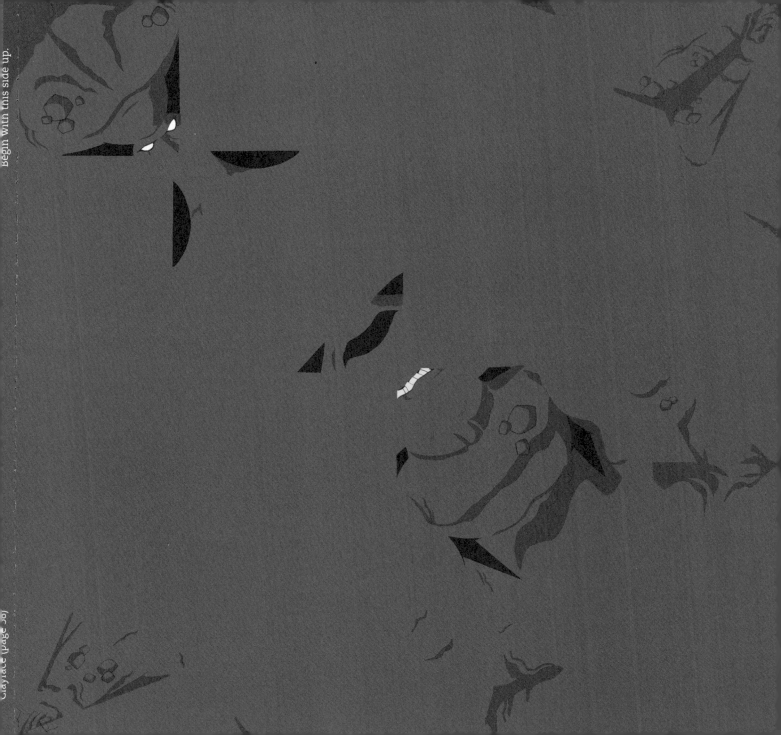

Photo (a)

Begin with this side down

Clawface (page 59)

DOG (616)

Begin with this down

Begin with this side down

DDC (515)

Robin (page 64)

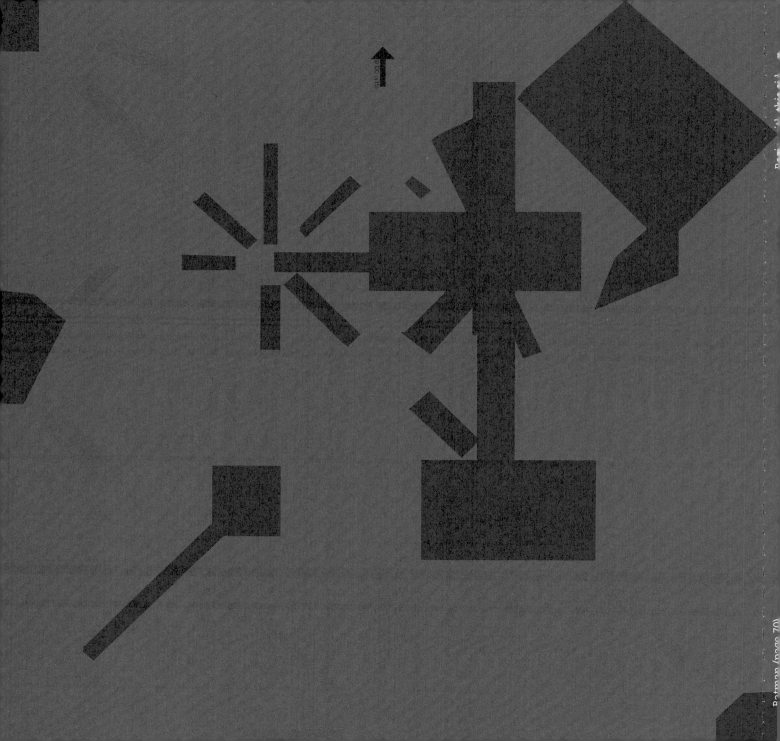

Begin with this side up

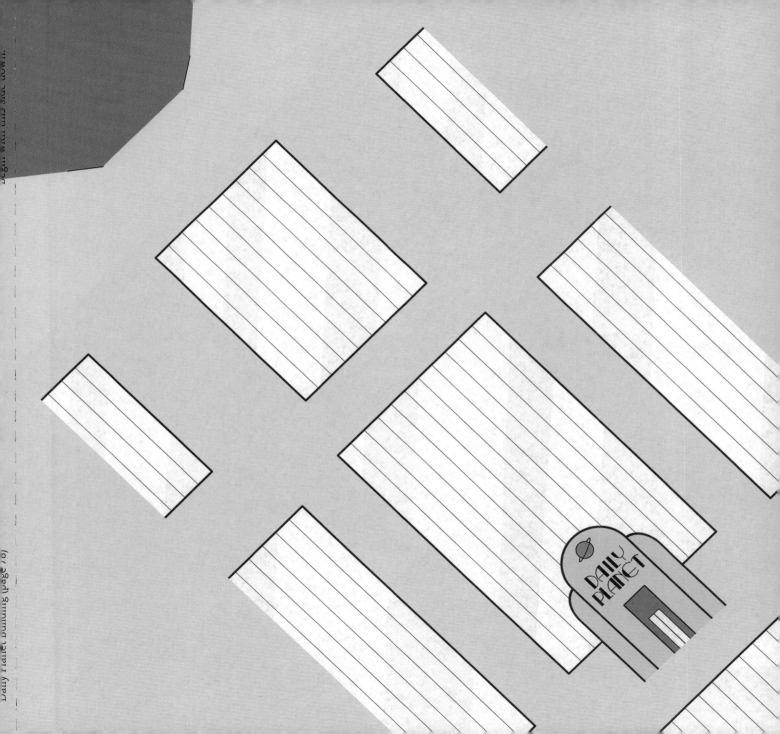

DAILY PLANET

Begin with this side up

TM

Fold (3)

Daily Planet Building (page 78)

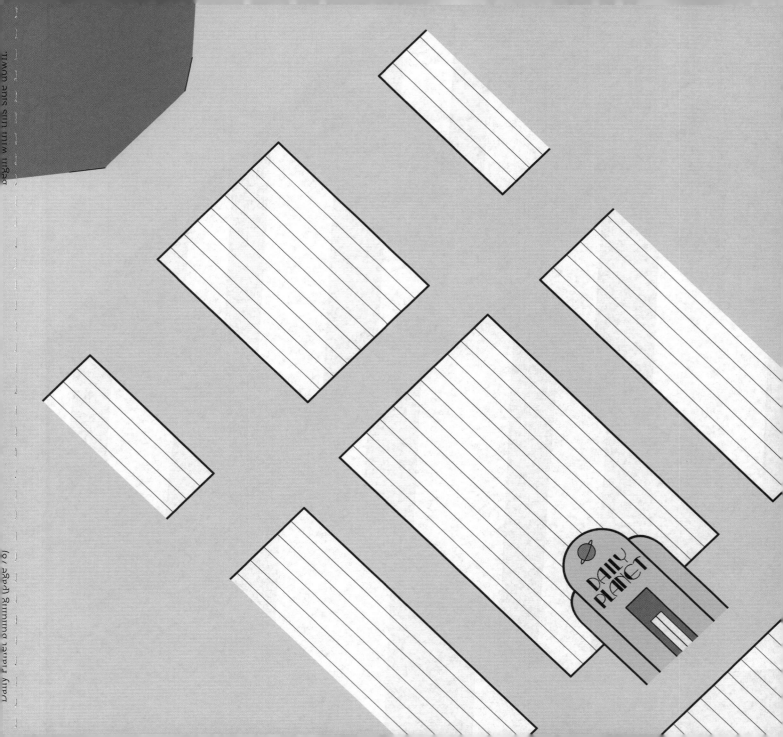

Daily Planet Building (page 78)

TM

© DC (s15)

DAILY PLANET

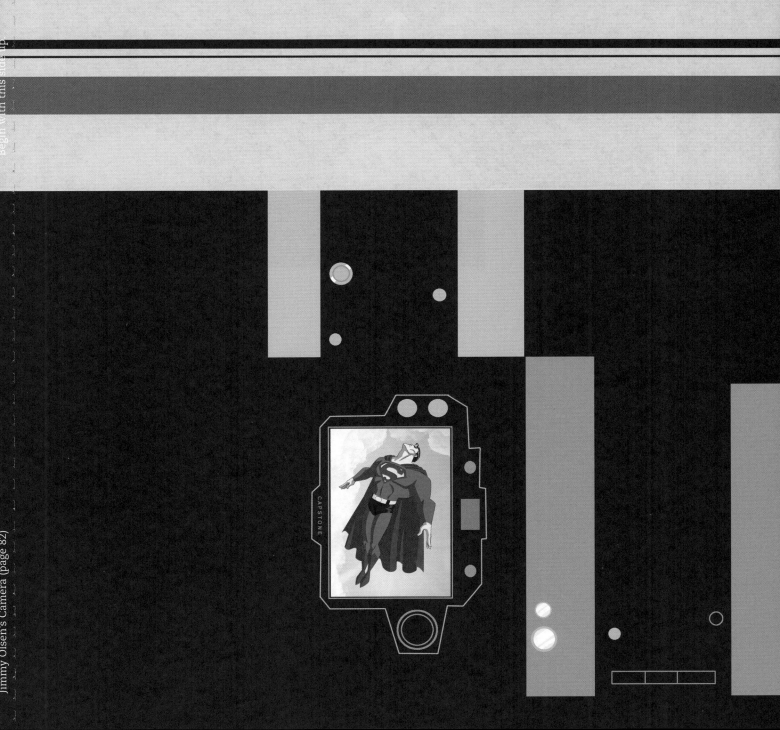

CAPSTONE

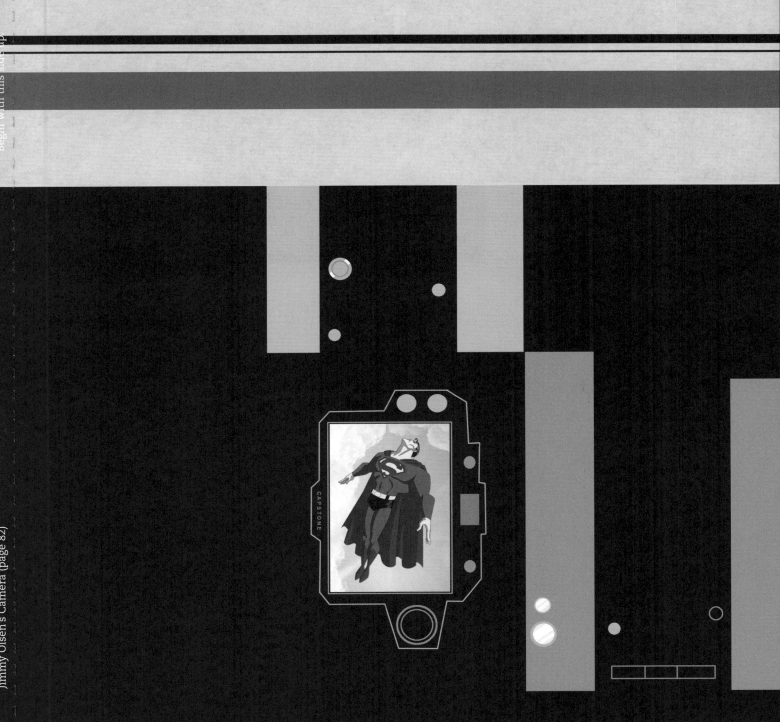

CAPSTONE

Begin with this side down.

Clark Kent's Glasses (page 80)

© DC(515)

begun with arms still down.

Town arm. sits um.

Kryptonite (page 90)

© DC (s15)

™

© DC (s15)

™

Begin with this side down

Fortress of Solitude Key (page 98)

™

© DC (s15

™

™

Picture 5 shield (page 108)

© DC (s15)

™

Begin with this side down

Bizarro ∫ shield (page 100)

© DC (STS)

Begin with this side down.

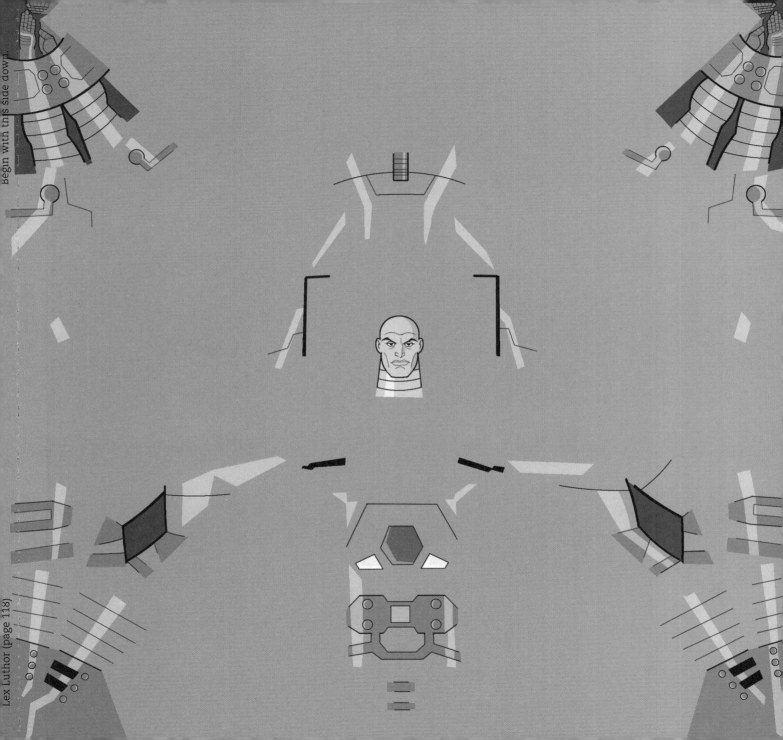

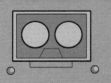

Begin with this side up

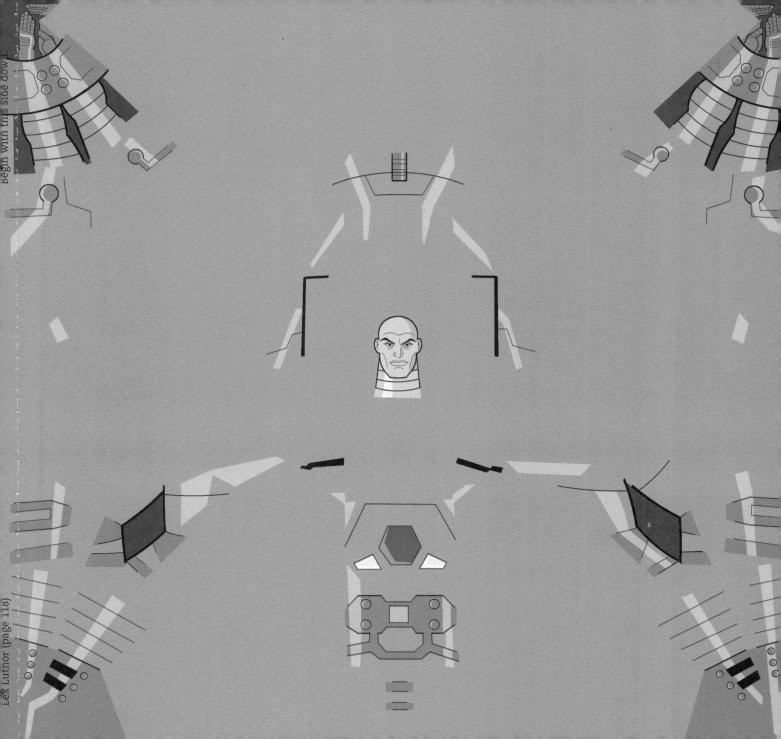

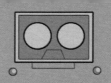

© DC (615)

Lex Luthor (page 118)

Begin with this side up

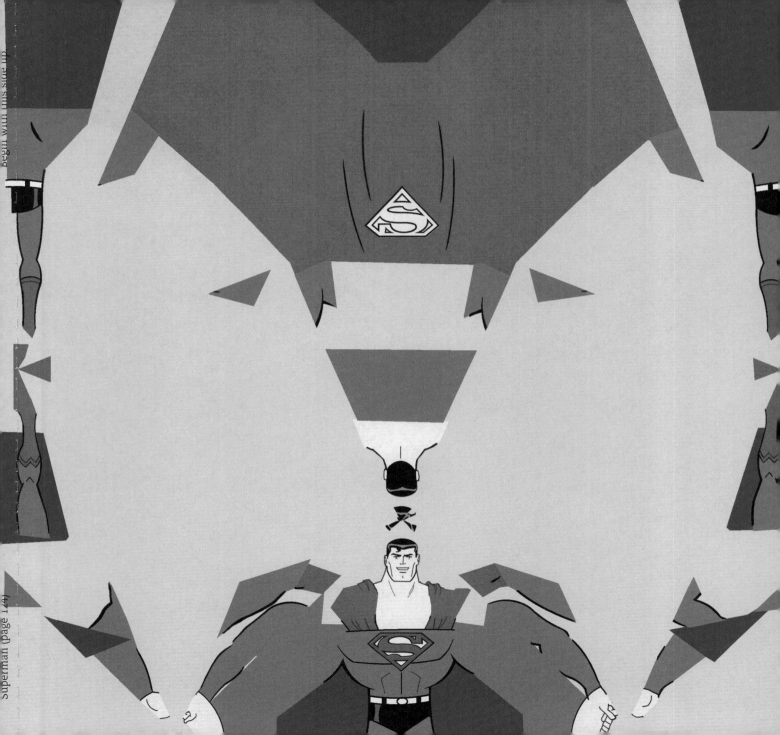

© DC (s15)

Begin with this side down.

Begin with this side down

Superman (page 124)

Begin with this side up.

Superman Flying (page 130)

© DC (615)

Superman Flying (page 130)

Begin with this side down.

© DC (s15)

Silver Bracelet (page 142)

Begin with this side up.

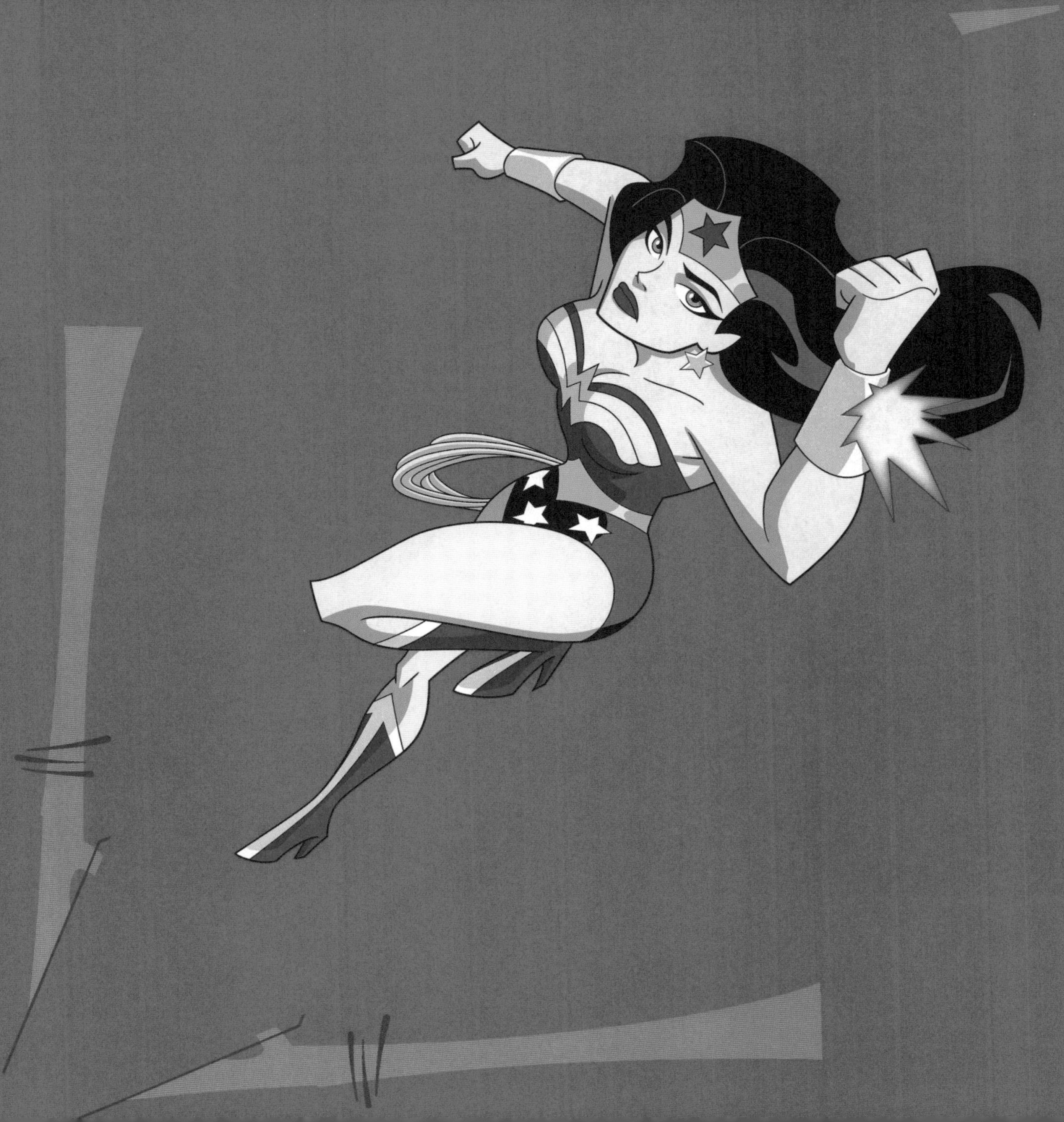

Begin with this side up.

Wonder Woman's Boot (page 146)

© DC (s16)

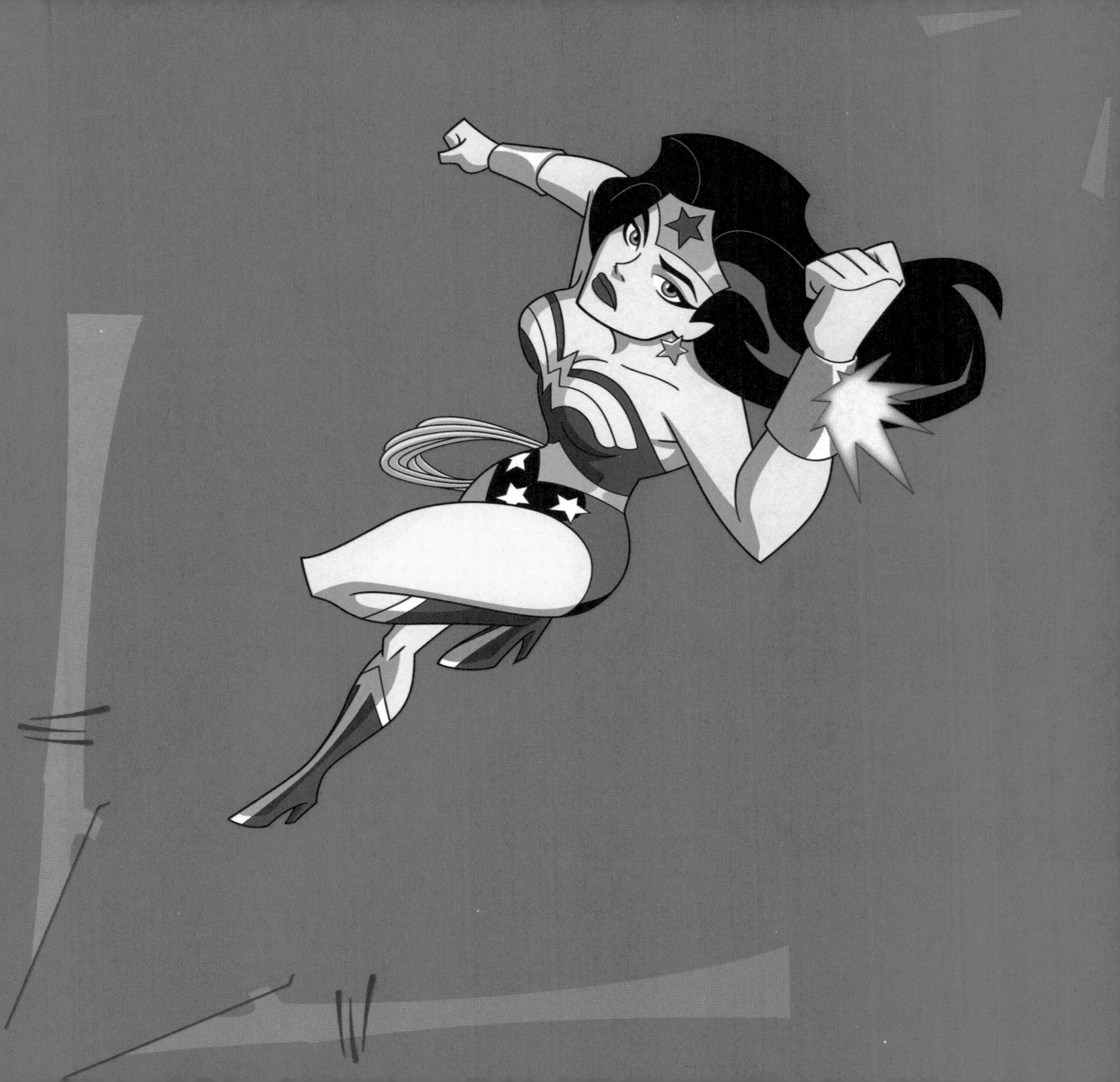

Wonder Woman's Boot (page 140)

Begin with this side up.

© DC (1915)

Wonder Woman's Boot (page 146)

Begin with this side down

© DC (815)

Star (page 150)

...won aros suu uuw uiseq

DDC (815)

© DC (s15)

Wonder Woman's Sword (page 150)

Eagle (page 162)

©DC (S15)

Eagle (page 162)

Eagle (page 162)

© DC (515)

Eagle (page 162)

Begin with this side down

Wonder Woman Symbol (page 168)

Begin with this side down.

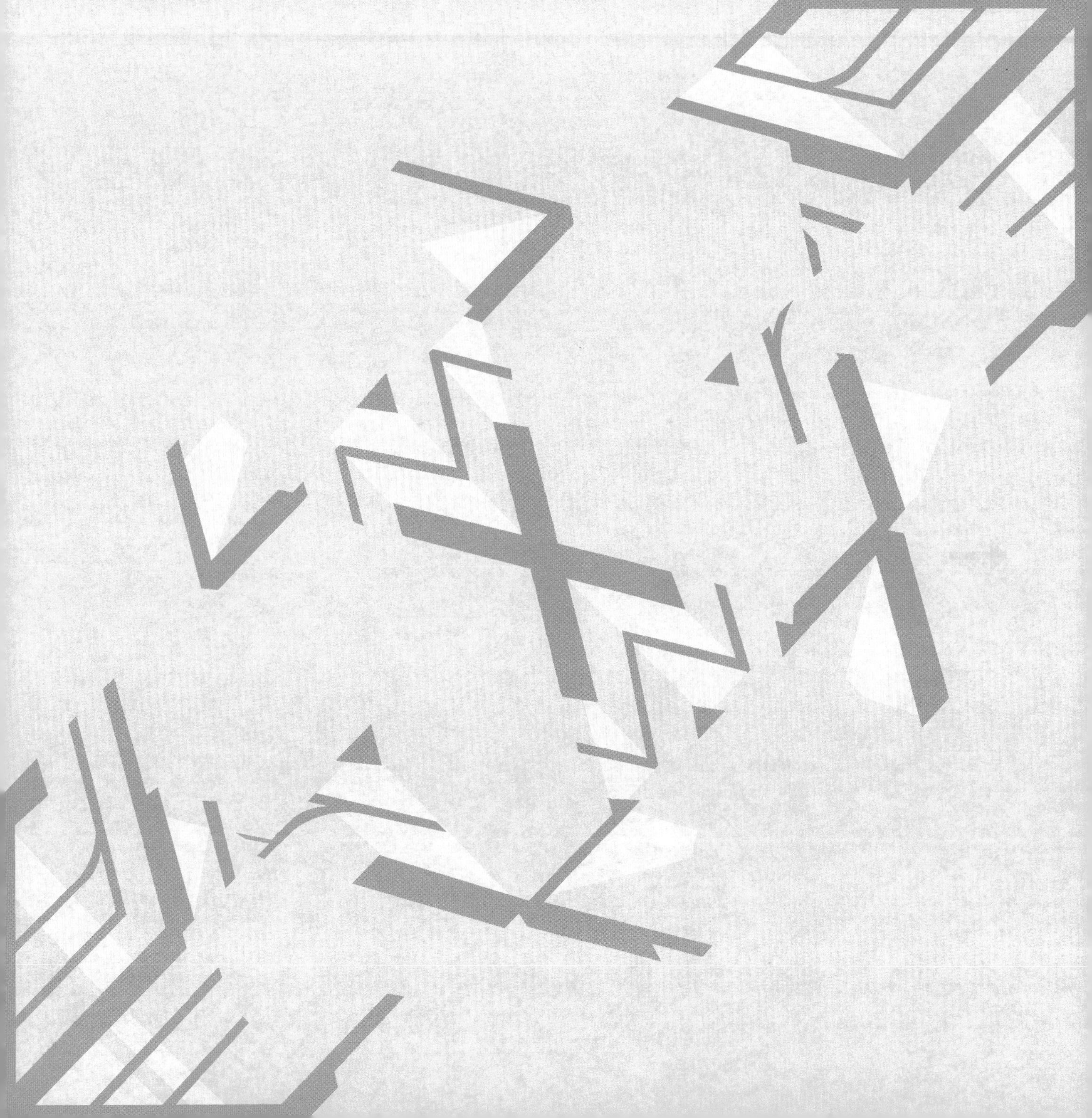

©DC (s15)

Wonder Woman Symbol (page 168)

Wonder Woman Symbol (page 66)

(or, begin with this same down-moon...)

© DC (s15)

© DC (s15)

Begin with this side up

Wonder Woman Symbol (page 168)

Invisible Jet (page 174)

Begin with this side up.

Jumpa the Kanga (page 180)

Begin with this side down

puzzles

Jump to the Kanga (page 190)

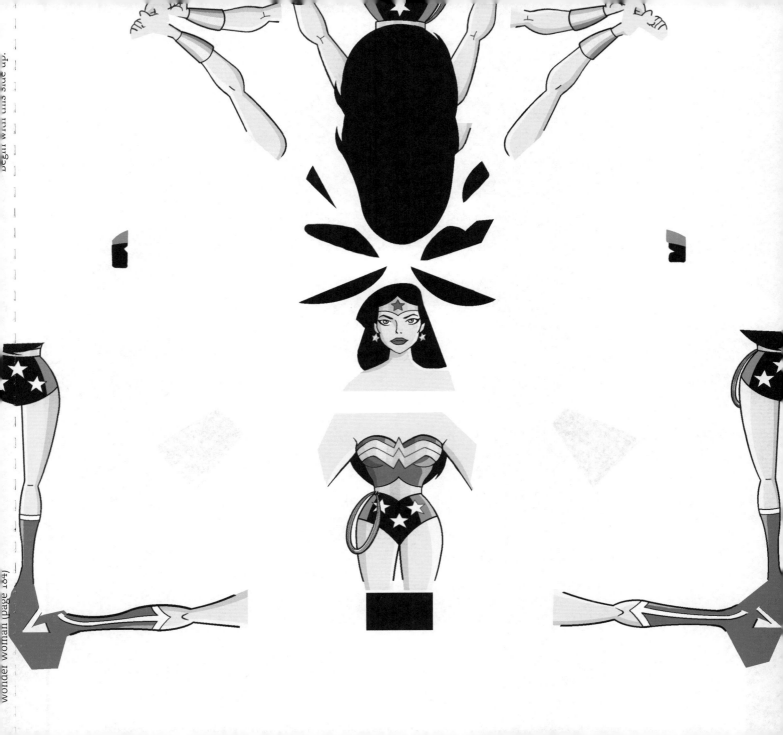

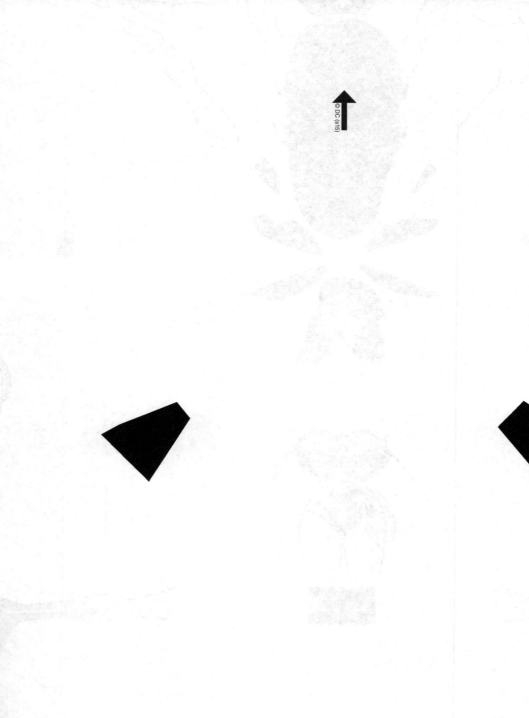

© DC (s15)

Wonder Woman (page 184)

Begin with this side down

© DC (s15)

Martian Manhunter Symbol (page 197)

Shazam! Symbol (page 196)

Begin with this side up

Begin with this side up

The Flash Symbol (page 200)

Begin with this side down.

The Flash Symbol (page 200)

© DC (s15)

The Flash Symbol (page 200)

Begin with this side up

© DC (315)

Green Arrow's Hat (page 204)

Begin with this side up

Green Arrow's Hat (page 204)

Begin with this side down

Green Lantern Symbol (page 208)

Green Lantern Symbol (page 208)

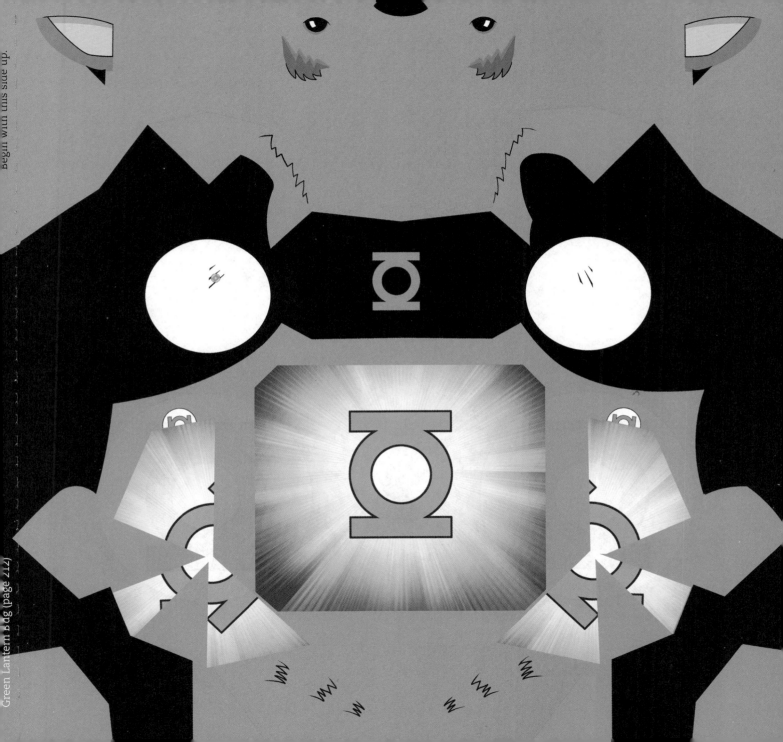

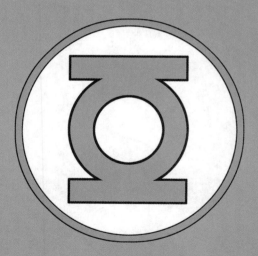

© DC (s15)

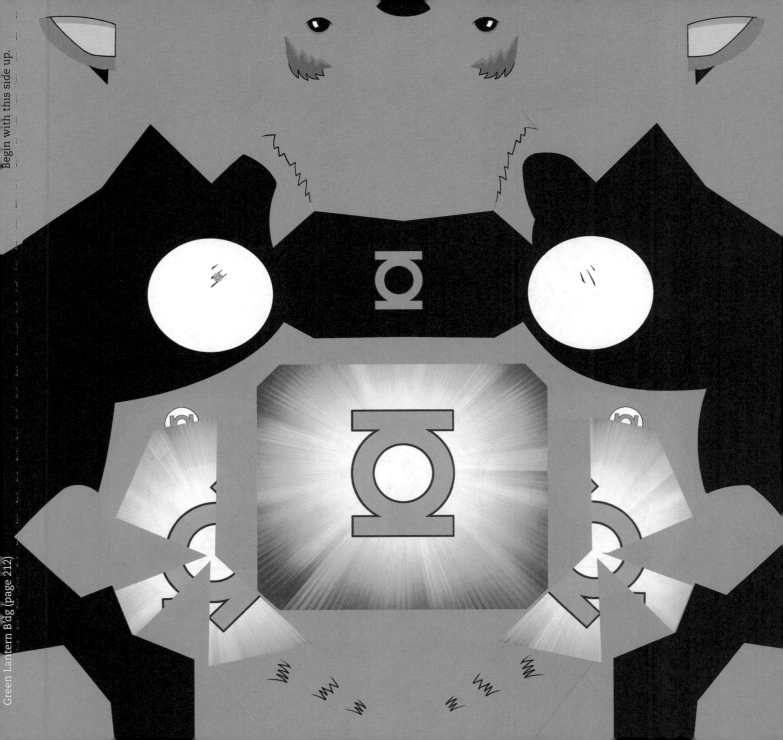

© DC (s15)

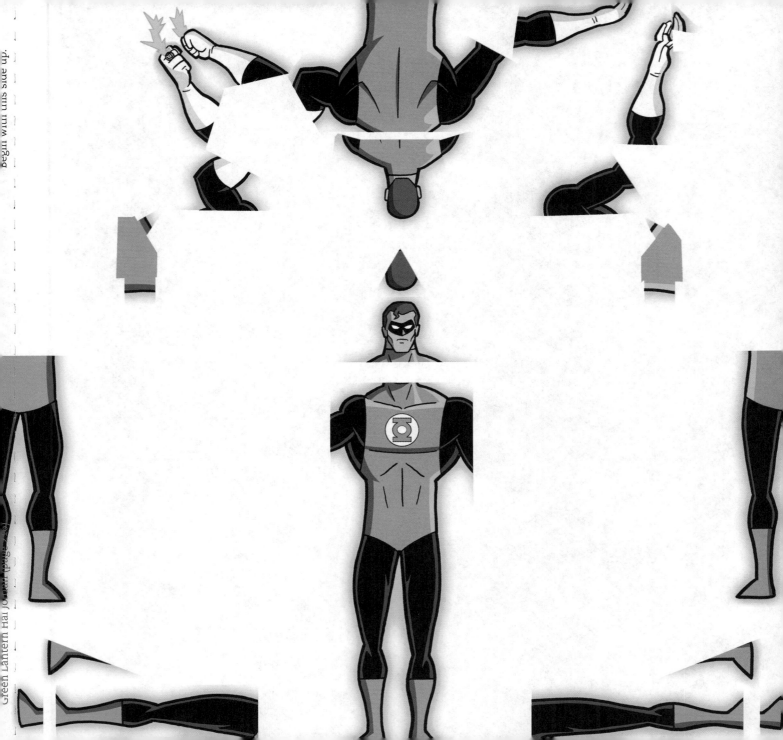

Begin with this side down

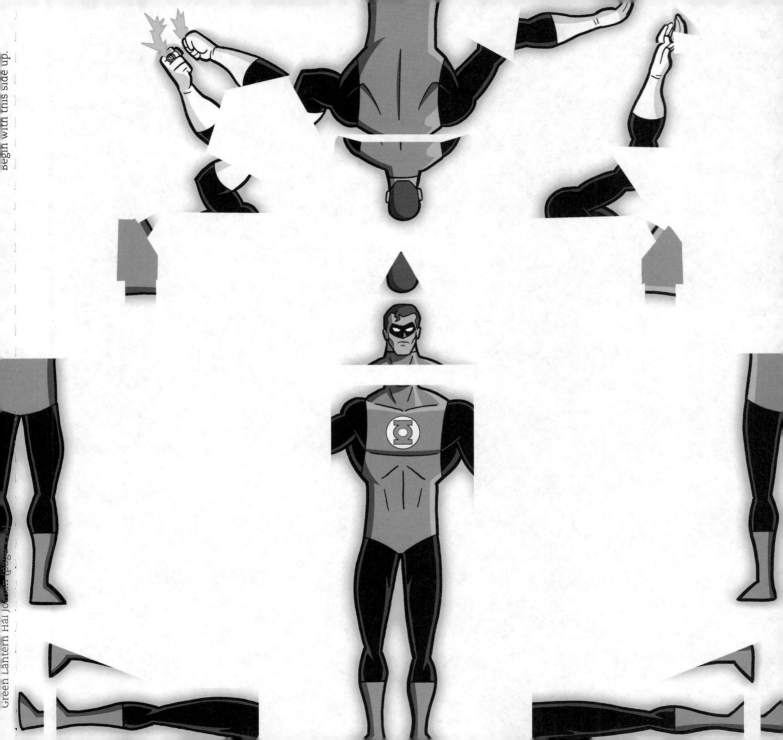

Begin with this side down

Green Lantern Hal Jordan (page 216)

Begin with this side down

(2 DC (s)s)

Storm (page 222)

Begin with this side down.

(page 515)

Storm (page 222)

Aquaman's Trident (page 276)

Begin with this seat down...

©DC (s15)

Aquaman's Trident (page 226)

Begin with this side down.

Aquaman's Trident (page 226)

Begin with this side up.

Aquaman's Trident (page 226)

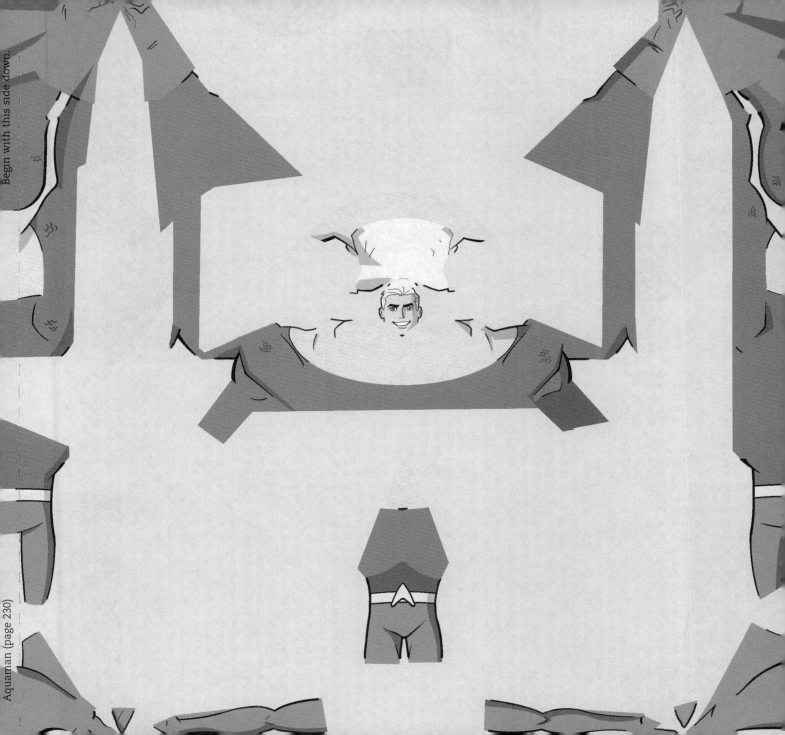

Aquaman (page 230)

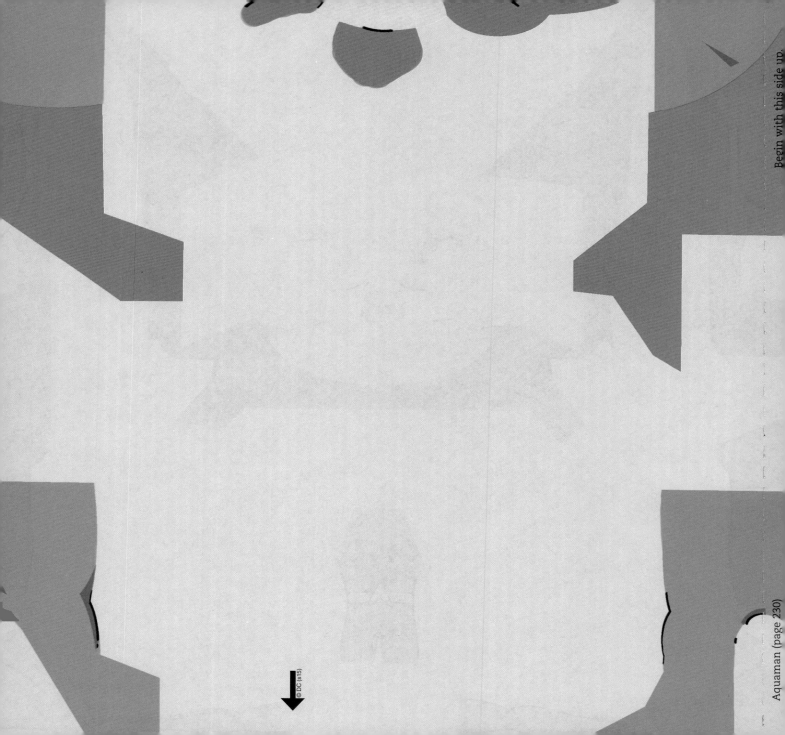

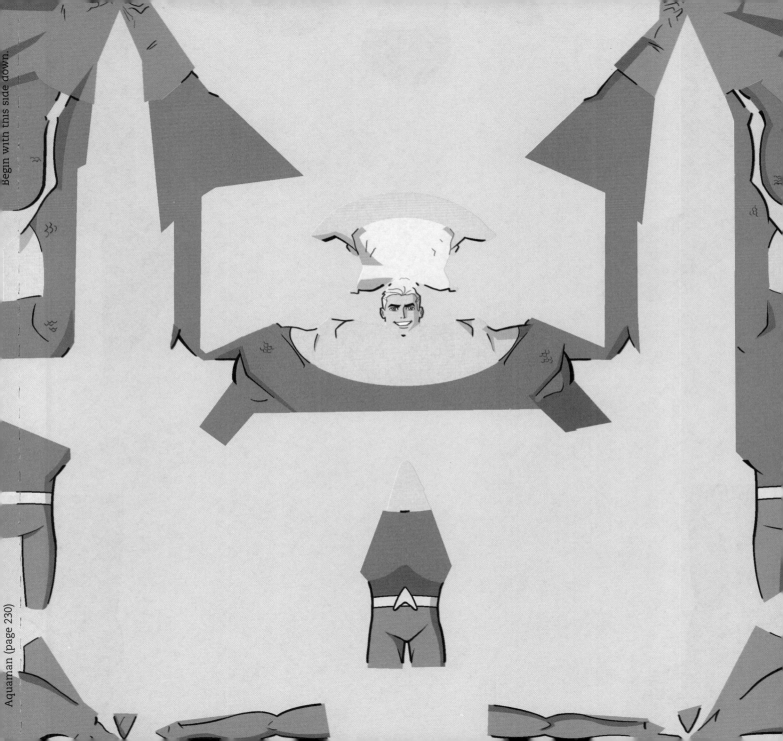

Aquaman (page 230)

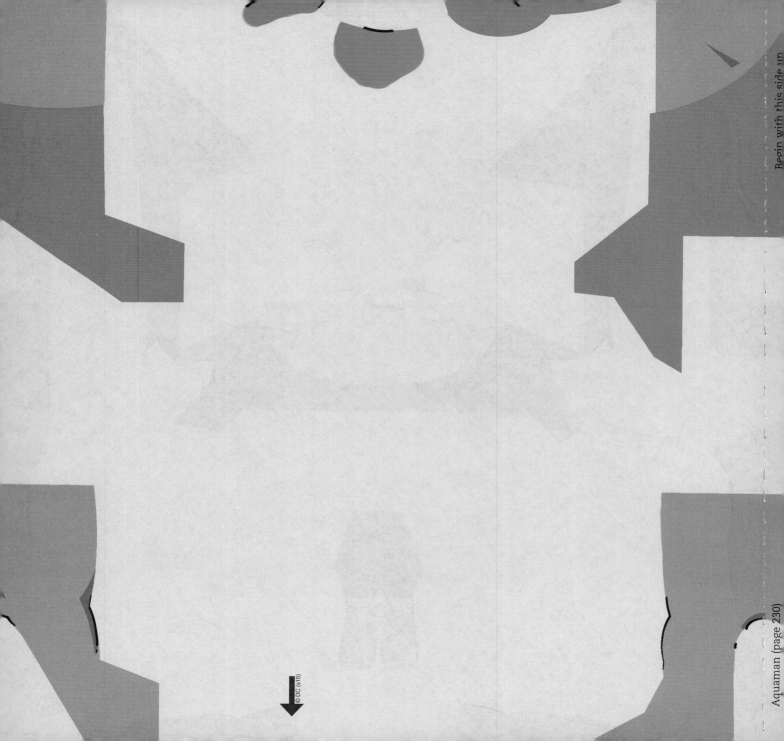

Aquaman (page 230)

Begin with this side up

Begin with this side down.

Hawkgirl's Mace (page 238)

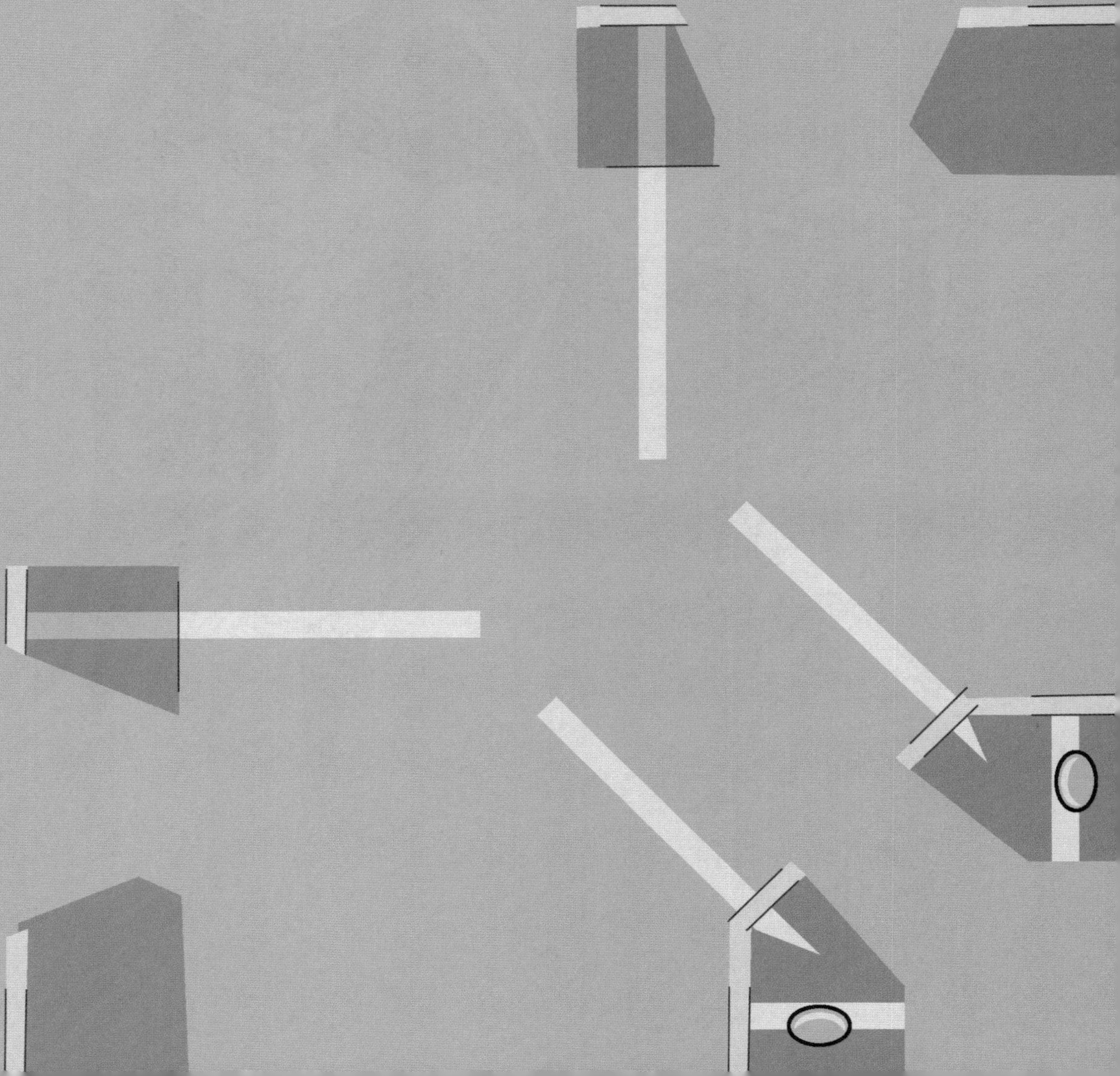

©DC (s16)

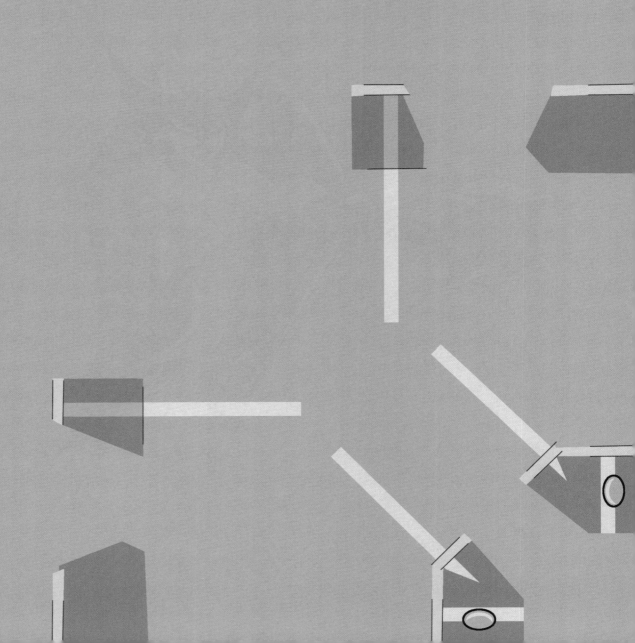

Hawkgirl's Mace (page 238)

© DC (515)

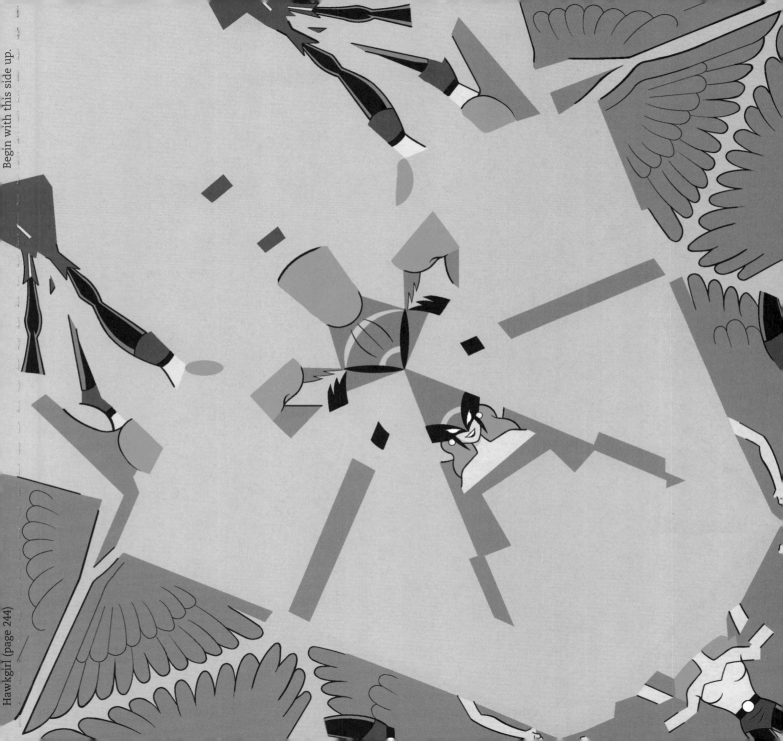

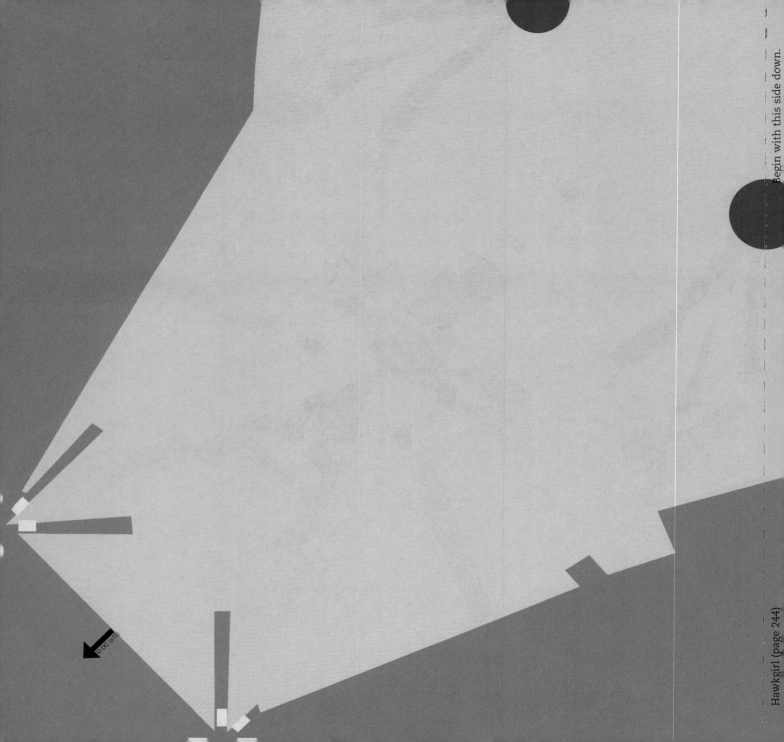

© DC (s15)

Hawkgirl (page 244)

Begin with this side down.

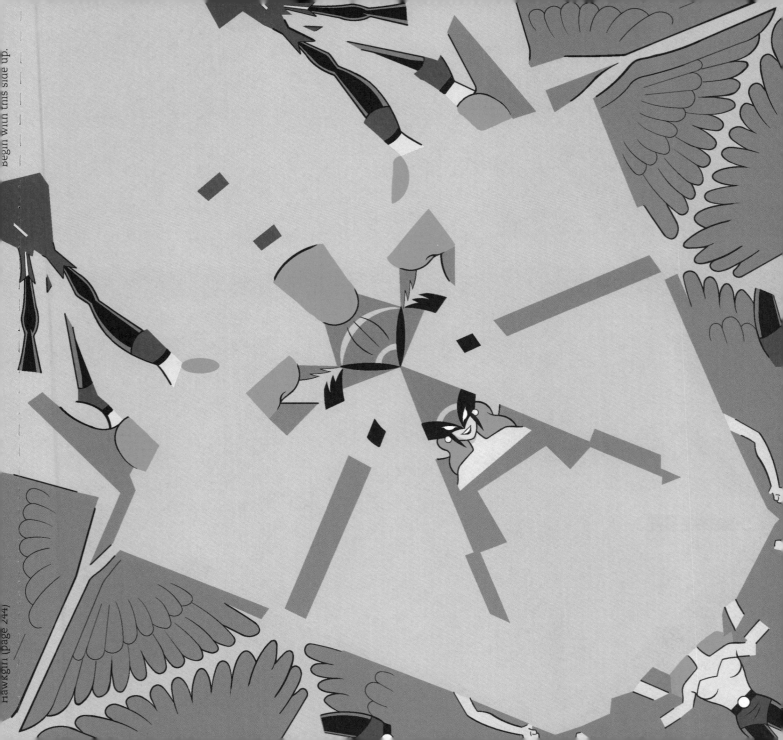

Hawkgirl (page 244)

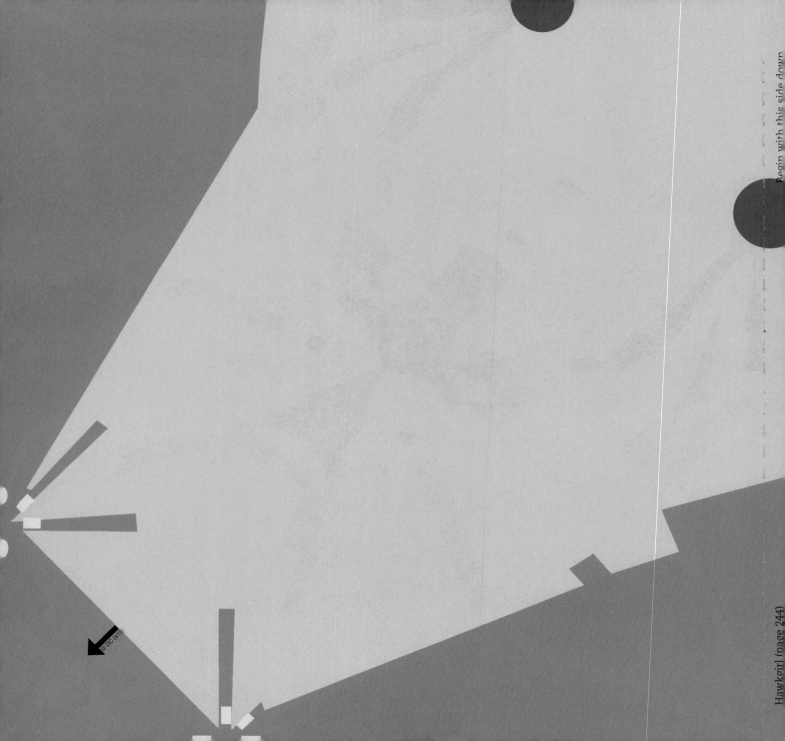

Hawkgirl (page 244)

Begin with this side down

© DC (S15)

The Atom (page 250)

Begin with this side down

(turn)

The Atom (page 250).

Begin with this side down.

The Atom (page 250)

@DC (515)